# GEORGE PREDDY
## Top Mustang Ace

Joe Noah and Samuel L. Sox, Jr.

First published in 1991 by Motorbooks International Publishers & Wholesalers,
PO Box 2, 729 Prospect Avenue, Osceola, WI 54020 USA

The essence of this book was previously published as *Wings God Gave My Soul* in
1974 by Charles Baptie Studios, Annandale, Virginia. It underwent two printings.
Illustrations in the original work were by John R. Beaman. Original Library of
Congress Catalog Card Number: 7481677. All rights reserved. Copyright 1974, 1991
by J. W. Noah

Library of Congress Cataloging-in-Publication Data
Noah, Joseph W.
    George Preddy : top Mustang ace / Joe Noah, Samuel L. Sox, Jr.
      p.  cm.
    includes index.
    ISBN 0-87938-531-6
    1. Preddy, George Earl, 1919-1944.  2. United States. Army Air
Forces—Biography.  3. World War, 1939-1945—Aerial operations,
American.  4. Fighter pilots—United States—Biography.  I. Sox,
Samuel L., 1933-  .  II. Title.
    D790.N63 1991
    940.54'4973'092—dc20          91-10060

*On the front cover: The markings on
George Preddy's* Cripes A'Mighty 3rd
*were perfectly rendered on this re-
stored P-51 Mustang owned by Kermit
Weeks.* Michael O'Leary

*On the back cover (clockwise from
upper left): George Preddy's fifteenth
victim, an FW 190 (USAAF); a portrait
of Maj. George Preddy (USAAF);
Preddy in the cockpit of the original*
Cripes A'Mighty 3rd *(P. Grabb).*

Printed and bound in the United States of America

# Contents

*To Betty, my wife, and to my children—Robert, Judy and Susan—for all their understanding and forbearance since this effort first started in 1955.*

*Joe Noah*

*To my wife Sarah, who showed uncommon devotion and understanding during the days and nights I spent preparing the photos for this book, which was imme-diately preceded by the* 352nd Fighter Group History.

*Sam Sox, Jr.*

# Acknowledgments

I owe my gratitude to Aunt Clara, Uncle Earl and Rachel who made available vital information about George and Bill and about the family. Without full use of the diaries kept by George, this book would not have been possible in its present form. The family photos and letters enhance the meaningfulness of the final book immensely.

We are deeply indebted to those in the US Air Force who have helped during the many years since 1955. A few people with whom we have had direct communications include: Maj. James F. Sunderman, USAF Book Program; Dr. Maurer Maurer, Air University; Col. Raymond F. Toliver who wrote in 1959 that George Preddy's official score should have been 28.83, a score which included one Japanese victory; and more recently Capt. Joe T. Reams of the Air University.

The many friends and associates of the Preddy brothers who provided us information and insight are mentioned in the body of the book. We are most thankful to them for their memories. We are especially grateful to Tom Ivie, Bill Hess, and Bob Powell who encouraged us to continue this effort and who provided answers to some very important questions having to do with the official record for George Preddy, John Meyer, Bill Whisner and others. Tom Ivie read the manuscript before and after the proofs; Bob Powell also agreed to read the proofs. Several errors were corrected as a result of their help. However, the authors accept full responsibility for the contents of this work.

Of extreme importance to the authors was the suggestion Tom Ivie made that we contact Motorbooks International as a potential publisher. We did, and they were interested! I am most grateful to Greg Field of Motorbooks International for his diligence and enthusiastic help as we made progress toward a final product.

4

# Foreword

## by General John C. Meyer

In the fall of 1942, Lieutenant Jack Donalson, hero of the Philippines and Humpty Doo and newly appointed Operations Officer of the squadron I commanded, came to me and solicited my efforts to get Lieutenant George Preddy into our squadron. We were preparing to go to war and I wanted fighters to lead our pilots and pass on their experiences to the young, new pilots who would carry the burden of our future actions. Jack Donalson said Preddy was a fighter and that was good enough for me. We got George!

With this background, I was surprised when Lieutenant Preddy reported to me. If ever anyone looked like a nonfighter, it was George. He was small and slight, and physically unimposing. And his voice, words and demeanor did nothing to modify the impression given by his appearance. He spoke softly, without even a hint of braggadocio in word or tone. I later asked Jack if he was sure we had the right Preddy. He said we did; and we did!

I have yet to meet a man with such single-minded and dedicated purpose, with such intense desire to excel, not for himself but for his squadron and for

*John C. Meyer said, "George Preddy was the greatest fighter pilot who ever squinted through a gunsight; he was the complete fighter pilot." USAAF*

5

his country. Above all, always, for his country. His appearance and conduct on the ground belied his skill, tenacity and fighting heart in the air. But his achievements confirmed them. George Preddy was the complete fighter pilot.

Joe Noah writes of Preddy's exploits with accuracy and flair. But especially, he captures the total flavor of the man—the core of steel in a largely sentimental soul, the coolness under fire, the professional with his passion for essential details. It is remarkable how this perception has been wrought from the records and memorabilia. That Joe could do this speaks nobly of his skill as a writer, does justice to this story of a brief yet full life, and makes me proud once again that George Preddy, my comrade in arms, was my friend.

Every man should read this to reacquire the bright vision of his youth and remember again the hope and glory of America. And every high school student should read this book. For they will find spark there to light the fires of their dreams—the dreams that will make certain that our America will endure.

*John C. Meyer, General, USAF*
*Commander in Chief*
*Strategic Air Command*

*May 24, 1974*
*Offutt Air Force Base, Nebraska*

# Preface

Research for this book has been done intermittently since World War II; the bulk of it was accomplished during the period from 1955 through 1960. The task was undertaken for two essential reasons. First, George Preddy was the leading active ace in the European theater of operations (ETO) when he was killed in action on Christmas Day in 1944. Second, the authors discovered a difference among authoritative records regarding Preddy's score. Early research uncovered documentary evidence supporting a claim for one aerial victory not recognized by the official Fighter Victory Credits Board, which had been convened after the war to review and compile a list of credits for the destruction of enemy aircraft.

As a result of research conducted in the 1950s, the first edition of this book, *Wings God Gave My Soul,* was published in 1974. A new study published in 1978 by the Office of Air Force History—*USAF Credits for the Destruction of Enemy Aircraft, World War II*—gave George Preddy credit for the omission, bringing his official score to 26.83 aerial victories.

It is often said that in measuring one's success in life, it is not how many years a person lives but rather what is accomplished with the time he or she is given. If success is to be measured by decorations, George Preddy was most successful. He earned the Distinguished Service Cross (second only to the Medal of Honor), the Silver Star with one oak-leaf cluster, a Distinguished Flying Cross with eight oak-leaf clusters, and an Air Medal with seven oak-leaf clusters, and was posthumously awarded the Purple Heart and Belgium's croix de guerre. If his success is to be measured by job proficiency, twenty-seven air and five ground victories rank him the best among those flying his type of aircraft, third among all ETO aces. No one scored more victories in the North American P-51 Mustang. He was the best he could be to his life's end. The true measure of his success is the fact that he gave his country—by way of his dedication to duty—his all! While doing that, he flew 143 combat missions, accumulating 532 combat flying hours.

Appendix B on Aircraft was researched and written by Samuel L. Sox, Jr., who—with the aid of John Beaman—prepared a similar appendix for the first version of this book. There have been some changes since the first book was published. For example, Art Snyder, the crew chief on Preddy's last Mustang, was located and he gave us details about the markings we didn't have before. Also, there have been some new revelations regarding the paint scheme for *Cripes A'Mighty 3rd.* Sam Perry, the artist for the 487th Squadron, was located in Miami in time to authenticate the markings and paint scheme on Kermit Weeks' restoration of his P-51D. The scheme depicts the Mustang as it appeared the day following Preddy's record-setting mission of destroying six enemy fighters in a single engagement.

# Introduction

On Christmas Day in 1944 one of America's greatest fighter pilots took off from a small improvised airstrip near Asch, Belgium, to meet the enemy. He was flying his Mustang fighter named *Cripes A'Mighty* on a patrol near Coblenz.

When the uneventful patrol was nearly finished, his headset blared a report of bandits southwest of the Coblenz area. Major George E. Preddy, Jr., turned his P-51 and led his squadron toward the vectored position. As he approached the enemy formation, Preddy picked out a target, closed in and started turning with his opponent. After several turns he managed to gain an advantage on the enemy aircraft he had selected as his first target; but just then another Me 109 cut in front of him. Quick thinking led to quick reaction; a short burst from Preddy's guns found the mark, causing the enemy pilot to jettison his canopy and bail out.

The slight interruption caused the Major to lose his advantage on the first Me 109 only momentarily; a few more turns and Preddy was on his tail again. He gave a long burst, netting numerous hits, then pulled up sharply to avoid debris from the splintering enemy aircraft.

At this juncture Preddy became the leading active ace in the European theater of operations with 27.5 aerial victories. He also had five on the ground while strafing but these did not count toward acedom; only aerial victories counted. His greatest single addition to this score occurred on August 6, 1944, when he knocked down six Me 109s in less than five minutes.

Receiving a new vector over his radio, Preddy headed for Liège where more enemy fighters were reported near the deck! Only two other Mustangs were with him now. As the three P-51s approached Liège, Preddy spotted an FW 190 at about 1500 ft. altitude. The 190 dived to treetop level as Preddy pressed the attack. Lt. J. Gordon Cartee was flying the ace's wing and they both were skimming the deck in hot pursuit of the enemy aircraft. As Preddy closed on the 190, he noticed intense ground fire coming up at him in one large barrage. He broke off the attack in a sharp chandelle to the left but not in time to escape the wall of fire put up by Allied ground troops eager to shoot down the enemy aircraft they heard coming! At about 700 ft. altitude, the canopy came off and *Cripes A'Mighty* nosed down, still in a turn . . . .

## Chapter 1

# "I *Must* Become an Aviator"

*Had my first real airplane ride today. Hal Foster took me to
Danville with him in his little '33 Aeronca. It took us 30
minutes to make the trip. I see now how great the airplane
is. That trip was the most wonderful experience I ever had.
I must become an aviator.*

George Preddy
November 13, 1938

To fly and fly and fly was his greatest desire. The fulfillment of this desire
carried a grave price—to kill and kill and kill and finally be killed. War is a
holocaust of impersonal madness. Seldom does the conqueror know the
conquered. Seldom does he care!

War soon becomes another sport. It becomes a game that is played for
keeps, and as in any game the score becomes all-important. The number of
games won is to the big-league pitcher as the number of enemy aircraft
destroyed is to the fighter pilot. Just as there is no appeal from the umpire's
decision in the game of baseball, there is also no appeal from the will of God in
the game of fighter pilot versus fighter pilot.

Competition enters the game of war in a big way: competition for the
highest award, the most recognition, the greatest number of victories and for
life itself. Competition for life, or the art of self-preservation, is pursued by
men in different ways. Some men fight for their own lives, others fight for the
enemies' lives. A common trait found among the top aces was their utter
disregard for their own safety while pressing the attack—usually against great
odds.

It's impossible to know how many men he killed while glorying in the
fight, but glory in that fight he did. It's also impossible to know how many
enemy aircraft he destroyed, but destroy many he did! He was aggressive,
tenacious and eager and most of all he worked hard at the task at hand. It
made no difference what the task was—killing or playing basketball, rescuing
crippled bombers or target practice, studying or dancing.

His start was not a flashy one. He was in and out of combat for almost two
years before he scored his first aerial victory. Less than thirteen months after
destroying his first enemy aircraft, he destroyed his last and was himself
destroyed.

Young and dark-headed, small and reserved, he loved girls and a good
time and had plenty of both. He was a handsome and likeable fellow with a
yen to enjoy life. He was one to not waste a minute and his efforts were not

without dividends to his country—or to himself. He lived a full life in his short span of twenty-five years.

His name was George Earl Preddy, Jr.

George was raised in Greensboro, North Carolina, a medium-sized Dixieland city famous for its O. Henry, writer of many books and short stories, and more recently for another native, Edward R. Murrow. The family lived in a small, brown-shingled home near the stadium which was built in memory of World War I dead.

Dearer to his mother than the rows of decorations won by her oldest son George, dearer than the multitude of commentaries made about her son and his record-breaking achievements, are the fond memories of the love shared between both of her fighter pilot sons and herself—a closeness in mind and spirit seldom equalled in any family or between any persons. She was a truly remarkable woman with right to be saddened by the cruelty of the passing years, but with a courageousness found through her faith in God and complete trust in mankind. Her trust was sometimes interpreted as gullibility. Perhaps on some issues and at some times it was.

Besides George and his younger brother Bill, the family included Jonnice, who was the oldest, and Rachel, who was between the brothers in age. Mother Clara knew heartbreak long before the United States entered World War II. In 1939 Jonnice died while giving birth to her first child, a son named John Faircloth. To a family so full of love for one another, the news of Jonnice's death came as a bomb out of the silent night. For the first time there was a deep sadness in the Preddy household—a sadness that would be repeated twice more within six years with the deaths of George and Bill.

Descending from a line of German ancestors, Clara Noah Preddy gave birth in Greensboro to her first son on February 5, 1919, and named him George Earl Preddy, Jr. George was a strict individualist, as was his father, whom the family called Earl. Growing up, George developed a strong competitive spirit, a desire to excel and a pride in winning.

By most standards the southern city of Greensboro was quite small. During George's time the population never exceeded 50,000. The industries providing a livelihood for most of the people were an outgrowth of the farm crops grown in North Carolina—tobacco and cotton. George never worked the tobacco fields, but he did work in a cotton mill for the year immediately following graduation from high school.

George was an intellectual, a competitive intellectual with innate athletic abilities subdued by his small size. Tipping the scales at a bare 120 pounds and measuring less than five feet, nine inches during his high school days, he didn't participate in organized sports at school. He definitely cannot be characterized as the typical all-American athlete, a trait often represented as common among our heroes.

To satisfy his natural urge to compete and his insatiable desire to build his body, George resorted to sports not then demanding of size, such as basketball and tennis. He also subscribed to exercises designed to improve his physique and build his muscles. For basketball, George and several others organized a team and played at the YMCA. At one point they became overly optimistic about their abilities and challenged the high school team. They lost, but not too badly!

Tennis presented less of a problem for George to play. He lived within one block of the tennis courts at the Memorial Stadium. He opened a soft drink concession at the tennis courts to make a little money while taking on all comers during the summer. George named his stand the "Mouse Hole," an appropriate name inasmuch as his nickname was Mouse. Many of George's friends had nicknames. But George's nickname described him in two ways: it depicted his small size and his large ears. With the maturity and status achieved during the war, George's new friends changed his nickname to Ratsy connoting a somewhat larger size.

George met Robert "Bozo" Boaz while playing basketball at the YMCA. After becoming good friends George learned that Bozo's mother had died five years earlier and, as a result, Bozo had been living at the YMCA since that time. George asked his mother if Bozo could come to live with them, and she said, "If you and Bill will share your room with Bozo, we would love to have him come here to live." After much persuasion Bozo gave in to his inner desires and came to live with the Preddy family. He lived with them for the next five years and was like a brother to the children and like a son to the parents. He referred to George's mother as Mother Clara.

To George an education was a means to an end, not an end in itself. He doubled up on his courses in high school so he could graduate early. Because of his high grade average he was exempted from taking history and chemistry. As a result he finished high school at age sixteen but didn't go directly to college. Rather, he spent the first year working in a cotton mill earning $15 a week.

George was able to save a little money toward his college education while working at the mill and to continue some of his high school social activities. George had served as president of a social club while a senior in high school; it was called the Greater Union of Brotherhood Club, or GUB Club for short. And that was before acronyms became so popular! The GUB Club sponsored dances, primarily, and its membership included some of George's best friends: "Bozo" Boaz, Clyde "Otto" Gaskins, Arnold "Goat" Mathews, and so on. The club had only twenty members.

George, playing tennis and basketball at a feverish pace but with an ability to take losses within his stride, also became a self-taught gymnast. He put up a horizontal bar in his backyard where he practiced by the hour. One of his favorite stunts was called "around-the-world." In this one he would leap up, take hold of the bar, pull his feet and legs straight up until he was balanced on his hands in a vertical position. Keeping his body straight, he would start spinning around the bar. With his wiry build he was able to master many stunts on the bar.

He and Otto Gaskins built a tree house and hung ropes from several of the trees. This is where George first learned to fly—but without wings. The two of them moved through the trees like monkeys. George was a bit smaller than his football-playing friend Otto. Although the best of friends, they were forever scrapping. George could usually hold his own when the two tussled but he was seldom able to get the best of Otto. Nor was Otto able to get the best of George. Otto said many years later, "He was a great little scrapper and he would never give up."

It was no different later when George became a fighter pilot and entered combat against seasoned Japanese flyers who had been fighting for several years. Nor was it any different when he went up against the Germans and he himself was a seasoned combat pilot. He never gave up!

The air battles of World War II were less intimate than those of the First World War. During World War I it was not uncommon for the victor to know the victim by name and reputation, but during World War II it was practically unheard of. But that doesn't mean the fighter pilots of World War II had any less respect for the foe, or any less mercy. George said that he felt great relief on a number of occasions when he saw his victim bail out before his aircraft burned or exploded.

Clara Preddy had not raised a killer but she had raised a glorious fighter pilot—two of them in fact. As was the case with most of our fighter pilots who knew their job a bit better than the opponent, they gloried in their victories with humility because they knew that invincibility was a function of time and not theirs forever!

After his sister's death, George wrote a poem about Jonnice. According to Earl Preddy, he wrote the poem the day Jonnice died.

What is this thing?
This trance I'm in?
I know not what death brings.
I know she's gone,
Her soul has fled,
But to me her sweet voice rings.
She lingers in this very room,
She directs me in my role.
I know she dwells not with the dead,
She lives within my soul.
—George E. Preddy, Jr.

He wrote this poem on a three-by-five index card, tossed it on the coffee table and walked out of the living room without a word. Earl picked it up and read it, then put it away. George never saw it again, but Earl preserved it.

George was interested in college primarily because he thought it might make it easier to fulfill his ambition to fly. As it turned out, he was right. During the years immediately preceding World War II the armed services required some college education as a prerequisite to becoming an aviation cadet.

His was a purpose, a purpose he knew very early in life, and he worked hard to reach his goals. The success he achieved during the war was due in large part to his strong determination and singleness of purpose. Some men never learn their purpose in life. They struggle along aimlessly either being pulled by the social current or swimming viciously against it. But not George Preddy. He wanted to fly and he learned this at an early age. He never once strayed from that aim!

He reached his decision in high school when he started reading about famous flyers and flying stories. But it was not until three years after he graduated from high school that he took his first airplane ride. One beautiful Sunday afternoon George went to the regional airport as he did on many occasions to watch the planes and talk to the pilots. Hal Foster, a friend of the family, asked George if he wanted to ride along to Danville, Virginia, which was just about fifty miles north. The flight to Danville and back in Hal's 1933 Aeronca changed George's life. From this point on, he knew he ". . . *must* become an aviator."

12

# Chapter 2

# Obstacles Along the Way

*I remembered the dream of the days of the youth*
*Of my flying, that burst of glory, and how the world*
*And my shining youth itself shone with the radiance*
*Of it. It was my Creator.*
*It created life for me, for Man shall not live by bread alone. Man cannot. Only*
*His dreams and his vision sustain him.*
                                                              —Jimmy Collins

Also found in his early scrapbook, this quotation succinctly expresses the feeling George had for flying. Within just a few months after his first flight in the Aeronca, George learned to fly. He had made the transition from his backyard aerial circus to the real thing! His agility on the horizontal bar was now being concentrated on the vertical stick of an airplane.

His flight instructor, Bill Teague, owned a Waco which he operated out of a small dirt strip near Vandalia, just six miles south of Greensboro. Bill had named his Waco *Wanda C* for his wife, Wanda. After George soloed, Bill suggested that they invest $75 each and buy a second Waco and go on a barnstorming tour. The Waco (pronounced wahco) was the product of George E. "Buck" Weaver, one of three founders of the Weaver Aircraft Company. Buck was a barnstorming pilot whose principal contribution to the company was to obtain financing for two struggling engineers who used the money to buy surplus JN-4 Jenny parts and OX-5 engines to build "new" biplanes. This was in 1919. It was one of these early models that Bill Teague and George Preddy bought. It had an eight-cylinder, 90 hp engine which, on a good day, permitted a speed of 80 mph.

Bill Teague managed an A&P grocery store during the late thirties when he taught George to fly. Bill had been taught to fly by one of the more famous Tarheel pilots, Johnny Crowell of Charlotte. Crowell taught many to fly during the 1920s and 1930s and thrilled many spectators with his stunts and aerobatics. He gave rides in his World War I Jenny—one dollar a ride. Many who took him up on the offer came down too frightened to ever fly again; others loved it and hired Johnny to teach them to fly. Bill Teague was among the latter group. Crowell died at age ninety after having been an active aviator into his seventies flying transmission lines for Duke Power Company.

George started accumulating flying time and practicing aerobatics for the barnstorming tour in the Waco, but not without incident. It was during one of these early flights that he was first introduced to blind flying and it happened purely by accident, or perhaps purely by the lack of a proper preflight inspection!

After completing the normal run up and mag check, George started his takeoff roll down the dirt strip at Vandalia. All was going well; he cleared the trees at the end of the runway with a few feet to spare. Then the engine noise changed abruptly; next there was a banging noise. Suddenly he lost all forward vision! The cowling had blown off the engine and was now lodged against the leading edge of the upper wing directly in front of the forward cockpit. George was in the rear cockpit, as is usual when flying solo in the Waco, and couldn't reach the cowling.

Now he was barely at treetop level and unable to climb because of the terrific wind resistance caused by the large surface of the cowling. Very carefully George wheeled his Waco around, just skimming the treetops in a desperate effort to get back to the airstrip. He couldn't see ahead, but he could see to either side. He soon decided that it was folly to try to get back to the field with so little altitude. Knowing the surrounding territory quite well, he decided to head for a cornfield directly ahead and try to set the plane down before he clobbered a tall tree. Here he made his first blind landing; it was bumpy but no damage was apparent.

After securing the engine cowling back in place, and chastising himself for not conducting a proper preflight inspection, he took off and flew back to Vandalia where he and Bill Teague carefully inspected the biplane for damage. None was found! Perhaps it was this incident among others which served to convince George that good maintenance was critical to safe flying. It instilled in him a lively respect for maintenance crews during the war.

The war between China and Japan had begun long before George started his flying career, the career that would lead him into combat against superior pilots and airplanes in the Far East, into combat for which he was ill-prepared because his country's leaders swapped foresight for complacency. As early as July 1937 fighting between Chinese and Japanese troops broke out at Marco Polo Bridge near Peiping (now Beijing). As the general situation deteriorated in the Pacific, too few of our people were able to recognize its seriousness. The "minor skirmish" at Marco Polo Bridge became known as the Sino-Japanese Incident, a turning point in history. It erupted into a bloody and savage full-scale war between the two combatants calling on a major part of each nation's industrial and economic strength.

By the time George had learned to fly in early 1939, Hitler's naziism was also showing its ugly head. German troops crossed the Czechoslovakia frontier and Hungarian troops annexed a portion of Czech territory. In the two years since the incident at the Marco Polo Bridge, the Japanese had taken vast portions of China and the sea lanes were theirs.

Not realizing that he was preparing himself to fly against enemy pilots on two far-flung battlefronts, George laid plans with Bill Teague for their summer barnstorming tour of North Carolina. Covering the Tarheel state from one end to the other, the two spent the summer hopping passengers and putting on exhibitions of stunt flying.

The Waco, a two-seat open-cockpit biplane with the normal undercarriage of the times—a tail-dragger—was difficult to taxi because the nose of the plane blocked the pilot's forward view. So, the procedure for taxiing was to fishtail the plane as it moved forward. This procedure was less than fail-safe. Near the end of the summer's barnstorming tour, George landed at Vandalia and started his fishtailing to the tie-down area. He was unaware that Bill Teague was taxiing out for a takeoff. As it happened, both were looking out the opposite sides of their respective airplanes as they passed one another. Their wing tips met with the ripping sound of fabric and the cracking twang

14

of ribs breaking. Fortunately, the accident occurred near the summer's end; the tour had been a successful experience for both. The winter weekends of 1939-40 were spent repairing both damaged planes in preparation for next summer's planned barnstorming tour.

On September 1, 1939, Hitler's armies marched into Poland touching off World War II in Europe. Within the next ten days Great Britain, France, Australia, New Zealand and Canada declared war on Germany. Although the United States proclaimed neutrality, George, sensing our neutrality would be temporary, decided he wanted to fly with the military.

Not yet twenty-one and still eligible for passes on the railroad, George asked his Dad to get him a pass to Pensacola, Florida, where the Naval Air Training Center was located. Earl, not one to hold his children back, accommodated the request and George went to Pensacola to take the rigid physical and mental exams required of pilots. He had the necessary college credits and he passed the mental exams with no trouble. But the physical problems seemed unsurmountable. There he learned for the first time in his life of some of his physical limitations. The navy doctors told him he had a curvature of the spine, he was too small and his blood pressure was higher than it should be.

Discouraged, but by no means ready to give up, George returned home and immediately went to see his family doctor. He was advised to continue his exercises and add some new ones to help straighten the spine. George had subscribed to the Charles Atlas Body Building Course long before going to Pensacola; he was interested in building his body for reasons other than his flying ambition. His doctor suggested he engage in stretching exercises, so George asked his brother Bill and his "adopted" brother Bozo to help him. One would hold him by his feet and the other by his arms, and they would pull in a stretching action. When Bill and Bozo tired of this, George would go to the horizontal bar and just hang by his hands until exhausted.

When George first applied for the Navy Air Cadet program, the quota was still quite small and the navy could afford to be very selective. And they were. As the world situation became more serious, the navy and the army relaxed their requirements—both mental and physical. But before that happened George took the navy exams two more times and both times was rejected. So he decided to spend the summer of 1940 as he had earlier planned and go on his barnstorming tour with Bill Teague.

After what seemed to be long and tedious preparations, the team of Teague and Preddy finally took off from Vandalia in their pair of Waco biplanes bound west with the blaze of morning sun at their backs. They flew a loose formation as they followed the railroad tracks through town and on to Walnut Cove where they found a field worthy of landing. They had very little money and needed to earn some soon so they could buy fuel and continue their tour. But when they landed there was no one in sight. After about an hour, there was still no one in sight. So George suggested they take off and fly down the main street in town at the lowest possible altitude and wake up some of the folks. They decided they would make three passes down Main Street and then show the people where their field was by going there in trail. It worked! Townspeople started coming out to see what all the commotion was about. And some had money enough to pay for rides; others contributed to the "gas kitty" in return for watching their aerial stunts.

*George's red and white Waco 10 in which he performed aerobatics and accompanied Bill Teague on barnstorm-* *ing tours. Pictured from left to right are: Bobby Boaz, Bill Preddy, Bill Teague and George Preddy.* W. Teague

That night Bill and George slept under the wings of their respective airplanes; they wanted to save their money so they could afford to stay in the YMCAs across North Carolina at least once every three or four nights. That would allow them to have a good shower and go swimming. And that's the way the summer went—barnstorming by day and sleeping under the wings by night with an occasional respite in the Y.

One of the most memorable events of the summer for George occurred about midway through their tour. He and Bill were operating out of a field near the small town of Valle Crucis near Boone, North Carolina. As George landed after a passenger hop, he noticed a police car with lights flashing coming out on the field. So George stopped his Waco, cut the engine and got out to see what he had done to stir the ire of the local police force. As it happened, he had done nothing. A local official—a state representative for that district—needed to get to Asheville in a hurry. Driving the 100 or so miles through the mountains in 1940 was at least a four-hour trip. The Waco could make the trip in a bit over an hour. They hired George to take the official and paid him handsomely for the trip. George never revealed just how "handsomely" he had been paid.

Another event about which he spoke very little also occurred in the mountains. A small girl was brought to the field from which they were flying; she was sick and needed hospital treatment not offered in Mount Airy, which was the closest town. Her mother asked that she be taken to Winston-Salem where a relative would meet them at the airport. George turned his Waco into an air ambulance before we had conceived of them. The girl—just ten years old—was strapped into the front cockpit with her mother and away they

16

went. The trip was uneventful, and the relative was waiting when George landed. He would not accept pay for this trip, but asked the mother to let him know how her daughter made out. A letter was waiting for him when he got home after finishing the tour. He learned the girl had recovered from her bout with pneumonia, and the mother had recovered from her bout with panic. She had diagnosed her daughter's illness as tuberculosis!

Now that the summer's barnstorming fun had ended, it was time for George to renew his efforts to get into military flying. Private flying had been loads of fun, but it was limited—limited mostly by the amount of money one could make while doing it. Also, George thought it would be great to fly faster and more powerful airplanes. So he decided to try for the Army Air Corps this time rather than a fourth try for the navy. Even though the United States was still neutral and the exams still rigid, George passed the army exams with flying colors the first time. It made him wonder about the navy. But he had put on some weight and some more muscle, so perhaps his family doctor's advice had paid off. In any event, he was accepted and placed on a long waiting list for a cadet class.

It was the month that Herman Goering initiated the German blitz on London, September 1940. The world situation was becoming grave and George did not want to wait at home for his class to start. On the advice of one of the Army Air Corps recruiters, he enlisted in the National Guard and was assigned to basic training with the 252nd Coast Artillery at Fort Moultrie, South Carolina. After completing the physically tough and demanding training involving difficult obstacle courses, rigid discipline, and fun on the rifle and pistol ranges, he accompanied his outfit to Fort Screvins, Georgia. From there he hoped to be called into the Air Corps, but he discovered that plans were being made to ship his entire battery to Puerto Rico within six weeks. He suspected that if the Air Corps failed to call him up before he shipped out, he would have little chance of getting out of the National Guard and into flying. So he wrote a letter to the Air Corps explaining the situation and asking that they intercede on his behalf—either hold him in the zone of interior until his next class started or put him in an earlier class. Naturally he hoped they would do the latter, but down deep he believed his letter to be a waste of time. He had to try for his own peace of mind.

As he suspected, he heard nothing from the Air Corps. Six weeks passed and still no response. But his outfit did not move out as planned, either. The schedule changed and George was grateful for the resulting delay. But as the new departure date approached, the troops were given their necessary shots, issued machetes and other gear peculiar to the tropical zone of Puerto Rico, and in general made ready for their change of station. George, frustrated, hurriedly dispatched another letter to the Air Corps following up on his first. Again he was afraid his efforts would be futile. On the day the 252nd was due to depart, George was packed and physically ready to go, but there was little consolation to be found in his disrupted plans. He still had not heard anything from his letters, both of which had gone out through appropriate channels.

Several hours before it was time to board the ship, the commanding officer of his outfit sent for George. When he reported—which was right away—the officer told him that he was cutting orders in order to have him transferred to a battery that was not being shipped out, at least not then. The officer had been aware of George's desires through the letters he had written and, unusual as it may seem to those who served in World War II, this commanding officer did something constructive about the situation. Before the other battery received orders to ship out, George received his orders to report to the Army Air Corps for flight training at Darr Aero Tech, a primary flying school southwest of Albany, Georgia.

That happened in April 1941 when the Germans invaded Greece and Yugoslavia and heavily and repeatedly bombed Belgrade, and the Italians announced they would act with all their forces in collaboration with Germany. In Asia, the Sino-Japanese conflict had become an all-out war, savage and vicious! Claire Chennault had been made brigadier general, and he returned to the United States to lobby for aid to China, basing his plea on the importance of keeping the Burma Road open. He was successful in reaching the sympathetic ear of President Roosevelt; he asked for aircraft and a volunteer force of experienced American pilots to fly them. He got both, and they became known as the American Volunteer Group, better known as the Flying Tigers.

Training in the primary trainer, the Boeing PT-17 Kaydet, was reminiscent of his barnstorming days in his Waco. Both were slow biplanes with open cockpits, and both performed aerobatics well. However, the PT-17 was larger than the Waco and had more power—220 hp—which gave it about a 20 mph advantage. Both were fun to fly! And of course George had no trouble with primary flight training since he had already accumulated about 300 hours in his Waco. But he was careful not to tell anyone, especially his instructor. Within three months George had completed primary and was transferred to a basic flight training field just nine miles south of the primary school. This was also a civilian school operated by Darr Aero Tech. Here he learned to fly the larger basic trainer, the Consolidated Vultee BT-13 Valiant, which had 450 hp. George found this monoplane to be less nimble in aerobatics than the PT-17 biplane. Perhaps this was at least partially due to the experience he had accumulated in biplanes.

George discovered that a pilot's career field is determined during basic training. The flight instructors decide who is suited for pursuit, for bomber, and for observation duty during this phase of schooling. From the very beginning George was determined to get into pursuit aircraft; his size was certainly in his favor. Now it was up to him to demonstrate to his instructors that he had the capability to fly pursuit aircraft. He thought the best way to do this was to excel in aerobatics and formation flying, and that is just what he did! There was really never any question about his ability to fly pursuit aircraft; the question was whether or not the army would assign him according to his desires and abilities, or whether they would assign him by the same random scheme which accounts for the fate of many soldiers during most wars.

During October 1941 George finished basic training, and the British had turned the London blitz into a Berlin blitz. They were raiding Brest, St. Nazaire, Benghazi, Tripoli and Stuttgart. The Germans were attacking Newcastle and Dover and launching their two-pronged assault against Moscow. George entered advanced training while the United States remained neutral.

He reported to Craig Field, Alabama, an advanced flying school for pursuit pilots. It was an old, established base with paved roads and grass and barracks made of concrete and stucco. The mainstay was the excellent North American AT-6 Texan. This was the future ace's first indoctrination into the many fine features and flying characteristics designed into the Texan, many of which he later found gave him an edge over the enemy while flying North American's P-51 Mustang through the skies of Europe.

As part of the advanced course, George's class was sent to Elgin Field in Florida for ground gunnery training. While there, he had the pleasure of flying his first real pursuit aircraft, the Curtiss P-36. This was a low-wing monoplane with 1050 hp and a maximum speed of over 300 mph. This aircraft was used by France and was probably the first American pursuit to go into action during World War II. Flying this speed demon was quite a thrill for George, but one flight in a real pursuit plane was hardly sufficient training for pilots receiving their wings and commissions as pursuit pilots. As many pilots soon discovered, their wings represented only their license to learn to fly more powerful aircraft in combat.

Just five days after the Japanese launched their surprise air attacks on US naval, ground and air bases in and around Pearl Harbor, sinking two battleships, completely disabling three and putting three others out of action, sinking three destroyers and damaging many other ships and bases, George and his classmates graduated from flying school. On December 12, 1941, his mother came to Alabama to proudly pin wings on his blouse during the graduation exercises. Outwardly she was oblivious to the dangers she knew he would face; her concern was that George had succeeded in completing the first phase of his lifelong dream. She would not spoil that for him!

With his newly won wings and commission as a second lieutenant, he took a short leave prior to reporting to West Palm Beach to join the 49th Pursuit Group. While at home he enjoyed the ovations of his close friends and relatives who were also quite proud that George had succeeded in getting something he wanted so badly. There was the idol worship of his younger brother and cousins, the respect and admiration of his friends, and the anguish of his sister and parents who fully understood he had won his wings just in time to be thrown headlong into the first battles of World War II involving the United States.

After the brief furlough George reported to his new assignment: the 49th Pirsuit Group, 9th Pursuit Squadron. The 49th Fighter Group had the new Bell P-39 Airacobra. This aircraft had 1200 hp, a maximum speed of about 375 mph, and a ceiling of 38,000 ft. The engine was mounted to the rear of the cockpit and it had a 20 mm cannon mounted in the nose. Many of these aircraft were engaged against the superior Japanese Zero during the early months of World War II in Southeast Asia; later many were sent to the Russians on lend-lease. However, George noticed something very strange about the P-39s when he got to his new base. After close inspection he discovered they had no propellers. So the new shavetails had to revert to flying primary trainers, since the PT-17 was all that was airworthy and available and those were in short supply. The shortage of P-39 propellers, however, had little to do with the lack of training received between graduation and the first combat assignment. The 49th was in West Palm Beach for only a couple of weeks before boarding a troop train for the West Coast, perhaps enough time for the new pilots to have checked out in the P-39, but that's all.

Priorities still given mail and passenger traffic by a yet complacent nation caused frequent stopovers and delays. George spent most of his time reading, a pleasure he enjoyed in spite of—not because of—the scenery. His fellow Carolinians heckled the Texans about the barren countryside; the Rebels joined together in verbal skirmishes with the Yankee boys as they relived their most imaginary mental picture of the Civil War.

Five days later the troop train rolled into San Francisco; officers billeted in a downtown hotel and enlisted men herded into San Francisco's famous Cow Palace, a livestock pavilion. The officers had to report to Cow Palace daily, but beyond that they had no official duties. George bought a camera and spent his time sight-seeing. On January 11, 1942, just three days after arriving, his holiday was cut short with orders to board the US Army Transport *Mariposa*, destination unknown!

*Chapter 3*

# From Zone of
# Interior to Combat Zone

*Though I've belted you and flayed you, By the living Gawd
that made you, You're a better man than I am, Gunga Din!*
—Rudyard Kipling

The last verse of Kipling's *Gunga Din,* that famous barrack-room ballad of the
regimental water boy for British soldiers, was one of George's favorite quota-
tions. Apparently the ballad became ingrained in his subconscious and he
actually lived by the spirit of it—perhaps it helps explain why he had the
highest respect for the ground crewmen who maintained his aircraft throughout the war.

During the first month after Pearl Harbor, the Japanese launched a major
attack against the Philippines, placing from eighty to one hundred thousand
troops in the Gulf of Lingayen. The Chinese at Hong Kong surrendered, Wake
Island was taken by the Japanese and an invasion of the Netherlands East
Indies was underway.

In the face of world war, the former palatial South Seas pleasure liner of
the Matson Steamship Company, the *Mariposa,* set sail on its first voyage as a
wartime troop transport. The lounges and ballroom were fitted with tiers of
bunks; extra bunks were added to all of the once spacious cabins. Temporary
latrines were constructed on the upper deck. The *Mariposa* no longer
resembled the luxury liner that had carried many famous people on Pacific
Island excursions. It was now carrying about four thousand soldiers, men who
made up the first complete expeditionary force of the US Army Air Corps.

As the *Mariposa* sailed majestically under the Golden Gate Bridge,
George took his parting glimpses of San Francisco and home soil, knowing his
date and state of return were most uncertain. In fog and heavy ground swell,
the *Mariposa* joined a sister transport, the *Coolidge,* a cargo ship named
*Monroe,* and a navy escort cruiser, the *Phoenix.* The destination was unknown
to the troops aboard; speculation during the first day of the voyage seemed to
center on Australia because the passenger list included some Aussie airmen.
The consensus was that those airmen were returning home from Canada. The
first night out George made his first entry in his wartime diary.

January 12, 1942—Monday
Left San Francisco harbor about 4:15 PM on the *Mariposa* for unknown
destination—possibly Australia. About 4,000 men aboard. Ship is armed with
50-caliber anti-aircraft machine guns and 3-inch guns. Also loaded with bombs

and P–40s. No radios or cameras can be used; blackout is in effect. Quit smoking cigarettes today; will resort to pipe if necessary.

George made entries in his diary without missing a day through the end of his voyage. He passed time reading, playing poker, attending briefings, talking to his peers and pulling less-than-pleasant extra-duty details such as mess and policing. On the twenty-seventh he wrote that he was in charge of policing the squadron area; apparently, he didn't get it cleaned properly and caught hell for it.

The convoy crossed the equator at a position approximately north of the French-mandated Marquesas Islands. The heat was unbearable in some parts of the ship. Enlisted men were crowded below decks and blackout restrictions reduced ventilation substantially. Going further south meant cooler weather was in store for the troops. To avoid detection by Japanese submarines, the ships in the convoy varied their course by sailing alternately south and southwest, continuing their blackout restrictions. Last holdouts finally conceded that Australia was most likely their destination.

One week into the voyage, George had lost all of his money playing blackjack and poker. About midway to Australia, the *Mariposa's* rudder became fouled causing the ship to list decidedly and travel in a tight circle. The huge liner narrowly missed the cruiser *Phoenix* in the dark as the overcast sky made it almost impossible to discern the other blacked-out ships in the convoy. George was unaware that the rudder problem was so serious. It occurred at night when most aboard were asleep, and all he knew was that they were safely underway soon after he discovered they had had a problem.

Ground school and briefings were held, and these were welcome ways to pass time. Pilots studied reports of aerial combat prepared by American observers who had been in England, and they were briefed on the secret radio aircraft locator used by Great Britain. Major Paul Wurtsmith, who achieved rank of major general and became commanding officer of General Kenney's fighter command, was on board the *Mariposa* and his first briefing was less than welcome. He ordered that all cameras be sent home. George had just spent $70 to buy his new Argus while in San Francisco and had taken only a half roll of film. George observed that he would have to give up not only his camera, but possibly his radio-phono and his diary as well. He said, "Things are coming to a bad state when you can't own a thing but military clothing and issue. Probably it is best. If it will increase our chances for success, I'm all for it." At least he still had a few books to read. George read Hemingway's *For Whom the Bell Tolls* and James Hilton's *Random Harvest* among others.

Proceeding south from the Marquesas Islands, the convoy passed the island of Tutuila southeast of Samoa, then took a course just south of the Fijis, crossed the international date line, then passed through the Tasman Sea between New Zealand and Australia. They were met in the Tasman Sea by a large Australian cruiser whose duty was to escort the plodding cargo ship *Monroe* on to a separate destination. Once relieved of the slow cargo ship, the remainder of the convoy stepped up the pace for southern Australia; the troops still didn't know their exact destination but it had been narrowed down to a toss-up between Sydney and Melbourne.

With each day that passed the tales grew wilder of that wonderland called Australia where the food was fresh and scarce, the liquor excellent and plentiful, and the girls beautiful and available. It was the place where things were upside down—where it was summer during the winter, spring in the fall and fall in the spring. It claimed strange animals like the duckbilled platypus, the kangaroo and the koala bear. It was the land where citizens had to pay *not* to vote.

The *Mariposa* anchored in Melbourne's bay on February 1. The troops were allowed to use their radios but were not allowed to go ashore until the ship docked the next morning.

February 2, 1942—Monday
Docked this morning and took a train to Camp Darley, about 30 miles from Melbourne. Had to walk five miles from the train station to camp. We got a good welcome from everyone. Some men threw cigarettes off the boat and the Aussies fought over them like a pack of hungry wolves. They have trouble getting cigarettes here now and very few drive private cars due to shortage of petrol.
Went into a little town called Bacchus Marsh tonight and picked up a girl. Went to bed on the floor about midnight.

George wasted no time finding female companionship after two weeks aboard ship. He was in Melbourne on the 4th, and on the 5th his entry read, "Celebrated 23rd birthday tonight with McGee, Smitty and our dates at one of the girl's flats. It was a beautiful place on the water, and we topped things off with a glass of champagne. Afterwards we went to a club and came back and sat on the beach. Smitty had the pick of the lot of girls. Expect to be here another week. Would surely like to move now and start flying."

Lt. Lawrence P. "Smitty" Smith was one of George's closest friends from the time they both entered flight training together. In response to my letter written to him in 1957, Smith wrote his impressions of George. He said, "To me, he was a happy-go-lucky type, maybe on occasion even a hell-raiser, who made certain he got the maximum out of life. He was in no sense immature, however. He was what we considered superior fighter pilot material and I think he proved that. I'll wager also that he made an excellent commander in the European theater of operations. He used to recite a poem that I'd give my right arm to have a copy of. It concerned a lecture on sex by the president of a woman's club (to her club) and George accomplished it with much emphasis and many gestures; it was a priceless performance."

Major Wurtsmith took over command of the camp and selected George to serve as his acting adjutant. George was happy about the duty for two reasons: it gave him something to do while waiting to move out, and he learned quite a bit from the job. However, he said the work didn't compare to flying! The job didn't last long, either. George was relieved by the permanent adjutant and left Bacchus Marsh on February 15 by train. He had a comfortable trip of about 450 miles and plenty to eat. Some of their food was provided by women volunteers who served them all along the way to Bankstown, a suburb of Sydney. They arrived at their new airfield the next day and George saw an airplane for the first time in about a month. The quarters and food were much better than he had found at Camp Darley.

To the Americans who raised the first stars and stripes over Australian soil, the move from Melbourne to Sydney unveiled an astonishing change in scenery. Melbourne's streets were unbelievably beautiful; the streets in Sydney were treacherous. Like London, except prettier, Sydney consisted of many small towns banded together amassing a population of about 1.5 million. Bankstown was one of those small towns. It later came to be known as, what else, "Yankstown."

*One of the airstrips near Darwin, Australia, where the 49th Fighter Group* *first saw combat, 1942.* R. Preddy Harris

Melbourne's streets were three times as wide as those in Sydney, with flowering strips of beautiful exotic trees down the middle. But the spectacle of Sydney Harbor was unsurpassed even by Acapulco. The Harbor comprised a beautiful body of water surrounded by little houses with red roofs placed neatly amid the rolling hills.

One thing the two cities had in common was the habitat. The Australians of both Sydney and Melbourne consumed more beer than milk and defended their White Policy with fanaticism. Demanding that no one with nonwhite blood be allowed citizenship, Australia enforced their policy with brutal consistency. The White Policy was initiated as an answer to the Chinese influx into the gold mines and to the Solomon Island slaves into the sugar fields. Being from Dixie, George was very well acquainted with his own people's policy of segregation; it seemed a weak measure in comparison to Australia's policy.

Butter, tea and sugar were rationed and price controls were strictly enforced. But the Americans found the usual black market flourishing. Grocery stores doled out nice, big, ripe tomatoes to customers who would pay double. You could buy anything for cigarettes. Drugstores were, and are, called "chemists," and streetcars were "trams." Restrooms usually had coin-operated doors requiring a penny; and thus the origin of the phrase "I'm going to spend a penny." Also, the Aussies had a blue law just as the GIs from the southern United States had grown up with and learned to disregard. The law fixed it so you couldn't get a drink, go to a dance or even go to a movie on Sunday. But, like the southerners from the United States, the Aussie girls had learned how to make Sundays pleasant for the visiting soldiers in spite of the blue law.

It was now six weeks since George had flown an airplane; he had never flown a P-40, yet that was the type he would be flying in combat in the very near future against the Japanese, who had steadily gained momentum. After occupying Manila, their fierce push carried them to Rabaul and Gasmata in New Britain, and to Balikpapan in Borneo. Australia waited tensely for the

24

threatened attack but was determined to hold the industrial southeastern section of the continent at all costs. They concentrated almost exclusively on preparations incidental to a strategic plan of defense along the "Brisbane Line," a line of resistance halfway down the east coast. In line with this policy, the northern cities including Darwin, Cairns and Townsville were being prepared to evacuate all civilians as rapidly as transportation would permit. Port Moresby in New Guinea was also to be evacuated.

In the meantime American flyers—most of whom were green—were hurriedly being prepared to protect the soon-to-be evacuated cities. Perhaps the greatest bottleneck encountered in carrying out these plans was the Australian transportation system. It was inadequate to meet the demands; for example, the railroad network on the journey from north to south varied from standard- to narrow-gauge tracks to no tracks at all! Loading and unloading from one train to another and from trains to trucks practically doubled the length of any Australian trek.

While high-level plans for defense were being laid, George was finally getting back to what he loved most—flying. But it was not with the frequency he would have liked, nor was it in the kind of aircraft he would have preferred. There were two Wirraways (the Australian version of our AT-6) for about fifty officers. George checked out in one of them on the 16th.

The Japanese bombed Darwin for the first time on the nineteenth of February, then on the twentieth they invaded Timor. Both incidents came as a prelude to the battle of Java Sea and the subsequent invasion of Java. In an effort to meet the onslaught, extensive training in the P-40 was ruled a luxury for the green pilots, not a necessity. On February 22, two P-40Es arrived on the field and George spent two hours just sitting in the cockpit getting familiar with the arrangement of instruments and controls. He said it was the best arrangement he had ever seen. Two days later he was pulled out of bed at 5 A.M. to fly the P-40 for the first time. He put in 1.5 hours, then caught a train to Brisbane to ferry one back to the field.

Inexperience, the long layoff and new surroundings all added to the hazards faced by the American pilots fresh out of flying school, now in Australia to be combat airmen. Further complicating their plight was the task of quickly making the transition from the advanced trainers to the faster and trickier Kittyhawk. As one would expect under such conditions, a rash of training accidents occurred. Fred O'Riley received only a lip injury when his P-40 ripped up 50 ft. of fence before coming to a stop in the kitchen of a civilian home two miles from his field; Don McGee was not injured when his aircraft left the runway, hit a hole in loose sand, and turned over on its back. And there were many other accidents, some due to forced landings resulting from pilots getting lost and others from mechanical failures. Fortunately, during this period when the accident rate was quite high, most of the pilots escaped serious injury, but the scarce P-40s were becoming even more scarce.

Not all pilots in Australia were inexperienced, however. Capt. Boyd D. "Buzz" Wagner, one of the very early aces in the theater, scored his fifth victory against the Japanese on 16 December 1941. He scored two of those victories while on a one-man reconnaissance mission out of Clark Field in the Philippines; he attacked a Japanese airfield at Aparri, strafing the planes he found on the ground. He discovered, much to his surprise, that five of them had gotten airborne and were coming in on his tail as he pulled up from his second pass. He immediately put his P-40 into a dive knowing he could outdive, and hoping he could outrun, the Zeros at sea level. Only two Zeros followed; the other three stayed up as top cover. Wagner soon learned he could not outrun the Zeros; they were slowly overtaking him as he skimmed the treetops. Just as the enemy aircraft came within firing range, Wagner chopped his throttle and watched the Zeros whiz past. With both of them now in front of him, he opened fire simultaneously kicking his rudder first right and then left destroying both enemy aircraft.

Just three days later Wagner and two other pilots—Church and Strauss—flew to Vigan Field where they planned a dive-bombing and strafing attack against enemy fighters and bombers, hopefully caught on the field. But remembering the five enemy aircraft that had gotten airborne over Aparri and bounced him with vigor and surprise, Wagner wisely ordered Strauss to provide top cover while he and Church made their attacks on the field. As the two made their first run, Church's fighter took several direct hits from enemy ground fire and immediately burst into flames. Although mortally damaged, Church held his dive, released his bombs and completed his strafing pass across the field before crashing into the ground just beyond his targets.

Wagner continued his attack in the face of intense ground fire; he made a number of passes, blowing up several planes while setting others on fire and finally igniting a fuel dump. For this action he was awarded the Distinguished Service Cross. Several days after the attack on Vigan Field, Wagner scored his fifth aerial victory and became the first American ace in the Pacific theater in World War II. Pilot Officer William R. Dunn, an American flying with the Royal Air Force, became the first American World War II ace in August 1941.

Wagner deserved the respect of the younger pilots by virtue of his recent exploits, and perhaps even more so by virtue of his training. He was a graduate aeronautical engineer with an intense interest in flying and in aircraft. Quick to give him the credit and respect he deserved, George also wanted to give him some competition.

George was grabbing every opportunity to fly the P–40. He found formation flying in the P–40 to be much more difficult than in the AT–6. He was trying hard to acquire the habit of looking around in all directions for other aircraft, aircraft which soon could be enemy aircraft. He was convinced that surprise in the air could well be the difference between victory and defeat. George, like most of the top aces, had excellent eyesight but his ability to spot enemy aircraft was something he developed.

Captain Selman was transferred to the 9th Pursuit Squadron to take over as their commanding officer. George had talked to Selman in February about his desire to join the 9th. He reminded the captain of his desire when Selman was made commanding officer. The very next day, on March 5, George was assigned a P–40 to fly to Williamstown just north of Sydney where he joined the 9th. That evening Captain Buzz Wagner talked with the pilots of the 9th, and George was quite impressed. He wrote in his diary, "He knows airplanes and tactics inside-out. He is certainly no lucky pilot—he's the real thing! I have a lot of respect for a guy like that."

On March 7 twenty-three P–40s and one B–17 left Williamstown for Brisbane on the first leg of their journey to Darwin, about 450 miles north. After flying three-fourths of the way, the entire flight was forced to return due to bad weather. Only 1½ percent of the Australian continent had been mapped at the outbreak of World War II. Because of this and the unreliable compass used in the Kittyhawk, it was deemed necessary to use a mother ship such as a

B–17 to lead the small pursuit aircraft across the vast expanse of barren desert lands between Brisbane and Darwin.

On the tenth they tried for Brisbane again. George thought they would have to turn back because they were flying just over the top of the ocean to stay below the overcast. Even so, all ships continued on to Archer Field near Brisbane. Soon after arriving George noted that Brisbane had a bevy of beautiful girls and that if he should ever get leave he would spend it there.

The 9th Squadron stayed at Archer Field until all the P–40s could be fitted out with necessary equipment, new plugs installed, and other necessary maintenance performed. George flew his P–40 to Amberly to get the guns boresighted. On the thirteenth they left Brisbane for Charleville, about 400 miles west. They made this leg of the trip without incident. On the fourteenth the entire flight left Charleville for Cloncurry, over 500 miles northwest. Soon after departure, George's fighter developed an oil leak, forcing him to turn back. The leak was repaired quickly, and he followed a DC–2 most of the way to Cloncurry. He was most happy to be following another aircraft; the country he flew over was so desolate it was scary. He made his destination several hours behind the others. All of them were forced to spend the next day in Cloncurry because the B–17 mother ship had engine trouble. George noted that Cloncurry was like an oven all day long, and flies continually used humans as targets.

On the sixteenth, they flew to Daly Waters, another 600 miles northwest. George thought Cloncurry was bad until he arrived here. He said, "That's the worst place I've ever seen. It's just an airfield stuck out in the middle of nothing. The heat and flies are terrible. Luckily, the mosquitoes aren't bad; I had to sleep on the wing of my plane tonight. They told us we would be living with our airplanes, but I didn't expect it to mean this close!"

The lack of training in the P–40 proved to be a great hindrance to the 9th Pursuit Squadron. Of the twenty-five ships that left Williamstown headed for

*Preddy's housing at Darwin. A clearing cut out of the forest was typical for the area. Preddy can be seen inside his tent. One became very familiar with some of nature's strangest creations. Boots became overnight lodging for spiders and various types of snakes. R. Preddy Harris*

Darwin and the battle zone, only thirteen arrived safely on the seventeenth. The majority of those that didn't make it met with some accident attributable to lack of training. Some didn't make it due to mechanical failure.

And, coincidentally, on the day George reached Darwin, General MacArthur also arrived from the Philippines. His B-17 landed at Batchelor Field, sixty miles south of Darwin. Hearsay had it that the General brought two truckloads of furniture and a Chinese servant rather than some of the evacuating pilots and trained mechanics who were needed so badly. Perhaps more reliably, it has been reported that Capt. Frank Bostrom, a veteran B-17 pilot from Bangor, Maine, picked up the general and his party—comprised of his wife and son, the child's Chinese nurse, and Generals George and Sutherland—at Mindanoa and flew them to an airfield near Darwin. More about General George later.

Coming through the training period unscathed, George Preddy was now a full-fledged combat pilot. And that's what he wanted! Fortunately for the war effort, he and many others were eager to get into combat early. At this point, the new pilots averaged about fifteen hours of flying time in the Kittyhawk, hardly enough for the enemy to expect them to pose a real threat. The enemy was in for a real surprise.

By this time the Japanese had been successful in capturing refugees from Java in an air raid on Broome in western Australia. Lae and Salamaua in New Guinea had been seized; Rangoon had been evacuated by the British. Things were not going well for the Allies, to say the least!

George and the 9th moved to Batchelor Field on the eighteenth and had an alert soon after arriving. They all took off and flew back up to Darwin to intercept bombers, but it turned out to be a false alarm. The first night George slept in the woods near his P-40, the second night he slept in the rear end of a truck. The second day at Batchelor he scrambled to intercept seven Japanese bombers. It was *not* a false alarm this time; but the 9th got there about fifteen minutes too late to make the interception.

The air-raid warning system was still in the developmental stage—it worked fine in theory but not so good in practice. The radio locator was supposed to give an eighty mile warning, but due to technical difficulties, it was usually not functioning when needed. That allowed enemy bombers to slip in without detection. Warning of an air raid was more often than not sounded by antiaircraft guns firing.

Radar was nonexistent at this time, but American ingenuity and self-reliance was abundant. However, it was not until after George's tour that the Air Corps persuaded the army to place a ship equipped with radio about 150 miles off the coast of Darwin in the Timor Sea to transmit warnings of approaching enemy aircraft. With the new system, the slow-climbing Kittyhawks were able to get off the ground and obtain sufficient altitude in time to make interceptions possible. Sometimes, however, the enemy came in at altitudes beyond the effective capability of the P-40s. At 22,000 ft. the P-40 had to labor at full throttle to avoid a stall and was not responsive to the controls. Lt. Lawrence Smith, or Smitty as he was called, wrote about the high-altitude limitations of the Kittyhawk. He said, "I can recall sitting at 27,000 feet indicating 90 miles per hour and walking the stick all over the cockpit to keep from stalling out while an entire Japanese formation blithely sailed over Darwin three to five thousand feet above us. If you pulled the nose up for a squirt, the guns would surely stall you out!"

To make it even more difficult, the enemy fighter escort always came in above the bomber formation to ensure the altitude advantage. Tactics for the most part had to be limited to an occasional quick shot at a Zero after he had been decoyed down to an advantageous altitude. To stay with a Zero in a high-altitude dogfight was suicide. The Zero was far more maneuverable than the P-40; hence a defensive tactic called for a maximum speed dive which usually left the enemy behind. If he followed to a low altitude, as some occasionally did, he was usually met with an aggressive attack by a very maneuverable Kittyhawk in its own element.

By the end of March the pilots had set up tents to serve as their quarters. The 9th was still being called out on alerts, some of which were false. They also flew short patrols over Darwin and the adjoining coastline. On March 22, three veteran pilots who had already seen action in the Philippines and Java joined the 9th. Joseph J. Kruzel and Andrew J. Reynolds both became aces. Kruzel scored three kills in February while with the 17th Provisional Squadron before joining the 9th, and 3.5 more while with the 361st Fighter Group in the European theater in 1944. Reynolds had registered four in February with the 17th Squadron and added six more while with the 9th—all ten victories were scored in 1942. Ben S. Irvin was credited with two victories in February while with the 17th Squadron.

Lt. Clyde L. Harvey, Jr., and Lt. Stephen Poleschuk shot down a Japanese recon aircraft on March 22, 1942, the first aerial victory for the 9th Pursuit Squadron, sometimes known as the Iron Knights. Stephen Poleschuk was given full credit for destroying the recon aircraft, his only victory of the war. Clyde Harvey was credited with three victories, one on March 28, 1942, one on July 30, 1942, and his last on March 28, 1943—exactly one year from his first.

Capt. James C. Selman led his squadron on a wild flight hedgehopping all the way to Darwin. Upon their return to Batchelor Field, the 9th gave two correspondents from Sydney a good air show. Selman advanced rapidly, becoming a colonel when he took command of the 49th Fighter Group in July 1943 and holding that command until January 1944. (The 49th Pirsuit Group was redesignated 49th Fighter Group in mid-1942.)

On March 24 the squadron moved their aircraft to Royal Australian Air Force (RAAF) Field in Darwin and their officers to an evacuated hotel in Darwin. All civilians had evacuated and left hotels and apartments fully furnished. Now they had all the conveniences of home including running water and refrigerators. A large radio-phono was left in George's flat. He had had to dispose of his radio-phono earlier. Improvement of the camouflaged revetments for parked aircraft at RAAF Field, coupled with the better living conditions offered by the city, were the determining factors in the decision to move back to the port area. To avoid complete vulnerability, half the airplanes were flown back to Batchelor Field each day to stand alert.

The first ten days in the Northern Territory had been packed with excitement for George and colleagues. They had been called out on false alerts, delinquent on real alerts due to the poor warning system, and had flown a number of patrols over Darwin and the coastal areas. They had faced some real encounters, but George had yet to encounter the enemy. Others in the 49th Group had, so George was getting anxious.

The 7th Squadron, operating out of Horn Island just off the northernmost tip of Queensland, drew first blood for the 49th Pursuit Group when on March

*Unlike the European theater of operations (ETO) where most airfields had at least one building for service maintenance, all aircraft upkeep was performed in the open. Note the camouflage net above* Tarheel. R. Preddy Harris

14 one Japanese bomber and four Zeros were brought down in what sounds like a miraculous dogfight. The astonishing part of the battle occurred when Lieutenant A. T. House, wingman for Capt. Robert L. Morrissey, engaged his second victim for the day. With the Zero in his sights, House fired a short burst only to have his guns jam. As reported by the press, House then maneuvered his P-40 over the enemy aircraft and dipped his right wing tip into the enemy pilot's cockpit. The Zero plummeted to earth while House returned to base with about three feet of his wing tip missing. House, in the end, destroyed four enemy aircraft—the two just described and two more a year later while still assigned to the 7th.

While the 7th Squadron was making news in Queensland, the 8th was flying patrol missions around Melbourne in anticipation of air attacks on a huge convoy unloading in the harbor. Reports of a Japanese aircraft carrier operating somewhere in the waters south of Australia promulgated the patrols, which may have been an effective deterrent—the attacks never materialized!

Within the next month, all three squadrons of the 49th were flying together out of the Darwin area with all getting plenty of action—action against superior planes and pilots in vain efforts to prevent further bombing of the port area. Although the Kittyhawk boys found it almost impossible to stop the enemy bombers before they dropped their bombs, they were able to bring many of the enemy aircraft down by chasing them out to sea and catching them at lower altitudes. With their lives hanging in the balance, most of the green pilots were getting salty in a hurry. They were learning from the older and more experienced pilots, but actual experience against the enemy was clearly their best teacher.

30

Saburo Sakai, Japan's greatest fighter pilot to have survived the war, said in his book *Samurai!* that the Allied pilots were always screaming in to attack, regardless of the odds. He said that our fighter planes were clearly inferior in performance to their Zeros and that almost all the Japanese pilots at that time were skilled air veterans. He said, "The men we fought then were among the bravest I have ever encountered, no less so than our own pilots who, three years later, went out willingly on missions from which there was no hope of return."

The edge of Japanese superiority was fast waning, both in pilots and in aircraft. Our pilots were learning how to take advantage of the superior characteristics of the Kittyhawk—few as they were—and to avoid situations where she was at a distinct disadvantage. The encounters during the month of April provided ample evidence of these facts.

*Chapter 4*

# The Iron
# Knights of Darwin

Barely three months after graduating from flying school, George and his colleagues were involved in a struggle for supremacy over and revenge against the Japanese. Not only were they fighting against superior odds, in both Japanese pilots and aircraft, they were fighting the horrid environment of the Darwin area. The shoreline of that tropical region was fringed with impassable mangrove swamps; crocodile-infested tributaries extended deeply into the jungles from the Timor Sea. The ground crawled with huge ants, and mosquitoes bearing the germs of malaria, dengue and yellow fever filled the air.

During the dry season it was hot and dusty, during the wet season it was hot and muggy. There was no relief from the elements. While operating out of RAAF Field and living in Darwin, the elements of greatest concern were those exported by Japan—bombs dropped from Japanese bombers flying in high over the Timor Sea. At times the bombers stayed out of reach of our fighter interceptors, and at other times they came in undetected until it was too late to intercept.

March 28, 1942—Saturday
Seven Jap bombers hit RAAF Field at 12:30 PM. My flight was at Batchelor for the day and did not see them, but the boys at Darwin intercepted them on the way back to Koepang and knocked down two for sure and possibly disabled two more so that they didn't get home. Nobody was hurt by bombs.

Standing alert at Batchelor, George missed out on the action when Lt. Mitchell Zawisza led a flight of four P-40s from RAAF Field to intercept an unescorted flight of seven Japanese twin-engined bombers over Darwin. Again, the Kittyhawks were unable to prevent the Mitsubishi Type 97 bombers from dropping their payload, but as the bombers lost altitude in an effort to gain speed and make a fast departure from the target, Zawisza and his flight gave chase and caught the enemy about four miles out over the Timor Sea. The fight that ensued netted the American airmen credit for three bombers destroyed; Harvey got one and shared honors on a second with Sells, and Zawisza and Vaught shared credit for the third enemy casualty. US Air Force Historical Study Number 85, published in 1978 by the Office of Air Force History (hereinafter referred to as Study 85), gave Lt. Clyde Harvey, Lt. William Sells and Lt. Robert Vaught each credit for one victory on this mission. However, Lt. Mitchell Zawisza got his first official credit about one month later, 27 April 1942.

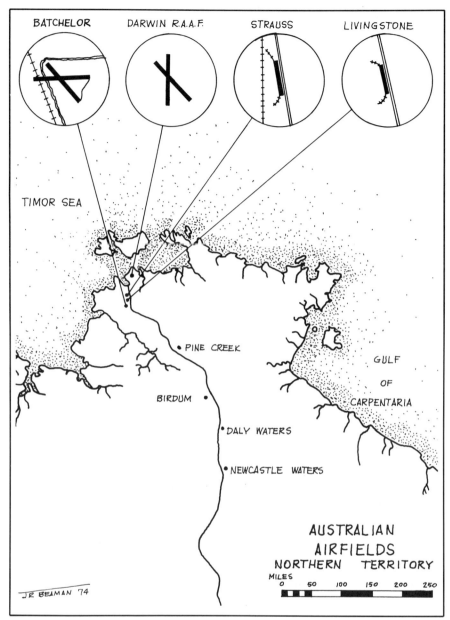

BATCHELOR    DARWIN R.A.A.F.    STRAUSS    LIVINGSTONE

TIMOR SEA

• PINE CREEK

BIRDUM •

GULF

OF

CARPENTARIA

• DALY WATERS

• NEWCASTLE WATERS

AUSTRALIAN
AIRFIELDS
NORTHERN    TERRITORY
MILES
0    50    100    150    200    250

JR BEAMAN '74

*Australian Airfields, Northern Territory:*
*Batchelor, Darwin RAAF, Strauss and*
*Livingstone.*

March 30, 1942—Monday
    RAAF Field was bombed again today. We went up about 15 minutes before
they arrived to intercept them, but were hit at 11,000 feet from above by a flight
of Zeros. Neither side lost anything, but McComsey had to bail out. I had a
perfect shot at a Zero, but missed by not turning one gun switch on.

Even the green pilots of the 9th Squadron were proving to be too much for unescorted Japanese bombers. After losing almost half their flight of bombers on April 28, the Japanese decided to send along an escort of six Zeros on the thirtieth. That encounter was the first for the 9th against the superior Zero fighter. The tactic proved valuable to the Japanese; they didn't lose a fighter or bomber on the thirtieth and succeeded in destroying one of our P–40s and damaging two others.

Here's how the squadron later reported the action. George and seven other pilots of the 9th took off at 1400 hours and patrolled for thirty minutes, then returned to base for refueling. While being refueled, they received an alert and took off again to intercept the approaching enemy formation. One of the eight P–40s returned to base with engine trouble. At 11,000 ft. the other seven Kittyhawks were hit from above by six Zeros. While the Zeros occupied the American fighters, the enemy bombers dropped their bombs and made a successful escape. During the dogfight, Porter's tail assembly was badly damaged by enemy fire, McComsey had to abandon his bullet-riddled plane, and the ship flown by Sells was also damaged by enemy fire. McComsey bailed out, landing in the swamps, and made it back to the base—but only after a frightful night. Sells and Porter got their planes back to base safely. George and three others escaped the wrath of the more experienced Zero pilots, a skillful feat in itself.

March 31, 1942—Tuesday
   Seven bombers and about 16 Zeros hit here. The field was bombed again but no damage was done. Reynolds shot a Zero off somebody's tail. McComsey came in after a harrowing experience in the swamps. Three bombers bombed for the first time at night.

Apparently the Japanese intelligence was functioning most efficiently in northern Australia, or perhaps coincidence was in their favor. The ground personnel and other support people assigned to the 9th Squadron arrived after a long overland journey. The last leg of the journey was by rail from Birdum to Batchelor where they unloaded the trucks and drove to Camp Connelly, a part of the RAAF complex. No more than five minutes after most of the trucks arrived, bombs began dropping on the airfield. The bombers were escorted this time by ten Zeros; only one was brought down and by one of the more experienced American pilots, Andrew Reynolds. Ack-ack thrown up by Aussie ground forces accounted for one bomber.

April 2, 1942—Thursday
   Experienced first raid from close range. Japs couldn't see the field due to cloud cover so dropped their load in town. We were in a slit trench in back of the house, and several bombs fell near us. Had a meeting of all pilots tonight.
   Sanford came in after two weeks in the wilderness. He went down in water near Thursday Island after an attack on Zeros and was picked up by the missionary and aborigines.

Clarence E. Sanford had bailed out of his P–40 during the incredible dogfight over Horn Island when A. T. House rammed a Zero. Sanford was picked out of the water some 300 miles southwest of Horn Island by aborigines and, with their help and the assistance of the missionary serving the area, finally made it back to camp. The aborigines were described by the first white

34

men who studied them as the "miserablest on earth"; Sanford was undoubtedly among the first white men to challenge that opinion!

April 3, 1942—Friday
Maj. Hutchinson flew in with Lt. Prentice and two pilots who were in the Philippines. The captain who was along was shot down in the Philippines and has quite a story about coming down in a river in his chute and Zeros blazing away at him all the way down, even in the water. Japs were on one side of the river and Americans on the other, so he swam to the American side while the Japs took pot shots at him.

April 4, 1942—Saturday
We gave the Japs the prettiest surprise they ever had today. When they came over with seven bombers and three Zeros at 23,000 feet, we had a flight of seven P-40s at 26,000 feet waiting for them. When they left there were only two bombers and one Zero. Reynolds is becoming quite an ace, adding a bomber and a Zero to his credit. Gardner was hit by our own ack-ack and bailed out. Livingstone overshot on a forced landing after the combat and was killed when his engine cut out.

One of the airfields—34-Mile Strip—was later named for Lieutenant Livingstone because he was the first pilot killed in action there.

After missing his first chance at a Zero a few days earlier by failing to turn on one of his gun switches, George missed his second opportunity by being in the right place but at the wrong time. His flight was airborne but too late to contact the enemy.

During the next several weeks enemy action slowed to a trickle. Easter passed almost without notice. The group commanding officer, Wurtsmith, was promoted to lieutenant colonel and arrived in Darwin. George said in his diary, "We can expect to see things running in good fashion now." The lull allowed time for walking on the beach, swimming, playing tennis and volleyball, training flights and other fun things. George was pleased to be transferred into Joe Kruzel's flight just before the 9th Squadron moved out of Darwin to 34-Mile Strip. A camp had been built while the pilots operated out of Darwin. The camp was built in the woods next to the airstrip. George shared a tent with McComsey, Driver and Smith. They brought beds and other furnishings from the hotel in Darwin and made their tent fairly comfortable. But, as luck would have it, they started getting heavy rains in the Northern Territory during the so-called dry season. The pilots were getting bored.

April 25, 1942—Saturday
Japs raided RAAF Field this afternoon with 24 bombers and nine Zeros. The 8th Squadron caught them on the way home and shot down eight bombers and two Zeros. The 7th accounted for one Zero—we got none! None of our pilots was lost although one of our planes cracked up while landing.

Again, George missed out on the action, the first action since April 5 when the Japs came over so high the P-40s could not reach them. On this, the largest raid on Darwin since the opening onslaught in February, the Japs sent their formations of twenty-four bombers and nine Zeros directly into the face of a recently augmented American force. With the addition of the 7th and 8th squadrons to the Darwin area, there were fifty Kittyhawks ready and waiting to bounce the enemy aircraft.

Tarheel *was later numbered "85." The name was removed from the right side of nacelle and a fire-breathing dragon was added. All members of Capt.*

Joseph J. Kruzel's "Dragon" flight *sported this unique scheme. Preddy's crew chief was Corporal Yates.* E. R. McDowell

Two flights from George's squadron returned from a patrol just five minutes before the enemy formation was reported. A third flight of five P-40s from the 9th, just finishing their patrol, spotted the enemy. The Kittyhawks were so short of fuel they were able to make only one pass before returning to base.

The other two flights from the 49th were more fortunate. The 8th won the honors by destroying ten bombers and one Zero; the 7th downed one Zero. No American pilots were lost, but Lieutenant Morehead had to make a belly landing when his gear failed to extend after the melee. After destroying three bombers, the most for an individual pilot that day, Morehead's skill and luck didn't fail him. He was not injured in the crash.

At this point in his combat career, George was becoming disturbed. His buddies were knocking enemy planes down while he sat on the ground, was in the wrong place in the air, or made a mistake! He had botched his first chance at a Zero, and so far hadn't gotten another. He took little solace in the fact that there were more pilots in George's category than were in the victorious class; he wanted very badly to get another crack at an enemy aircraft—a successful crack.

April 27, 1942—Monday
Japs raided RAAF Field about noon. We sighted the bombers and headed to intercept them when Zeros hit us at 19,000 feet. I was engaged in two different fights with them but could not get a decent shot at them. Zawisza and Taylor both knocked down Zeros. Total for the Group was six bombers and three Zeros. The 8th lost one pilot and possibly three more. Andrew is unaccounted for in the 7th.

George took off on alert at 0900 hours with Kruzel's Dragon flight of four ships only to find they had been sent out on a false alarm. At 1140 hours, they were again ordered off with another flight, eight P-40s in all. This time there was nothing false about the alert. Two waves of nine bombers each escorted by an equal number of Zeros—thirty-six enemy aircraft—made the attack. The enemy was met by the entire 49th Group. George encountered the enemy at 19,000 ft. where he engaged two different aircraft and damaged both. But he couldn't get off killing shots at either one of them. Zawisza got one for sure and Taylor was given credit for a probable.

This time the 49th didn't escape unharmed as they had two days earlier. Owen Fish of the 8th was killed when his damaged aircraft crashed into Fanny Bay; Captain Strauss died when his P-40 crashed near Swires Bluff in the port area. The airfield from which the 8th Squadron operated was later named in his honor. Lt. Stephen W. Andrew of the 7th Squadron bailed out into the sea about five miles from shore after an engagement with a Zero; Lt. Harold J. Martin made a forced landing near the beach after being attacked by two Zeros. Both pilots were rescued. Against this relatively heavy toll, the 49th accounted for three bombers and four Zeros in the final tally.

April 30, 1942—Thursday
Probably one of the best pursuit pilots and greatest authorities on pursuit in the world, Brigadier General George was killed at Batchelor late yesterday afternoon along with Lt. Jasper and a war correspondent for LIFE and TIME [Melville Jacoby] when a P-40 ran off the runway on takeoff and hit them.
Sid Woods is back after a month in the hospital due to a crack up at Daly Waters.

Brigadier General George and Melville Jacoby were in a transport plane, having just arrived for an inspection of the Darwin area. Lieutenant Jasper, adjutant and weather officer for the group, was parked in a jeep near the transport plane. The P-40 hit both the transport plane and the jeep. Gen. Joe Moore was the pilot of General George's plane, and Lt. Jack Donalson was flying co-pilot. Donalson said they pulled off the runway onto a hardstand to await the takeoff of two P-40s. One of the P-40s hit their plane and killed General George, Jacoby and two others. Donalson joined the 9th Pursuit Squadron at this time.

April was marked by the dismal surrender of General Wainwright's forces on the Bataan Peninsula, and by the air battles over Darwin; the latter captured much less attention than the escape of Wainwright's remnant force to Corregidor. Later in the month, Doolittle made his famous raid on Tokyo, an accomplishment that did much more for the spirit and morale of the American troops—and citizens back home—than it did damage to the largest of Japanese cities.

Gaining much valuable combat experience during his first month and a half in the battle-stricken area of Darwin had brought George face to face with death and the horrible realities of war. The experience was destined to pay off against the Germans rather than the Japanese. George managed to subjugate the verity of it all, a quality necessary to a sane mind. His singleness of purpose accounted in no small measure for his ability to keep harsh reality subservient to his desire to fly.

All three squadrons of the 49th Pursuit Group were now in the Darwin area. George and the 9th Squadron were occupying a strip cut out of the jungle near a cattle ranch named Humpty Doo. The 7th and 8th squadrons were near ranches called Koolpinya and Burrundie. All three strips were located near the road running south from Darwin; for this reason the airstrips picked up names indicating their distance from the port city. For example, 34–Mile Strip was near Humpty Doo.

The camp at Humpty Doo was hacked out of virgin brush. The runway ran parallel to the road with inserts for parking the Kittyhawks on either end of the airstrip. The center of social activity in the camp was the Officer's Mess, a hut with a concrete floor, tin roof, open on all sides for ventilation, mess table and benches, and some easy chairs looted from Hotel Darwin by persons unknown. George contributed his phonograph and records when they arrived. They had a radio, cards, cribbage board, checkers and chess game. Dispersed under the trees for safety were the tents, each housing three or four pilots. Also cunningly blended with the jungle verdure were the landing strip and inserts.

There were four pilots in each flight and each pilot had an assigned aircraft. The schedule of operations called for one flight to stand by for immediate takeoff, a second flight to be ready for a five-minute alert, a third prepared for a fifteen-minute alert and the fourth flight was off duty for the day. Each flight had its alert hut located near the inserts where the aircraft were parked. The huts were equipped with field telephones; a short ring they answered, long rings were drowned out by the roar of Allison engines as pilots scrambled to gain as much altitude as possible before encountering the enemy. Every second counted. Life or death often hung on a thousand feet more or a thousand feet less—five seconds sooner or five seconds later.

The worst air tragedy to date occurred about ten days earlier when a transport plane carrying ten enlisted men, a pilot and copilot crashed and burned six miles from Burrundie. The aircraft, bound for Darwin from Archer Field, arrived after dark and was unable to locate RAAF Field before running out of fuel. All men aboard were killed in the crash.

May 4, 1942—Monday
Shorty, Duck-Butt, Woods and I took a flight this afternoon. Did some formation flying, rat-racing and shooting. Had a good bull session in the tent over a bottle of scotch.

James Watkins was nicknamed Duck-Butt in flying school. As he relates it, he was in a flight of six to eight students in primary flight school and had "a little old Yankee flight instructor named Clipson from Cincinnati who was 5 feet 4½ inches tall." Watkins was the shortest man in his flight at 5 ft. 6 in. Watkins had never flown before primary flight school, but several other students had. So those who had prior flight experience soloed before Watkins. And just as Watkins built up enough flight time to solo, he caught a bad cold and was put in the infirmary for a couple of days. When he came out of the infirmary, the other students in his flight had soloed. But Watkins had to take a couple more rides before his instructor would let him solo.

He was walking out to the flight line with Clipson, who was carrying his parachute with straps slung over his shoulder and goggles up on his forehead. Cadets who had soloed were also allowed to put their goggles on their foreheads and their parachutes up over their buttocks so the chute wouldn't bump the backs of their knees. Cadets who had not soloed had to wear their goggles slung around their necks and their parachutes slung below their buttocks. So here was Watkins walking out to the airplane with his chute bumping the backs of his knees and his goggles hanging down his back, when a guy behind him named Shubric—an awful crass Yankee-type person as described by Watkins—said, "Hey, Shorty." Clipson said nothing and Watkins said nothing. Shubric called out again, "Hey, Shorty," and Clipson told Watkins to answer him. Watkins said, "That's not my name, sir." Then Shubric said, "Hey, Duck-Butt," and Clipson said to me, "You better answer him, mister, because I know damn well that's not me." So Watkins had to turn around and answer the crass Yankee, and everybody on the flight line saw and heard the exchange. So it was Duck-Butt from then on for James Watkins.

Watkins went on to become one of the leading aces of the 9th Fighter Squadron with twelve victories. He got his first one in December 1942 and his last one on 2 April 1945.

May 5, 1942—Tuesday
The funny thing about the war for us here at Darwin is that for two or three days the Nips keep us busy as hell and fighting like mad; then, for two or three weeks we are seemingly forgotten and this is the most peaceful place in the world. We don't have enough to do at these times and get lazy eating, sleeping and lying around. It has been a life of ease for the past week. The weather hasn't been too hot during the day, and has been wonderful at night.

May 18, 1942—Monday
Ran patrols all day due to a number of B–17s being at Batchelor. They left this morning on a mission, probably to bomb a Jap harbor. Our flight ran two patrols getting a total of two hours and twenty minutes. Ship isn't running as good as it should. Certainly not Yates' (his crew chief) fault. Probably a piss-poor engine to begin with.

May 19, 1942—Tuesday
OD today. It's a merry job carrying lunch to the pilots and picking them up after they land. Band from 147th Field Artillery played here again tonight.

Hutchinson sat in on the drums and did a beautiful job. Saw a lot of pilots from the 7th as they were sleeping at Headquarters. They had given their beds to the B–17 pilots. Nine B–17s raided Koepang yesterday and did slight damage. They are leaving before dawn tomorrow for another raid.

Donald R. Hutchinson took command of the 49th Fighter Group in November 1942 relieving Paul B. Wurtsmith. Both remained in the air force after the war and retired as major generals.

May 20, 1942—Wednesday
Was up over Batchelor nearly two hours on patrol. We sighted a single ship at 27,000 feet but were unable to catch him. Believe it was a P–40. Spent the morning washing. Some job!
B–17s bombed Koepang again today. Got a bomber on the field and possibly a ship in the harbor.
May 26, 1942—Tuesday
Pilots played the Armament Section in softball this afternoon and beat them 16–8. Gardner ran into Donalson fielding a ground ball and is believed to have broken Donalson's nose.

I. B. Jack Donalson played an important role in George's career as we will see later. He also became an ace with five victories. He got three kills while with the 21st Squadron flying out of the Philippines—two on 8 December 1941 and one on 9 December—immediately following the disaster at Pearl Harbor, Donalson was flying one of the last two aircraft out of Bataan the night it fell to the enemy. Gen. Joe Moore flew the other one; they flew south as the Japanese approached their field. When they reached Australia, Donalson was assigned to fly copilot for General Moore. His last two victories came in June and July of 1942 while with the 9th Squadron.

When asked about his recollections of George Preddy in 1981, Donalson had many. He said, "George liked to gamble. He'd get loaded and join a game of craps. He liked craps especially. And that's when George used the expression, *cripes a'mighty*. He'd roll the dice and holler *cripes a'mighty*. He lived like tonight was going to be his last night, and that's just the way he lived. He was wild; when he got drunk he would get mean. But I could always handle George. We were good friends in the Pacific and I pulled him out of the jungle when he crashed." (More will be said about this incident later.) "So when George would get belligerent I would say, 'Now George, you've had enough'; he'd want to fight but I'd get him off to bed. The next morning he was raring to go and sorry he had caused any trouble. You know, he was kind of a little guy, but tougher than a boot. He could lick the world, especially when he was drunk. When I saw he was getting in trouble, I'd say, 'Come on now, George, let's straighten up,' and he would. I think George looked on me as his big brother, or something."

May 30, 1942—Saturday
Had a good squadron flight first thing this morning. Flew over to Darwin at 10,000 feet with 15 other ships. After we landed, Fighter Sector called and said the anti-aircraft were loaded and getting their range to fire when we turned away. Would be humiliating to be shot down by your own ack-ack.
June 3, 1942—Wednesday

On alert today. Spent an hour and forty minutes diving, bombing and strafing machine gun pits in and around Darwin. It was lots of fun and darn good practice. Learned more than I have in the past month.

Driver got orders to report to a transport outfit. Hate to see him leave, but if he doesn't want pursuit, he's doing the right thing.

Taylor is back from Melbourne and is now in our flight in place of Angel. Kruzel and Taylor had a dog fight with Mike and I this morning. We were up on patrol this afternoon when Ed Miller was killed. His ship dived into the ground, apparently caused when he passed out from lack of oxygen.

June 8, 1942—Monday

Had another squadron flight this morning. The more I fly with Kruzel the better I like him as a flight leader. Not only a good pilot, but a good leader and a good man to have nearby in combat.

Final claim off Midway Island is 15 Jap warships. Fleet was forced to withdraw to home base.

George recognized a good man when he worked with him. Joseph J. Kruzel joined the 361st Fighter Group in the ETO after completing his tour in the Pacific. He became the group executive officer there, and destroyed three and a half more enemy aircraft, bringing his total credits to six and a half. He went on to become a major general before he retired in 1970.

It had now been over one month since George had encountered the enemy. During this time, he had been up on a few alerts and patrol missions, but most importantly he had gained some valuable flying experience in the P-40.

The Japanese concentrated their raids on Port Moresby and Chittagong during May and part of June; Allied raids during this period included targets at Rabaul, Gasmata, Koepang, and Rangoon. With the slackened pace caused by the enemy's diversionary tactics, George found time to relax—too much time—but he made good use of it. Besides the time he spent writing—writings that have never been found—he read, played games and worked out on the horizontal bar.

A major event during May was the Battle of the Coral Sea. Naval and air battles of the Solomon Islands resulted when the Japanese invasion fleet was

*Rare in-flight photograph of George in his P-40E, named* Tarheel *for his native state of North Carolina. Artwork ap-* *peared initially on both sides of aircraft.* USAAF via E. R. McDowell

41

intercepted by US naval and air forces. The battle moved to the Coral Sea where it lasted for two days until the Japanese withdrew to the north, presumably to join their main forces. Seven major enemy combat ships were sunk and about twenty were damaged. The United States lost the aircraft carrier *Lexington,* one destroyer and one tanker.

While the Japanese attacks were being directed toward targets other than Darwin, the 49th Pursuit Group changed its name to the 49th Fighter Group. The breather also allowed time for them to tally their victories:

|           | Zero | Bomber | Recon | Total |
|-----------|------|--------|-------|-------|
| 7th FS    | 6    | 1      | 0     | 7     |
| 8th FS    | 3    | 13     | 0     | 16    |
| 9th FS    | 4    | 10     | 1     | 15    |
| 49th FG Total | 13 | 24   | 1     | 38    |

Not a bad score for such a short period of combat and so little training. Better than the score of victories is the other side of the balance sheet—the American losses. Not counting the many noncombat losses, the 49th had lost seven aircraft and three pilots in combat action.

At this time in his flying career, George could lay claim to damaging two enemy aircraft, a Zero and a Mitsubishi bomber which he encountered on April 27. He hadn't even started his march toward acedom because damaged aircraft didn't count.

The American system of recognizing pilots' accomplishments during World War II varied among the combat areas around the world. The Flying Tigers in China and the Eagle Squadrons in Britain counted only airplanes shot down in air-to-air combat. The American units taking over the Flying Tigers' job in the China-Burma-India theater and the Eighth Air Force units receiving the Americans of the Eagle Squadrons credited enemy aircraft destroyed on the ground and in the air. The reason for giving credit for aircraft destroyed on the ground was that the enemy—both Japanese and German— often refused to send their fighters up to meet the Americans, saving their planes for special missions. Consequently, the Americans changed their tactics; they started strafing enemy planes parked on their airfields. And we soon discovered that while the parked enemy aircraft were sitting ducks, the intensity of flak and antiaircraft defenses made the dangers of this task greater than those faced in air-to-air combat.

The procedure adopted in the European theater of operations (ETO) required all pilots encountering the enemy to write a report describing the circumstances and any peculiarities noticed during the engagement. It was on these reports that pilots registered claims for enemy aircraft destroyed or damaged. In the isolated battle area of northern Australia during the first few months of the war, the Army Air Corps had not organized themselves sufficiently to have such procedures. Written statements or even verbal comments were made a matter of record for special missions netting a loss of aircraft on either side. But damaged enemy aircraft were ignored for scorekeeping purposes.

During the long lull since the last action against the enemy, the pilots of the 49th got more flying experience and training in fighter tactics—both badly needed. But the keen edge honed by continuous combat had worn dull. George, for one, took advantage of all opportunities to fly and that gave him experience that would eventually pay off in the ETO.

June 13, 1942—Saturday

Japs raided RAAF Field at noon with 27 bombers and 10 to 12 Zeros. Our flight was unable to intercept them. The 8th came within two thousand feet of the formation but were chased away by the higher Zeros. The 8th lost four ships but they believe all pilots are safe. Johnson took five bullets in the left arm and shoulder. Captain Van Auken is missing. Quite a 'MacArthur Day' celebration.

Lt. Clarence T. Johnson, Jr., of the 7th Squadron was found after five days in the mangrove swamps without food. He was picked up by a navy boat he spotted coming down the river. Van Auken returned safely, although he received burns when he bailed out. He landed on Melville Island and was brought back by the aborigines on June 17.

June 14, 1942—Sunday

Reynolds' flight was up on patrol when they spotted about 20 Zeros at 19,000 feet. They made one pass from 26,000 feet and Landers and Donalson each got one. Our flight was up twice but didn't make contact.

Gave my new engine a 15-minute hop this afternoon. She's a honey!

John D. Landers had a highly successful Army Air Force career; his final tally was 14.5 aerial and 20 ground victories. On April 4th he got two aerial kills that escaped George's notice in his diary. Landers scored a total of six victories while with the 9th, and the remainder in the European theater. The last four aerial victories were claimed with the 78th Fighter Group, three in March 1945. He finished his career as a colonel commanding the 78th, flying the now-famous *Big Beautiful Doll* which is memorialized as a restored P–51D in the aircraft collection at the Imperial War Museum, Duxford Airfield, England.

June 15, 1942—Monday

Heavy bombers, about 27 of them, dropped their load on the town at noon. Our flight went in to attack just before they reached their target but we were attacked from above by several Zeros. We were forced to dive out but Manning's flight caught them from above. After the enemy turned west, Manning and McComsey got one Zero each with Peterson and Fowler getting one between them. Taylor damaged one and the 7th got another. My ship was hit in three places. Otherwise the squadron received no damage.

June 16, 1942—Tuesday

Again, 27 bombers with Zero escort attacked. Zawisza, Porter, Ball and I followed them about 50 miles out to sea but did not hit them. Reynolds claimed two bombers and Landers and Sauber each got a Zero. Reynolds was forced down with a bullet through his oil cooler. McComsey landed wheels up with his rudder and trim controls shot up and hydraulic system shot out. Also, he had a bullet through his seat pack. Three pilots are missing from the 8th.

Six of our pilots left for a 10–day leave this afternoon.

The month-long period of peace and tranquillity was broken by four days of heavy concentrated attacks on Darwin. With the exception of the second raid, which was a reconnaissance mission by Zeros only, all attacks were made by twenty-seven bombers with Zero escort. These were the heaviest raids since February. The downtown and dock areas bore the brunt of the bombing with the loss of two oil storage tanks, the Bank of New South Wales, railroad spurs, electric lines and several buildings, including the newspaper office.

During those four days, George encountered the enemy only once. That time came very close to being his last. Although not intentional, the flight George was in acted as decoys by drawing the Zeros down from their advantageous altitude. But with the Zeros coming in from above, his flight had to take the prescribed evasive action—dive for the deck! That's when Manning's flight hit the attacking Zeros from above. But as George's P-40 screamed for the deck in a power dive, one of the pursuing Zeros put three bullet holes in *Tarheel*. The damage was not serious and he had no problem making it back to the field safely.

June 19, 1942—Friday

Apparently we didn't do a bad job when the Japs visited. Tokyo admits to loss of 17 planes during the four-day engagement, so evidently lots of their ships didn't get home that we didn't know about since we only claimed 12 enemy aircraft destroyed. We lost 12 ships and one pilot from our Group. Our Squadron lost two aircraft, Reynolds' and Mac's.

Got a letter from home. Bill [Preddy] enters Texas A&M this month.

It was quite unusual during World War II to have the enemy (Germany or Japan) admit to more losses than the Allied pilots claimed. On the contrary, both Allied and enemy pilots usually claimed more than they actually got. The reason is quite simple, especially in Europe. A victim's aircraft often disappeared into clouds after being hit, perhaps leaving a trail of smoke. But occasionally that aircraft would make it to safety.

June 20, 1942—Saturday

Had a good flight this afternoon with just the four ships in our flight.

Crew of five who had been given up for lost wandered back to civilization the other day after almost two months in the wilderness and hostile Abo country.

Harris was in the bush three days before he was picked up. He had begun to eat grasshoppers and was seriously considering owl meat.

June 26, 1942—Friday

General Brett and three lesser generals plus colonels and all kinds of other rank were here today. We had a good bull session tonight at Headquarters led by two colonels just over from Washington. They gave a general picture of the Air Corps set-up and types of airplanes being produced. Also, they gave us the low down on the Midway battle and the Tokyo bombing. Learned that Tokyo was bombed by 25 B-25s which took off from aircraft carriers and landed in Russia and China.

June 27, 1942—Saturday

Found out yesterday that December (1941) was a pretty fouled up month in the States. Among other things, the Army now finds it was a great mistake to send green pilots just out of school into combat. I am thankful I lived through the first stage as I feel now I am a little better prepared having learned from actual experience how to take care of myself up there. There is something to be learned on each combat mission and I am just a beginner.

June 29, 1942—Monday

Woods and Lanier were in Batchelor today flying co-pilot on B-17s. Saw them tonight and had quite a session. They flew over here coming by way of Africa and India. They were in Java during the latter days of that fracas. Tomorrow they go on a mission 700 miles north of the Celebes. Their target is a field with 75 Zeros and 25 heavy bombers, so they say. Here's hoping for some good hits.

George noted on July 1st, "The B-17s found 150 planes lined up wing to wing in the Celebes. They blasted hell out of a third of them. It's a pity there were only five B–17s. Should have been ten times as many. One pilot came back on two engines and a third one failed 30 miles out from Batchelor, so he piled up and two enlisted crewmen were killed. The ship burned." Compare this raid to some launched in the ETO from England—hundreds of bombers with fighter escort were dispatched on many of those missions. For example, the first large-scale American daylight raid on Berlin was made on 6 March 1944—814 heavy bombers (B–17s and B–24s) with 943 fighters (P–38, P–47s and P–51s) were launched.

Sidney S. Woods went on to fly 112 missions from Darwin, Port Moresby and Buna, destroying one Zero and one Betty bomber. Like George, he was transferred to the European theater of operations following his tour in the southwest Pacific. He joined the 479th Fighter Group in England in April 1944 and flew one tour; he got one ground victory during this time. He came back for another tour of duty in February 1945 and joined the 4th Fighter Group. This was his most successful tour; he got five FW 190s in the air and four more enemy aircraft while strafing. Sid Woods was shot down in April 1945 while strafing near Prague, Czechoslovakia. He was taken prisoner.

July 8, 1942—Wednesday
General Brett was here today and awarded medals for distinguished service. About six DFCs and a dozen Silver Stars were given. Kruzel, Reynolds and Pvt. Garvey got Silver Stars. Two Purple Hearts were given for wounds received in combat.

After concentrating almost solely on Port Moresby during May, the Japanese divided their offensive about equally between Moresby and Darwin in June. Besides Koepang, enemy-held cities of Rabaul, Lae, Salamaua, Tulagi in the Solomons, and others received the attentions of Allied bombers.

With the increasing intensity and frequency of Allied attacks on enemy strongholds, it appeared unlikely that the Japanese would get back to Darwin with an appreciable force. Therefore, plans were being laid for a possible change of station—probably Port Moresby. And George was hoping to take a leave in southern Australia before the change occurred.

# Chapter 5

# The Sun Is My Undoing

It happened at about dinnertime. George went up on a training mission with his flight of four. He and Lt. Richard Taylor were the guinea pigs; they simulated enemy bombers while Lt. Jack Donalson and Lt. John Sauber made practice passes at them.

Donalson was flying Sauber's wing when the accident occurred. On one of his passes, Sauber's P-40 collided with George's, hitting it just behind the cockpit. Sauber had misjudged his attack; perhaps the sun got in his eyes. Donalson later recalled that Sauber was too close to George when he started his pass; he should have been a bit higher and farther away. Whatever the cause, Sauber was unable to get out of his aircraft but fortunately George bailed out of his—but with some difficulty.

Donalson and Taylor circled until George landed. Then they returned to base to lead help to the crash site. Back at 34-Mile Strip, Capt. Ben Irvin had gotten word of the accident over the radio. He jumped into a crash truck with a war correspondent, the famous Lucien Hubbard, Hollywood producer and originator of the *Andy Hardy* series. Hubbard was there on sabbatical leave at the request of some Army brass. Donalson, Taylor, Irvin, and Hubbard raced to the crash site.

They charged off along a dirt road through the bush, missing tree trunks by mere inches. They knew that only about thirty minutes of daylight remained and the crash had occurred about twenty miles northeast of the Strip. If they were to get George out that day, they had to do it before dark. There would be little chance of finding him without daylight.

Irvin finally turned off the dirt road and went through real bush country for some distance until they couldn't go any farther. Irvin jammed on the brakes and the four jumped out and started running to the spot where a plane was circling overhead to mark George's location. There were only a few more minutes of daylight remaining. The rescue party ran for at least a half mile through the bush. Carabaos and kangaroos crashed off through the jungle in alarm. Then they caught a glimpse of something white halfway up the ridge and raced for it. It was George lying on his parachute. He had landed in thick bush not thirty feet from a huge anthill. He had come down through a tree, hitting a branch on the way down. The branch gouged a deep hole in his calf and cut his hip and shoulder badly. Immediately after disentangling himself from his shroud line, his greatest worry was the nearby anthill. They grow large ants in Australia, and what they can do to a wounded man is frightening to think about.

He was bleeding badly but was not unconscious. He had bandaged himself using his first-aid kit. His first comment to Irvin was, "Looks like you owe me dough, Irvin. I bet I'd be the first one to date one of those new nurses down at Adelaide River."

Lt. John S. Sauber was killed when his
P-40 collided with George's P-40 on
July 12, 1942, during a training flight.

Note that the censor has overpainted
forward canopy area to obscure details
of the gunsight. E. R. McDowell

Upon Hubbard's return to the States, he wrote about the accident in an article entitled "The Fighters at Humpty Doo." A condensed version of the story was published in *Reader's Digest* giving George his first taste of international publicity.

John Sauber, according to Hubbard, had been reading *The Sun Is My Undoing* the day before the fatal accident. Maybe it was. Maybe the sun got in his eyes as he simulated that last dive on George from 20,000 ft. In 1987 a retired RAAF airman, now an aviation historian, R. N. Alford, set out to find the remains of Preddy's P-40 called *Tarheel*, Serial 41-5509. He found it and also found Sauber's aircraft. At our request he sent relics from Preddy's aircraft to the Greensboro (North Carolina) Historical Museum where they are displayed.

July 13, 1942—Monday
    What a day this has been! Just lying in bed cut all up and stiff as a board. At least, I'm thankful to be here at all. Sure sorry about Sauber. My right hip is cut about off and there is a big gouge in my left calf. Also my right shoulder is cut up. Sure lucky!

Just how much of the damage was done by the tree and how much was done during the crash and subsequent escape from his aircraft was not even clear to George. It all happened so fast and his survival reactions were undoubtedly driven by adrenaline racing through his body.

With nothing to do but lie on his cot in the tent, George had lots of time to think—time to reminisce and time to plan for the future. Less than satisfied with his past, he wanted to improve the future! While waiting to be transferred to the hospital, George wrote in the back of his diary thirteen rules he wanted to live by:

1. No smoking at any time or under any circumstances.
2. Drink intelligently and sparingly.
3. Eat sensibly.
4. Exercise regularly and diligently.
5. Learn all possible about flying or any other job at hand.
6. Always be willing to go out of the way to learn something new.
7. Always try to give the other man a boost.
8. Fight hardest when down and never give up.
9. Don't make excuses but make up with deeds of action.
10. Learn by experience.
11. Listen to others and profit by criticism.
12. Live a clean life.
13. Trust in God and never lose faith in Him.

George E. Preddy, Jr.
July 18, 1942

George, six other patients, a doctor and an orderly took off from Batchelor on July 20th, making it as far as Alice Springs where they spent the night in an Australian hospital. The following day they flew to Adelaide; they spent the night in an old warehouse which was being used as a hospital. There was no heat whatsoever, so the patients were kept warm with layers of blankets and hot water bottles. The following day they made the last leg of their long journey arriving in Melbourne where they were taken to a big new hospital that had been taken over by the US Army. George remained bedridden until July 28. That night the nurses helped him get in a wheelchair so that he could go downstairs and watch a movie. The hospital provided regular entertainment for patients including movies, concerts, and plays.

*The multiple wounds George sustained to his leg were most painful. It would take George three months to recover sufficiently to be transferred home for R and R. R. Preddy Harris*

George made daily entries in his diary during his recuperation period. Each entry was brief, but when taken as a whole the entries are quite interesting. They tell a story of what a wounded soldier on the mend in Australia thought about, what he read, and the company he kept. That story is summarized below.

During his first two weeks in the Melbourne hospital, he met Joan Jackson and her friend June. Joan and June made frequent visits to the hospital to cheer up patients and take them goodies. George also kept up with news of the war and other things. He noted in his diary that for the first time since the 49th Pursuit Group arrived in Darwin, the alert of a raid came sufficiently in advance to allow the P-40s to take off and gain an advantageous altitude. This permitted them to intercept the enemy bombers before they made their bomb run, and also made for a good ratio of enemy to friendly losses.

As a result of the large daylight raid and continuing night raids, plans to move the 49th to New Guinea were postponed. The 49th hadn't attempted an interception of the small night raids on Darwin up to this time; however, the 23rd Fighter Group of the China Air Task Force (CATF)—made up of pilots from the disbanded American Volunteer Group (Flying Tigers) and crew members of the Doolittle Raiders—pulled off their first successful night interception.

It was about 2:30 A.M. on the morning of July 30 when Maj. David "Tex" Hill, commanding officer of the 75th Squadron, got word that Japanese bombers were approaching Hengyang. He sent two of his pilots—Capt. Albert J. "Ajax" Baumler and Maj. John R. Alison—up to intercept. Each pilot knocked down two bombers, but the bombers put many shells into Alison's P-40, narrowly missing him. One bomber crashed within 100 yards of where Tex Hill was directing the fight over his radio. Alison, returning to the field with his severely damaged plane, made an approach which was interrupted by bombs dropping on the runway. He deliberately overshot the runway and landed in a nearby river in hopes that he would not lose the precious fighter. He escaped injury, and the plane was later salvaged by Chinese coolies who dragged it from the river on bamboo mats. Just as Alison was making his crash landing another wave of enemy planes came in, and Tex Hill jumped in a P-40 and went up to intercept but could not locate the enemy. However, this was the first successful night interception for the Allied forces in the Pacific.

August 10, 1942—Monday
Was out for a short while today and took snapshots, but the weather was bad and I couldn't stay out long.
Navy has begun an offensive in the Aleutians and Coral Sea off the Solomons. Details as yet are scant.

Recuperating from his serious injuries took three long months. Part of this time was spent in the hospital, part was spent more enjoyably. He met and dated several girls, only one of whom meant anything to him. That girl, Joan Jackson, won his heart from the beginning. They spent most of their time in sharp contrast to the way he entertained other girls. Joan didn't care for nightclubs and drinking. So they patronized the big amusement park on the beach in Melbourne. Dancing and riding the roller coaster provided the centers of attraction for the two.

August 25, 1942—Tuesday

News came today that Japs raided Darwin Sunday with 27 bombers and 20 Zeros. We got nine Zeros and four bombers without a loss. They can come every day if our boys can knock them down like that.

Russians are sure catching hell around Stalingrad! There is a chance they can hold out since the civilians in town are fighting, too.

Jack Donalson has been awarded the DSC for action on Bataan. I believe he really deserves it.

The day of the Japanese surprise attack on Pearl Harbor, military installations in the Philippines went on alert. Because the international date line lies between Pearl Harbor and the Philippines, it was December 8 on the Bataan Peninsula where Jack Donalson was operating with the 21st Pursuit Squadron. He was sent up on patrol when, in the words of Martin Caidin in his *The Ragged, Rugged Warriors*, all hell broke loose. As the P–40Es were circling Iba Airfield preparing to land, a gaggle of Zero fighters caught them at great disadvantage—low on fuel and low on altitude. Lieutenant Donalson immediately threw his fighter into the midst of the attacking Zeros and poured bullets into two of them. Before the one-sided fight ended, five Kittyhawks were lost and three others were forced to crash-land on nearby beaches when their fuel ran out. But Jack Donalson destroyed two of the attacking Zeros. The very next day he got another chance at the enemy and destroyed one more. Donalson was well on his way toward acedom by the time war was

George's fiancée Joan Jackson. G. Preddy

Portrait of 2nd Lt. George Preddy given to Joan Jackson. This photo was retrieved from an estate sale in 1990 by Steve Collins, an Australian aviation buff, also a police detective, from Melbourne. S. Collins

declared! But this is not the action for which Donalson received the Distinguished Service Cross.

During the next month the Japanese attacked Clark Field, completely destroying the remaining P-40s of the 21st Pursuit Squadron. Captain Donalson was given ten men and assigned to an infantry unit. He carried an old Lewis machine gun and wore an asbestos glove on his right hand so he could fire the Lewis from his hip. His unit made a landing behind a Japanese force on the beach and destroyed it; and for this action he was awarded the Distinguished Service Cross. In February 1942 he escaped from Bataan at the last minute in a P-40 and crash landed at Panay and made his way to Australia where he was assigned to the 9th Pursuit Squadron.

Now, back in Australia, the new warning system, using a ship equipped with radio and stationed 150 miles off the coast of Darwin in the Timor Sea, was working wonders. For the second time the Japanese were intercepted before making their bomb run. George was sorry to be missing out on the action. The loss of one plane and no pilots versus the destruction of twenty-four enemy aircraft with others probably destroyed and damaged was the score achieved during the last two raids. Increased experience on the part of pilots and the improved warning system combined to account for the uneven score.

It had been six weeks since Sauber and George collided. And that six weeks was riddled with medical operations, treatment, medicines, therapy, soreness and some mending. The next six weeks promised rest, recuperation and recreation. It also promised some boredom and frustration at not being able to get back into the fight.

September 6, 1942—Sunday
Finberg and Howk were in today. They will be in Melbourne a few days for oxygen school. They say that Colonel Wurtsmith has left the group and Colonel Hutchinson has taken over. I sure hate to see Wurtsmith go.
Had supper at June's new flat tonight. Took Joan home afterwards.
September 9, 1942—Wednesday
Had dinner at Joan's house this evening. It was a very enjoyable evening. Her Dad is a famous golfer and a very nice fellow. Also her sister is a clever girl and very attractive. I think I could love Joan.
September 17, 1942—Thursday
The days are still a little nasty. It was good enough this afternoon to play tennis, however. My leg stood up under it nicely, although I didn't do a lot of running around.
September 23, 1942—Wednesday
Flew for first time since accident this afternoon at Laverton. Drug a wing tip slightly by trying to taxi a Moth in a 30 mph wind.
Took Joan to theatre tonight.

Lt. Lawrence Smith was now in the hospital with George. He was recovering from jaundice. The two of them were able to get a Tiger Moth during the next week. They had fun flying mock dogfights and buzzing the countryside, but both wanted to get back into a real fighter. George continued to see Joan at every opportunity.

October 14, 1942—Wednesday
Landers, Blachley and Ball are in town on leave. They say Selman has left the Squadron and Irvin is now in command. Pilots and planes are now in Townsville.

51

October 18, 1942—Sunday

My orders came in this morning to report back to the outfit. Had supper at Joan's house and afterwards stayed there for the night.

George left Melbourne on the twentieth catching the train to Brisbane via Sydney. He learned from Joe Kruzel that his name was on a list of personnel to return to the States. In a way, he was disappointed he wouldn't get to rejoin the 9th where his buddies were having a field day. When he arrived in Brisbane he was greeted with two sets of orders: one set ordered him home, the other promoted him to first lieutenant. He found it difficult to be unhappy about not returning to Darwin.

October 22, 1942—Thursday

What a day! Arrived on train in Brisbane at 2:30 PM and received orders making me first lieutenant and sending me home in same hour. Reynolds and Donalson have already left, and I catch the next plane.

Saw Gignac tonight. His face is pretty well scarred up from a crash landing in a P–39.

Lt. Andrew Reynolds was at this time the leading ace in the Pacific theater of operations with ten victories. He was awarded a Silver Star for action over Darwin when he destroyed two fighters and one bomber on a single pass through their formation. He was officially credited with two of the three victories claimed on 4 April 1942. Reynolds got all ten of his victories between 5 February and 30 July 1942. He went on to win two more Silver Stars.

*A photo of Joan wearing George's wings. Joan has since donated the wings to a museum in Australia.* R. Preddy Harris

*Chapter 6*

# 21,000 Miles to the Jug

During the three months since George's accident, the Japanese had been very busy in New Guinea. They had captured Kokoda Airdrome there; they had seized the Kai, Aroe and Tanimbar Islands and landed at Milne Bay where they were finally repulsed. The Australians had stopped the Japanese drive across the Owen Stanley Mountains just 28 miles from Port Moresby, and started their offensive to push the enemy back.

To help meet the onslaught in New Guinea, the 7th Squadron was moved to Port Moresby in early October. Most of the pilots from the 8th and 9th were at various airdromes in Queensland getting their aircraft in shape before going back into combat. The pilots of the 7th were already escorting A-20s over Kokoda to bomb and strafe the recently-lost airfield. But here was George in Brisbane waiting to catch the next plane out for the zone of interior.

October 23, 1942—Friday
Ten of us from the good old 9th had dinner and a sing session at the Belleview tonight. I don't believe there ever was an outfit to touch that bunch!
Took off from Amberly Field shortly after midnight for New Caledonia in a B-24. Passengers are mostly pilots; a civilian, an RAAF pilot and two Army men who escaped from the Philippines in a sail boat are among us also.
October 24, 1942—Saturday
Landed in New Caledonia about 7 AM and had breakfast. Dropped a few passengers and picked up a Navy lieutenant and a painter for *LIFE*. Got off shortly after breakfast and landed at Nandi, Fiji about 2:30 PM. These are beautiful islands and the climate is magnificent.
Heard sad news that a B-17 was lost east of here with Eddie Rickenbacker aboard. Talked with a pilot who has been on a search mission for him; there are no signs of him or the crew.
October 25, 1942—Sunday
Sunday for 48 hours. Took off from Fiji this morning and landed at Canton Island this afternoon. Saw Carol Conrad from Greensboro. He is flying a PBY in search for Rickenbacker. Spent the night in Canton and took off at 4:30 this morning. Landed in Hawaii this afternoon and got a room in a hotel in Honolulu. This town has changed drastically. Instead of a playground, it is now a military base. Everything closes at 7 PM.

Rickenbacker and the crew of the B-17 survived a twenty-one day ordeal while living in life rafts.

October 26, 1942—Monday
Got up late and did a little shopping around town. Talked with several pilots in a P-40F squadron here who are pulling out soon. Had supper at the Hickam Field Officers Club and took off for San Francisco about 7 PM.

October 27, 1942—Tuesday

Arrived in Hamilton Field [California] this morning and checked in at Headquarters. The general commanding the Fourth Air Force talked with us for over an hour. Got a room at the Clift Hotel and after supper went to a movie with Ryan. Hope to leave for home tomorrow. Bet folks were surprised to get my telegram saying I'm in America.

George was back on home soil just nine months after departing on a very uncertain voyage. In some respects his return was sort of empty; he hadn't scored a victory. His injuries were sustained during training so he hadn't even been awarded the Purple Heart for his pain. But by now many fully understood that training was proving more fatal than combat, especially so during those first few months in Australia. His return was not totally empty; he had gained some very valuable experience—firsthand combat experience—and he had damaged two enemy aircraft in dogfights.

The first order of business now that he was back in the States was to get home and see his folks and his friends. His hopes for catching a ride on an Air Corps plane were dissipated when, in Salt Lake City, he was bumped off a transport plane to make room for cargo. George spent the night at the Utah Hotel and caught the *Challenger* out of Salt Lake City the next day.

October 30, 1942—Friday

Slept pretty good in coach last night and spent the day reading and riding. Story and pictures in *LIFE* about Kiser and his return home to Kentucky.

Capt. George E. Kiser had nine aerial victories by this time; he got his last one on the August 23. Kiser also knocked down three bombers on the April 27 mission when Preddy damaged two enemy aircraft. But what really set Kiser apart was his score of two victories while flying with the 17th Fighter Squadron in the Philippines on December 10, 1941, just two days after Pearl Harbor. He was awarded the Distinguished Service Cross for extraordinary heroism by Gen. George Brett, who flew from Melbourne to the Northern Territory to hold a ceremony honoring Kiser, Capt. Robert Morrissey, Lt. James Morehead and Lt. A. T. House. The ceremony was unique in that it was held on the airstrip in a combat zone from which the airmen being honored had flown their courageous missions. A large crowd of American and Australian airmen formed a square around General Brett and the men receiving awards. P–40s lined the field and a flight of Hudson bombers circled overhead while the awards were being made.

When Captain Kiser returned to Kentucky, he was among the highest scoring aces of the war to date; thus the story in *Life*. A two-page spread entitled "Hero's Homecoming" included photos of the large crowd in Somerset, Kentucky, a sleepy town of 6,154 people. Most turned out to see their star high-school halfback come home with his decorations and receive another from Governor Keen Johnson, who made Ed Kiser a full-fledged Kentucky colonel.

George finally pulled into North Carolina on November 1. He was quite surprised to see his dad board the train in Reidsville, about twenty miles north of Greensboro. His dad was very proud of his oldest son and wanted to see him before his attention was diverted by the entire family waiting at the passenger station in Greensboro.

The next nine days were spent visiting relatives and friends. Bill Preddy and Bozo Boaz took George to Winston-Salem to visit with Bill and Wanda

Teague. Bill Teague then flew George, Bill and Bozo to Charlotte and back in his Stinson Reliant—just for the fun of it!

George probably ate more southern fried chicken during his leave at home than he had ever eaten before in such a short span of time. According to his diary, all of his aunts and uncles had him over for chicken dinner. He was even taken out to the very popular family-style restaurant called Ma Benson's and had southern fried chicken there—Ma's specialty, of course.

George visited with Otto Gaskins and his wife Pat in Charlotte, and he went to Raleigh with his family to visit Bill Preddy at his fraternity. Bill was attending North Carolina State College at the time.

On November 10 he left Greensboro on the train for Oakland, California, via Washington, Chicago, Omaha, Cheyenne and San Francisco. He finally checked in with the Fourth Fighter Command in Oakland. Thus ended George's rest and recuperation at home. Now was the time to begin looking for an assignment. Little did he know how much travel would be involved, and how time-consuming that task would be. But it gave him the opportunity to fly several different types of aircraft—most notably the Lockheed P-38, the Bell P-39 and the Republic P-47.

November 14, 1942—Saturday
Finally got to San Francisco about 4:30 am. Checked in at the Hotel Mark Twain. Went to Fourth Fighter Command in Oakland and got a room there. Am trying to transfer to First Air Force.
November 15, 1942—Sunday
Slept late and had breakfast about noon. Went to a movie and went out to the airport about 2:00 PM. Flew an AT-6 for an hour and a half. Sure good to get back into the saddle. Am anxious now to get into a fast ship again.

During the next several days George battled with the bureaucratic maze in an attempt to get transferred to the First Air Force. He dealt with A-1 in San Francisco and A-3 in Oakland, both without success. On the nineteenth he took a break and went flying.

November 19, 1942—Thursday
Spent the day out at the field and checked out in the P-38. Flew it 45 minutes of the most enjoyable flying I ever did. That is a wonderful flying ship and fast as its name—Lightning—implies. Hope to put in several more hours on it this week.

He followed up his exciting flight in the P-38 with a flight in the AT-6 the next day. What a difference! However, he said he had a good look at the countryside around Oakland and San Francisco, and had a bit of fun buzzing. But he was hooked on the P-38; the following day he was out at the field clamoring for a chance to fly the Lightning again. He got it, and performed a few maneuvers in it this time. He was already getting comfortable with the remarkable P-38. He thought she handled nicely.

Orders came declaring that all pilots who had previous foreign duty were to report to a school in Orlando, Florida. The training was to last about ten days. Their TR (travel request) routed them through Denver, Kansas City, St. Louis and Jacksonville. George spent the day before leaving Oakland on the "Exposition Flyer" train at the field flying both the P-38 and the AT-6. The next week was spent on trains with four other pilots making their way to Orlando. They arrived about noon on the first of December and started ground school the following day. The next three days were filled with eight hours of daily instruction. The ground instruction was to be followed by a week of flying. His first day back in the cockpit was Pearl Harbor Day when he flew a P–40.

There just were not enough airplanes to go around. George noted that the situation seemed to be the same all over the country—about half as many planes as pilots. He was successful in getting a P–40 on December 8, and he gave it a good workout. But the next three days were spent trying to get an airplane without success. On the eleventh he heard that Buzz Wagner had been missing for several days. He had gone down somewhere between Eglin and Maxwell Fields. It was later discovered that Wagner was involved in a fatal crash after takeoff from Eglin. He became the first of a number of famous aces to die in noncombat flights after they returned to the States. Dick Bong was perhaps the most famous; he met his death when he crashed a P–80 jet on takeoff for a test flight. It happened August 6, 1945—just a few days before victory over Japan was achieved.

Even though the pilots had received inadequate flying time during the school, it ended as scheduled and George headed back to California on Saturday December 12. The train took him through Jacksonville, New Orleans and to Houston, where he went out to Ellington Field and tried to get a flight to San Francisco. No luck. So he caught the train to Dallas, Bakersfield and on to Oakland, arriving at Fighter Command on the eighteenth.

The next day he received orders to report to the 328th Fighter Group at Hamilton Field. He was assigned to the 326th Squadron equipped with P–39s. There were nine aircraft for fifty-nine pilots. The weather was so rotten the first few days with the 326th that the number of aircraft mattered little. It was Christmas Eve before he was able to check out in the P–39. He flew it for the next three days, perhaps because most pilots were on Christmas leave. George finally received orders to report to the First Fighter Command in New York.

December 30, 1942—Wednesday
Got orders to report to First Fighter Command at Mitchel Field. Believe this is a good move. Will probably have a chance to fly better planes and may get in a squadron with Kruzel, Reynolds or Donalson. Made arrangements to leave on the Challenger tomorrow evening.

December 31, 1942—Thursday
Well, here it is the last day of 1942, a year I will not soon forget. Here I am on a train setting out on my sixth crossing of the country since this time a year ago. Twice across the Pacific and up and down the continent of Australia have given me some great experiences. Hope by the end of next year I can have done much more for my country than I have this year.

He arrived in New York on 4 January and reported in at Mitchel Field. He met the colonel in charge who offered him a few days off. George declined the offer because he was anxious to get back in an airplane—he had had enough leisure. The next day he received his orders to go to Westover Field in Massachussetts where he was assigned to the 320th Squadron equipped with P–47s. Several of his old friends were there: Gignac, Rybak, Donalson and Drake. Weather was good, but the runways were too icy to fly during his first few days.

January 9, 1943—Saturday
Checked out in P–47 to tune of three hours this afternoon. She is a nice flying ship and one I believe we will be successful with in combat.

Andrew and I went in to Holyoke tonight and met a couple of girls. The tall dark girl was especially so!
January 10, 1943—Sunday
Flew two and a half hours today, some of it in formation. Am expecting to lead flights right away. Stayed around the BOQ tonight and read.
January 11, 1943—Monday
Weather was bad today so no flying. Saw Donalson and went with him to see the commanding officer of new 352nd Group. Looks hopeful that I may get in it. Sure hope so; I much prefer a tactical outfit to a training one.

George got about ten flying hours in the space of five days, more than he had had for a long time. He loved it, and wanted more. And there would be lots more before he shipped out.

January 15, 1943—Friday
Have been transferred to the 34th Fighter Squadron. The CO is a darn nice 1st lieutenant by the name of Meyer who saw service in Iceland. Jack Donalson is Operations Officer and was mainly responsible for me getting transferred. We are going to train as a tactical unit and will probably go across in a few months. Meyer says he is going to put me in command of a flight. I pledge now to do my best to make my flight the fightingest unit in the Army.

So, after several cross-country trips and little flying time, George had finally gotten an assignment to a tactical unit. He was delighted! At this stage in his career, he had flown—in addition to trainers—the P–38, P–39, P–40 and P–47. From his comments, it seems clear that the P–38 fascinated him more than any of the others. But he seemed to be satisfied with the P–47, and very happy with his current assignment.

*From left to right: Clara, Bozo, George, Bill and Rachel at the Capitol Building in Raleigh, North Carolina. R. Preddy Harris*

*In addition to a blue ascot, pilots of the newly formed 34th (later to be the 487th) Fighter Squadron stationed at Mitchel Field, New York, were required to carry a custom riding crop designed by their squadron commanding officer, 1st Lt. John C. Meyer. It had as its grip a highly polished .50-caliber cartridge. L. Hill*

*Chapter 7*

# In Preparation
# for the ETO

George was assigned to the 34th Squadron of the 352nd Fighter Group. First Lieutenant John C. Meyer was commanding officer of the 34th, and Lieutenant Jack Donalson was operations officer. As mentioned in his diary, Donalson was instrumental in getting George into the 34th/352nd. The group was slated to get a combat assignment after a few months training in the P–47, the fastest ship George had flown to date. George was quite happy now with his assignment and with the Thunderbolt.

While the remainder of the group stayed at Westover, the 34th moved to New Haven, Connecticut. The weather was generally poor during the winter months at both Westover and New Haven, but the living conditions were much worse at New Haven. Flying time and training suffered as a result of the weather, and many accidents were caused by ice and snow.

George and Meyer began flying together with Meyer taking the lead. They practiced formation flying initially. Meyer was checking George's ability to perform as a flight commander. An extra duty for the pilots was to work in the control tower, and George pulled his share of that duty during the first few weeks at New Haven. Republic's technical representative held ground school for the pilots when weather was too bad to fly.

On January 27, Don Dilling and George departed with two P–47s for the modification center in Evansville, Indiana. They made it only as far as Middletown, Pennsylvania, the first day due to poor weather. Then Middletown got their heaviest snow of the year which further delayed the pair until the thirty-first when they departed for Cincinnati. But they could get cleared only as far as Pittsburgh. They arrived in Cincinnati the following day where they had lunch with Dilling's folks who met them at the airport. After lunch they went on to Evansville where the modifications were completed the next day. The two then flew to Cincinnati where they had dinner and spent the night at Dilling's home. They left Cincinnati on George's twenty-fourth birthday, 5 February, and flew directly to LaGuardia Field where they had to land because New Haven was socked in. They took the train back to New Haven.

Weather was certainly a problem for the pilots preparing for the European theater. In fact, the ice and snow were far worse than they would ever encounter in the ETO. Low ceilings were common to both areas. On February 11, Lt. Gene F. Drake and three other pilots took off in their Thunderbolts from Providence, Rhode Island for Groton, Connecticut. The weather was poor. All four aircraft crashed somewhere along the coast killing the four pilots.

February 19, 1943—Friday

Flew a little today but the visibility was generally poor. Meyer, Donalson, Dilling and I got in a flight this afternoon. Gave Groton and Bridgeport both a good buzz job!

Germans are reported to have advanced on US in North Africa and have taken a couple of our airfields.

February 22, 1943—Monday

Went to Groton again this afternoon and finally got off with nine planes. Hamilton hit a truck on takeoff and made a crash landing minus one wheel. Luckily, he wasn't scratched. The gang sure flew a SNAFU formation so Meyer and I talked with them for about an hour after we landed.

Ralph Hamilton, during an interview for a videotape on Preddy's life, cited this event among others that were quite memorable for him. Ralph said, "George and I had gone from New Haven to Groton to bring two P-47s back. There was no radio in my airplane; both P-47s had been earthbound for some time. Preddy took off and I followed on his wing. Preddy cleared a truck that was near the end of the runway, but I hit the truck as I chandelled up behind Preddy. I was trying to catch up. When I hit the truck it damaged the left landing gear. I had no communication with the tower so I just brought it back in and landed. The Deputy CO chewed me out for not taking the damaged airplane to Windsor Locks where they had a facility for repairing P-47s."

Ralph said that one story he vividly recalls George telling was about the cow he shot while stationed near Darwin. George said that his squadron hadn't had any meat for quite a long time, so he took it upon himself to go hunting for meat. Thinking he was shooting wild game, he shot a cow instead. He had to pay the farmer for the cow, but at least the fellows had some meat on the table for a while.

February 23, 1943—Tuesday

Meyer, Donalson and I had a swell flight this afternoon in the unrestricted ships. It's wonderful to go 450 miles per hour and do acrobatics again. We sure buzzed the field properly and had an all-round hot flight!

February 26, 1943—Friday

Flew four hours and 45 minutes today. Led formation rat racing and making dry runs on ground targets. Sure a tired boy tonight but like to get in a lot of time. Bill [Preddy] reports to Miami for Cadet Training tomorrow. He and Bozo will both be there. Sure hope they get along okay. I know they have what it takes.

The squadrons of the 352nd Group were initially located at different fields. The 34th Squadron was based at New Haven and the remainder of the group at Westover. It was decided that the entire group should be located together, even if it meant locating at LaGuardia and living in apartments. George and his flight moved down to LaGuardia on February 28 and moved in to their quarters at Bay Manor Apartments. Civilians continued to live there also. Captain Meyer and the rest of the 34th Squadron flew down on March 2, just in time to be there when Gen. Hap Arnold came through to visit.

Many training flights, several interceptions, some gunnery missions, a few night landings, several trips to Mitchel Field, time in the oxygen chamber, and some very lengthy patrols followed Meyer's arrival. Although not typical, the following entry is indicative of how lengthy some of the patrol activity could be. It provided good training for the type of flying that would be done over Europe; six-hour missions were not uncommon.

March 22, 1943—Monday

Flew over six hours again today. Weather was pretty bad this morning. Was forced to bring the flight in two different times due to lowering ceiling and light snow.

April 6, 1943—Tuesday

Spent another full day flying. Major Baumler was on the field today. He just returned from China 10 days ago. Got six Japs while he was over there.

Berkshire and I went to the Orchid Room tonight, met some dames and took them home about 2:00 AM.

Major Albert J. "Ajax" Baumler was finally given official credit for five victories, all of which were claimed from June through September 1942.

April 8, 1943—Thursday

Flew two gunnery missions today. Shot 74 out of 155 and 91 out of 200. Must improve this a lot. Went on alert at noon and flew a mission with Meyer, McIntyre and Dilling late this afternoon. Left the line about 8:00 PM.

April 9, 1943—Friday

Ships were out most of the day for inspection. Had to test hop them all this afternoon. Had a couple of good individual combats while on test missions. Ran into Meyer and battled for about 20 minutes.

April 12, 1943—Monday

Flew a couple of missions today before it began raining. Fired a 21 in skeet and 91 in .22 rifle. Skeet is improving considerably.

Lt. Carl Luksic, Lt. Virgil Meroney and George Preddy turned out to be the best skeet shooters in their squadron, according to Luksic. When they got to England they made good use of their talent. The area around Bodney abounded in pheasant, and the three pilots went hunting on several occasions getting enough pheasant to serve all the pilots.

Skeet shooting provided valuable training for fighter pilots, aerial gunners and others who had to shoot at moving targets. It helped the trainees grasp a couple of important fundamentals about the speed of the target and the amount of lead necessary to intercept it. One huge difference is that the skeet shooter is standing still while his target is moving; the fighter pilot is moving while his target is also moving. But the concept of relative speed and deflection is amply demonstrated by skeet shooting.

April 18, 1943—Sunday

Flew early patrol and a gunnery mission this morning. Went over to see Colonel Ramage this afternoon about low acrobatics yesterday.

George and Lt. Clayton Davis, among others, were reported for performing aerobatics at an altitude lower than that required by the regulations—much lower. According to Davis, what they *didn't* get reported for was even worse. They had flown under a couple of the bridges which span the Hudson River. Colonel Ramage chewed them out and warned them not to fly aerobatics at altitudes below those prescribed by the regulations.

As a result of an inspection by General Royce, one of the ranking generals, and his conviction that LaGuardia was no place to train a tactical outfit for combat, George and the other officers had to give up their plush living quarters in the Bay Manor Apartments and move back to Mitchel Field. Two months in the relatively luxurious apartments soured the pilots on barracks life. Lt. Ralph Hamilton, who flew regularly with George while they were at Mitchel, remembers that General Royce's inspection was precipitated by the numerous air shows put on by the 34th for the residents of New York City. He also thought the tower operators may have had something to do with the inspection. Some of the pilots, on takeoff, would chandelle up and turn inside the tower which caused for much nervousness on the part of the tower operators. They were clearly concerned that one of the green pilots would someday miscalculate and come right through the tower, ruining their whole day!

April 27, 1943—Tuesday
...Powell went up on a hop at 1615 hours and as yet has not been heard from. Looks as if he tried to climb through a solid overcast.

An investigation concluded that Lt. Jerry Powell's Thunderbolt was probably lost due to a mechanical malfunction. He was sent up on a high-altitude mission from which he just didn't return. The investigators think that the fuel line came off the carburetor allowing fuel to escape into the accessory section. When mixed with hot exhaust gases, the P–47 simply blew up.

May 1, 1943—Saturday
Morning off. Stayed in town last night. Got out to the field about noon and flew until after 8:00 PM. Have been practicing some formations.
Gus Daymond, leading Allied ace now at Mitchel, flew for nearly three years with Royal Air Force.

Daymond was among those Americans who volunteered early to fly Hurricanes and Spitfires for the Royal Air Force. Their outfits became known as the Eagle Squadrons, and Gus Daymond was the Eagle's high scorer. He commanded No. 71 Eagle Squadron.

Clara and Earl Preddy, George's mother and dad, took the train to New York City to visit with George. They wanted to see him again before he shipped out to Europe. They stayed there four days while George took some time off from training. They visited Rockefeller Center, Radio City Theater, Central Park and the Observatory of the Empire State and had dinner at the Gay Nineties and a few other places. One day Clara and Earl came out to the field to have lunch with George. They got there in time to watch him land after a training flight. On their last day he took them to a radio broadcast and to the Paramount where they saw Harry James and his band perform.

May 7, 1943—Friday
Flew one mission this morning. Haven't many planes in commission. Sure getting disappointed in the P–47. Some of the high ranking officers in the Air Corps say it's ready for combat when they have never sat in the cockpit. Sure is a pity that some of our generals can't be in less responsible positions.

Another problem encountered with the early P–47s was the phenomenon called compressibility. Ralph Hamilton recalls that the first time he went into compressibility was when he started a vertical dive at full power from 38,000 ft. When he pulled out, the cockpit had steamed over, and he was at 1,500 ft. and climbing. He had grayed-out! Not much was known at this time about compressibility. It occurred only when pilots dived their planes at high speed. It was more mysterious than tail flutter, a problem common to almost every new fighter design during this era. Even the rugged Jug had tail flutter problems in the early models. Those early models earned a reputation as a pilot-killer when tail flutter frequently caused the tail to separate from the fuselage.

Ralph Hamilton said that while at Mitchel Field the idea was to get as much flying time in the P-47 as they possibly could, and to get checked out in firing the guns. They had ground gunnery practice at Fire Island. For air-to-air gunnery they were required to fire the guns above 40,000 ft. even though there was nothing up there to fire at; the tow planes couldn't pull tow targets that high.

May 10, 1943—Monday
Jamison [Lt. Robert O.] spun in landing yesterday afternoon while I was at Islip. Believe his engine cut out on the approach. A nice kid he was. Flew three missions today starting at 5:30 AM.
Allies are reported to be routing Germans out of Tunisia. Have captured 50,000 including four generals.

Ralph Hamilton also told about the case of mistaken identity. It happened when Lt. Marion Nutter mistook Roosevelt Field for Mitchel Field and landed at Roosevelt. His P-47 had to be disassembled and trucked back to Mitchel. Meyer was understandably upset about this case of mistaken identity. But Meyer had previously arranged to have a party for the pilots at a local brewery. At the party Meyer presented the first award to be given to anyone in the 34th Squadron. It was a pin of a flying ruptured duck with the wings outspread and "you know what hanging below." The Order of the Ruptured Duck was awarded to Lieutenant Nutter.

Lieutenant Colonel Ramage was relieved of his command and George hated to see him go. He thought Ramage was a good group commanding officer. Lt. Col. Joe L. Mason assumed command of the 352nd Fighter Group, and two of the squadrons were redesignated. The old 21st Squadron became the 486th, and the 34th Squadron became the 487th. People tend to resist change; this instance was no different. The redesignations were not accepted pleasantly. While officers of the 34th were stationed in the Philippines, they had incurred large debts at the officers club. It was thought that perhaps the new officers of the 34th did not want to risk having to assume those debts. In any event, the redesignations changed things not a whit. There were still some inspectors nosing around all day long. George was getting in plenty of flying time and lots of gunnery practice. His evenings continued to be most active as well.

May 19, 1943—Wednesday
Got most of my equipment together today and laid it out for inspection tonight. Met Dot Moore in Jamaica tonight and we went to the Boulevard Tavern with Button and Frieda.
May 20, 1943—Thursday
Because Button and I left inspection a half hour early last night, Meyer put us under arrest of quarters this morning and gave us restriction to post for rest of time we are in this country.
Took charge of packing today and worked all night.

After being restricted to quarters George got more evening rest. His restriction lasted until May 31. He helped supervise packing for the overseas move. He continued to get in plenty of flying time. He was called up on two scrambles one day, and the next day flew two alert missions in the morning and a cross-country flight to Westover in the afternoon.

May 26, 1943—Wednesday

Went down to the line rather late today; weather was too bad for flying. Group meeting for officers. Colonel Mason seems to be a good CO. Am getting more faith in him all along.

May 27, 1943—Thursday

This afternoon Button and I flew to Mitchel. Sure pulled a "head up" stunt coming back. Got lost and landed just at dark at Manchester. Button was nearly out of gas. After servicing ships we flew on to Westover.

Among George's records was a copy of his Individual Flight Record which summarized his flying time through May 27, 1943. It shows the following:

| Total First Pilot Time | Hours |
| --- | --- |
| This Month (May 1943) | 66.8 |
| Previous months this fiscal year | 237.9 |
| This fiscal year | 304.7 |
| Previous fiscal years | 310.4 |
| To Date | 615.1 |

George had flown as much during the first five months of 1943 as he had flown since he graduated from flying school.

June 2, 1943—Wednesday

Flew a mission this afternoon. Had a short combat with Dilling and Strickland. Returning to the field Strickland fell out of formation at 22,000 feet and went straight into the ground. Almost certainly due to lack of oxygen. He was surely a swell kid.

After being given his freedom once again, George started spending more of his evenings in town, often with Hayes Button and occasionally with Jack Donalson. However, all was not play at this time. On June 7th he got his instrument check ride with Lt. Clayton Davis in a basic trainer (BT). They were actually in the soup and flew the beam back to Westover. The next day he flew two gunnery missions and was still less than happy with his score. He continued to practice instrument flight at every opportunity.

June 9, 1943—Wednesday

Got in two instrument rides in the BT, and one squadron mission. The squadron mission was lousy. The pilots have been given so many conflicting orders about how to fly formation that they don't know which is right. Meyer sat down and wrote and diagrammed exactly the types of formations and signals we will use, so we can have an idea of what to do on squadron and group missions.

June 10, 1943—Thursday

Flew quite a bit today. Am still working on my instrument flying. Everyone in outfit has qualified for instrument cards but a pilot can never get too much practice. Led a squadron mission this afternoon and it went off pretty well.

George started flying so much that he was too tired to go into town at night. He played poker in the BOQ occasionally, however, and continued to lose. He made up some of his poker losses by playing solitaire with Button. The group was preparing to leave for the staging area, so much time was spent packing and writing home.

# Chapter 8

# 352nd Becomes Operational at Bodney

Notice of the 352nd's final staging came on June 14, 1943, with all leaves cancelled and everyone restricted to the post. All flying and combat training was now as complete as it would get. The group left Westover Field on the sixteenth arriving at Camp Kilmer, New Jersey, later that day. The next seven days were spent preparing for the final shakedown inspection and enjoying great steaks, private parties and shows in New York City. The 487th's final bash took place, oddly enough, on the second floor of the BOQ at Kilmer. Everyone who had a bottle of booze poured it into a big tub with two 25 lb. blocks of ice. John Meyer and George Preddy were both there. George said he took it easy; that probably meant that he didn't overindulge like some of the others did. However, according to Lt. Carl Luksic, George got involved. Bill Whisner was one of those who drank too much that night and got a bit out of hand. That's when George intervened. Carl said, "Preddy had Whisner by his ankles holding him out of the window threatening to drop him on his head from the second floor if he didn't straighten out."

> June 30, 1943—Wednesday
> Got all packed and boarded the train at 8:00 PM. We reached the dock a little before midnight and went on board the Queen Elizabeth. Have a stateroom with 11 others. The ship is very crowded and enlisted men are sleeping on decks and every available space.

Six days spent on the *Queen Elizabeth*, much of it in the officers lounge playing poker and reading, ended in the Firth of Clyde. After debarking, the 352nd boarded a train at Glasgow and headed south, arriving at their new station of Bodney, England, a deserted Royal Air Force (RAF) field. Located near the little village of Watton, Bodney is about ninety miles north of London.

The morning's first light revealed that the airdrome at Bodney was a 6,000 ft. crowned grass field. All buildings were dispersed and camouflaged. Much to George's dismay, combat aircraft were represented by a Miles Master and a lone J–3 Piper Cub! The realization that the new fighter group was finally in harm's way was evidenced by the daily overhead passage of B–17 and B–24 bombers joining up on their way to France and Germany. The occasional crack of ack-ack from nearby batteries fired at friendly aircraft failing to give proper recognition signals made permanent impressions on the newly-arrived pilots.

Within several days the first of eight P–47s arrived and training schedules were laid out. Ralph Hamilton recalled that the first P–47 received by the

352nd was immediately damaged. "A lieutenant who hadn't flown for several months made a poor landing and banged up the prop. We soon got another, so George took it up for a spin before someone else could damage it. He gave us a great buzz job; as he went across the field he pulled up into a barrel roll. There was no problem, but he soon discovered that his landing gear was still extended. I don't think he ever lived that one down!"

Initially all officers were housed in ten-man Quonset huts. On July 21 they were moved into Clermont Hall, a stately manor house on a large country estate which provided all the conveniences and comforts of home. Lt. Gordon Cartee said, when interviewed in 1987, that he had really looked forward to coming in from a mission, getting cleaned up, dressing in his battle jacket and enjoying a martini before dinner. Preddy observed in his diary after moving to Clermont Hall, "quite different fighting here and in Darwin."

There was still a great deal to learn before the unit would be considered combat-ready. Classes included lectures on gunnery and formation flying. The finger-four formation was adopted from the British. The formation is composed of two elements of two aircraft each—a leader and his wingman— and staggered just like the fingertips on one's hand. Each finger four was called a flight and three flights made up a squadron of twelve aircraft. Trailing flights were stepped down behind the squadron leader's flight so that pilots could easily keep him in view and follow his changes of course. The flights of a squadron were known as White, Yellow and Blue and the individual aircraft within a flight as Leader, Two, Three and Four. This scheme assisted radio communications in that each pilot in the squadron knew instantly from what position each call was being made. At times such information was vital. Each squadron in a group was issued a two-syllable call sign which preceded any radio call. For example, Crown Prince White Flight Three refers to the second element leader of the lead flight.

Cripes A'Mighty, *George's personal P-47, serial number 42-8500. Although he never scored a confirmed victory in this 'Bolt, he logged over 60 missions in it before his squadron converted over to the Mustang in early April 1944. The kill mark is for the victory he scored on December 1, 1943 while flying Lieutenant Hamilton's Frances B.* J. McVay

July 28, 1943—Wednesday
Flew down to Debden today where the old Eagle outfit is stationed. They sure have a good setup. The squadron I visited this afternoon was on a Ramrod mission this morning and accounted for five FW 190s to loss of two. Another group of P-47s shot down 16. This sure makes a guy want to get some action.

The Eighth Air Force adopted the practice developed by the Royal Air Force which used special code words to denote a particular type of operational activity. The word *Circus* referred to extraordinary fighter escort of a small force of bombers designed to provoke enemy fighters into coming up to fight. Escorting bombers to or from a target was called a *Ramrod*. A few fighters attacking ground targets, usually in poor weather, was referred to as a *Rhubarb*. And *Rodeo* was the code word for several squadrons carrying out a high-speed sweep over enemy-occupied territory to entice enemy fighters to aerial combat.

July 29, 1943—Thursday
Still having quite a few recognition classes. Otherwise little else of value. All of our planes are being painted with the new star insignia and characteristic P-47 markings.

The P-47 and the Focke-Wulf 190 both had radial engines and were often difficult to distinguish from one another. Therefore, recognition bands were painted around the nose and tail surfaces, and extra large white stars were painted under both wings. Special letters were assigned to each squadron; for example, HO designated aircraft assigned to the 487th Fighter Squadron, and PE to the 328th. Those letters were painted on the side of the fuselage just behind the cockpit. Each plane was also distinguished by a single letter painted on the side of the fuselage behind the star, a letter which usually represented the last letter of the pilot's surname. When invasion stripes were painted on the fuselage, that letter was moved to the vertical tail surface. Hence, Preddy's P-47 had HO and P painted on the side of the fuselage. Additionally, pilots named their aircraft and had the name painted on the left side of the nose section of the fuselage. Preddy's first P-47 was named *Cripes A'Mighty*, his habitual exclamation when shooting craps.
Preparing Bodney for operational status was no easy task. With the arrival of new Thunderbolts, adequate maintenance facilities for servicing aircraft had to be constructed and the old RAF base had to be upgraded so that it could handle the needs of a combat outfit. Soon, however, members of the group were more than casually anticipating the welcome break from their tasks and took advantage of an opportunity to visit London on a forty-eight-hour pass.

August 9, 1943—Monday
Got up early and walked around London. Had dinner at the Piccadilly Hotel. London is sure different from big American cities. The buildings are much older and streets are curved around all over the town. They seem to run toward a main square or circus. Parts of the town are pretty well bombed but it is surprising how little damage is seen after the German blitz of '40 and '41. Caught a train back to Bodney this noon.

Forty-eight hours pass by very quickly in London. George came back to Bodney and attended more classes on aircraft recognition, escape and evasion techniques, but no flying.

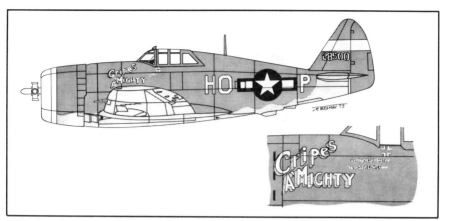

*Drawing of* Cripes A'Mighty *showing its markings more clearly.* J. R. Beaman

August 13, 1943—Friday
P-47s from some of the operational outfits are making some long range hops now. Using belly tanks, they are going almost to the Ruhr. The first time they went so far in the Hun was completely surprised and completely beaten.

In 1943 the Ruhr Basin, near the western border of Germany, was considered to be long range, but 1944 would see much longer escort ranges—all the way to Berlin and back. Preddy's desire to get back into action was reaching an all-time high for him. Just waiting for the unit to be declared operational was more than he could take patiently. Spending time enjoying London was not exactly what he had envisioned when he joined the 352nd Fighter Group. He was an experienced fighter pilot and wanted to do the job for which he was trained. He wanted to get on with it. His frustration is readily gleaned from diary entries which follow.

August 16, 1943—Monday
Flew P-47 down to Debden this afternoon in hopes they would get a show but they had it this morning instead. They got 17 destroyed for loss of one. Fighting took place right over Paris.

George had hoped to go on a mission with the 4th Fighter Group stationed at Debden. The mission he missed was one in which 246 B-17s were dispatched to bomb enemy airfields at Le Bourget, Poix and Abbeville, France. According to official history, the 4th Fighter Group scored eighteen victories that day, and their one loss was a crash landing at New Romney. They lost the P-47 but the pilot made it back to base safely.

August 17, 1943—Tuesday
Flew down to Debden again today with Dilling in a Tiger Moth. Stayed awhile and then went to Halseworth. They had a good show yesterday knocking down 18. Seems that they ran into several Me 110s and 210s.

The 56th Fighter Group was stationed at Halseworth, just eight miles from the Suffolk coast. The 56th became one of the most outstanding fighter groups in the Air Corps, and produced top fighter aces like Francis Gabreski and Robert S. Johnson. Their commanding officer, Col. Hubert Zemke, was thought to be one of the most brilliant of group leaders. On this day the targets were Schweinfurt and Regensburg—230 B-17s to the former and 146 to the latter. Fighters from the 4th, 56th, 78th and 353rd groups escorted the bombers—there were 240 P-47s in all. The 56th got final credit for seventeen victories and lost three of their own. This was the first battle of Schweinfurt.

August 18, 1943—Wednesday
Had camouflage classes all day. Most of it was pretty boring. We had quite a few ships to come in during the last 24 hours. Our squadron alone now has eight. Hope we can begin doing something soon. Getting rather fed up with sitting around when the other outfits are getting all the action.

No entries were made for August 19 and 20, just a diagonal line on each page. These were the first days he had missed since he started keeping his diary on January 12, 1942. On August 25, George noted that although the group now had a total of thirteen aircraft, he was still getting very little flying time. He concluded his diary entry for August 28 by saying, "Diary discontinued until something interesting happens."

It took only two weeks for something interesting to happen. It was noted in the history of the 352nd entitled *The Bluenosed Bastards of Bodney* that by the end of the first week of September 1943 the 352nd Fighter Group had completed all of its precombat tasks, pronounced itself combat-ready, and was waiting for its first call to duty. That call was not long in coming. During the evening hours of September 8th the teletype machines in group operations began chattering and quickly spit out the long-awaited orders for the group's first mission. These were relayed down to the squadrons and soon the entire base was buzzing with activity carrying out the many and varied tasks required before takeoff. When September 9 rolled around, the date of the group's first combat mission briefing, everything was ready—ready in the sense that the group could now execute their inaugural mission with a high probability of success. This was the moment for which the entire group had trained for several long and arduous months. There before them on the large briefing map was their route represented by a brilliant red ribbon running from Bodney east over the North Sea into enemy territory and back. It was a dramatic portrayal with the pilots seated in the darkened room, the map and group leader in the floodlights, blackboards showing the runway in use, wind direction, start-up times, order of takeoff, course to be flown, cruising altitudes, distances, checkpoints, and the course back home.

Watches were synchronized. With the call to attention, pilots filed from the briefing room with the knowledge that the mission was to support B-17s patrolling the English coast from Southwold to Felixstowe and to cover landings of Thunderbolts from the 56th and 353rd Fighter Groups. Forty pilots from the 352nd took part in this first mission. As Ralph Hamilton later put it, "We had no victories or losses on this milk run, but it certainly helped build confidence in all our pilots."

September 20, 1943—Monday
Am now at Goxhill for gunnery. Briefly, events of past few weeks: The Group became operational and we have been on three sweeps and one escort mission. As yet have not run into any action. Missions have taken us over Holland, Belgium and France.
Of course, Italy has surrendered but heavy fighting has been going on against Nazis.

*Esprit de corps was high in the 487th Fighter Squadron from its inception. The official squadron insignia of the "Little Bastard" so skillfully rendered by Sgt. Sam Perry was displayed throughout the unit's area at Bodney. J. Sabanos*

*Maj. J. C. Meyer, commanding officer of the 487th FS scored the unit's first aerial victory, an Me 109, on November 26, 1943 while flying his P-47 named Lambie, coded HO-M. Here he is photographed with Lieutenants Donahue, Hamilton and Meroney (left to right) describing how he scored his fourth victory. J. L. Slabe*

Goxhill, sometimes called "Goat Hill" by the Yanks, was used as an operational training base by the Eighth Air Force. It was located on the south bank of the Humber River opposite Kingston upon Hull. A bit over 100 kilometers north of Bodney, the 352nd flight leaders took turns taking their flights up for gunnery training. Robert S. Johnson commented on his stay at Goxhill in his book *Thunderbolt*: "Goxhill was an abominably filthy place, rundown and slovenly, and with an appalling layer of thick coal dust covering everything, including our mess tables and our beds." Air-to-air gunnery was practiced on a towed sleeve. A tow plane trailed a long, thin cable with the target—a fabric-covered sleeve—attached. If the sleeve was hit it would clearly show the impact of the bullets. As it turned out, the sleeve had a rather long life—hits were not too frequent.

September 30, 1943—Tuesday

Since I have let the daily notations pass, will bring the diary up to date.

I had a pretty fair gunnery score at Goxhill breaking the Group record on one training mission with a 29%. I was lucky enough not to miss any combat missions while we were up there, and got in on a show the day after my return.

The Group is now equipped with belly tanks and we've had 10 long range missions using them. With them, we can go pretty far into enemy territory and give better support to the bombers. So far, only a few of the pilots have encountered the enemy and we haven't destroyed any as yet.

On two missions our presence with the bombers was enough to keep the Hun fighters at bay.

The 328th was bounced on one occasion and Olson was shot up pretty badly. He was last seen over the Channel on the way home.

I now have nine bomber escort missions and five sweeps. On our last mission we were to escort B-26s over France but aborted due to weather.

I have seen only one B-17 go down while we were with them and that was due to flak.

Our longest mission was to Düren, Germany, where we picked up a task force of B–17s at the target and gave them withdrawal support almost to the Dutch coast.

Although George made no entry for the mission of October 14, he and the 352nd were among 196 fighters dispatched to escort 320 bombers on their second mission to Schweinfurt, a mission which has come to be known as Black Thursday. Because the first mission there in August resulted in heavy casualties, this one was expected to suffer also. The 352nd was assigned to the 93rd and 392nd bomb groups flying B–24s; the fighters and bombers rendezvoused as planned. But the bombers were diverted to a sweep of the Frisian Islands. The 352nd returned to Bodney without encountering the enemy, but others most certainly did. The diversionary raid didn't really work; sixty B–17s were lost and 594 men were listed as missing in action, five killed in action and another forty wounded. The 56th Fighter Group scored three victories and the 353rd was credited with ten. Several P–47s were lost when they crash-landed upon returning to England, but only one pilot was killed when he crashed at Herongate.

This second mission to Schweinfurt was immensely important to the Eighth Air Force. Knowing its importance and anticipating a repeat of the heavy defense put up by the Luftwaffe fighters during the first raid on Schweinfurt, an expert crew was assembled to fly the lead plane—the 96th Bomb Group's *Fertile Myrtle III*. The pilot was Capt. Tom Kenny, the copilot and task force commander was Col. Archie Olds (commanding officer of the 45th Combat Wing), the group navigators were Maj. Robert Hodson and Capt. Bill Jones, and the group bombardier was George's friend, Capt. John Latham. (See diary entry for November 19, 1943.)

The formation of bombers was under attack for an hour and a half by enemy fighters, but the lead Fortress escaped damage until the bomb run when a flak shell exploded close to the nose. Fragments hit John Latham in the head and legs and he was knocked away from the bombsight. Latham managed to get back on the sight in time to make an accurate drop on the bearing factories. *Fertile Myrtle III* was hit by another flak burst over Reims. Major Hodson was killed instantly, Latham was hit in the left thigh, Captain Jones was peppered, Colonel Olds was blown out of his seat, and Captain Kenny's legs were hit by Plexiglas fragments.

Kenny feathered engines two and three to extinguish the fire as he lost altitude, from 20,000 down to 11,000 ft. When he pulled out he found a flight of Me 110s preparing to attack his crippled Fort, and he knew his chances were slim at best. But his gunners claimed hits on two of the enemy aircraft giving Kenny a chance to find cloud cover. The Me 110s turned away while the Fort continued to lose altitude. They were down to 3,500 ft. when the B–17 reached the Channel, and their speed was just above stalling speed. Captain Kenny and Colonel Olds restarted one of the engines that had been feathered, but fire returned so they had to shut it down again. As they passed over the White Cliffs of Dover they were down to a few hundred feet so they selected the first airfield that came into view—Gravesend. Kenny made a safe but downwind approach. Some members of the crew received awards for their conduct on this mission; Latham received the Distinguished Service Cross. John Latham and George Preddy are among the very few Tarheel recipients of the Distinguished Service Cross.

Encounters with enemy fighters during the next several weeks were few and far between. Other than a brief engagement by Capt. Willie O. Jackson of the 486th on October 10, during which he claimed a probable victory over an Me 109, no further contacts with the Luftwaffe were experienced by pilots of the 352nd until late November.

November 3, 1943—Wednesday
Got a break in the weather today, consequently a mission! We supported B-24s on penetration. The target was Wilhelmshaven. We made no encounters with the enemy and no attacks were made on the bombers.

According to Roger Freeman's *Mighty Eighth War Diary* the November 3 mission comprised 566 bombers escorted by 333 P-47s and 45 P-38s. The 4th Fighter Group scored one victory, the 55th four, the 78th one, and the 353rd five. The only losses were sustained by the 4th; they lost two aircraft. Also, one of their P-47s crashed after takeoff and the pilot was injured.

November 5, 1943—Friday
Supported B-17 penetration to Ruhr Valley at noon. We were bottom squadron but made no contacts. I have never seen anything like the flak that was thrown up over the Valley. The Germans must be trying to protect something quite valuable.

The mission of the fifth was another large one with 503 bombers supported by 383 fighters. The B-17s went to Gelsenkirchen to bomb oil refineries and the marshalling yard, and the B-24s to Münster to hit their marshalling yard. The targets were indeed valuable to the enemy.

November 7, 1943—Sunday
Supported B-17s to Ruhr Valley again this morning. Again we made no encounter but I was in good position leading an eight ship section on roving detail up high.

On November 7 mission more fighters than bombers were dispatched—283 fighters (all P-47s) escorting 122 bombers. Targets included industrial areas at Wesel, Düren and Randerath. The 355th Fighter Group received credit for one enemy aircraft destroyed; the 56th lost one and the 355th lost five.

George Preddy and John Meyer took the train to London on a three-day pass. They enjoyed a bit of nightlife in the big city, and some camaraderie at the American Melody Club where they met and talked with a bunch of B-17 pilots and crew members. They did a little shopping before catching the train back to Bodney.

November 12, 1943—Friday
Did very little today other than test hop my ship. It is flying very well. Received letters from home. Bill [Preddy] is starting in primary. Bozo [Boaz] has soloed and also become a papa. Rachel [sister] has a little daughter.
November 13, 1943—Saturday
Gave withdrawal support for B-17s across the Z[ui]der Zee and out into the English Channel. Saw no enemy aircraft and very little flak.

Our bombers hit the port area at Bremen, their primary target. There were 390 fighters escorting 272 bombers, only 133 of which were effective. Some abandoned the mission due to bad weather at the assembly area. Severe winds limited the range of our fighters; the 55th Fighter Group flying P–38s got six victories but lost seven of their forty-five aircraft dispatched, and the 355th got three and lost two. All nine American pilots were listed as missing in action.

November 19, 1943—Friday
We went out to give withdrawal support to a task force of 180 B–17s coming back from Gelsenkirchen today but failed to make rendezvous. Learned later that they were unable to bomb target due to 10/10 cloud cover and were evidently off course and timing.

Snetterton was about twenty-five kilometers southeast of Bodney. The 96th Bomb Group was stationed there. Because Snetterton was conveniently located near 3rd Division Headquarters at Elveden Hall, the 96th Bomb Group often led major missions carrying commanding generals. Gen. Circus Lama, for example, led the famous Reconverts shuttle mission to North Africa. And the 96th also led the 3rd Division on the famous Schweinfurt mission of October 14, 1943—the mission for which John Latham was awarded the Distinguished Service Cross.

November 26, 1943—Friday
We supported 120 B–17s and 120 B–24s on withdrawal from Bremen today but I turned back at the Dutch coast. As luck would have it, my squadron bounced four Me 109s after I left and three were shot down. Meyer and Dilling destroyed one each, and Bennett and Berkshire shared one.
I know that my day is coming and I am going to do everything possible to be ready when I do meet that Luftwaffe. Starting right now I am going to get in top physical and flying condition.

This was another big mission—633 bombers in all were dispatched and 381 fighters provided escort. The bomber groups lost twenty-nine while their gunners claimed twenty-four enemy aircraft destroyed. The fighter groups lost four but destroyed thirty-four enemy aircraft. The 56th Fighter Group was the high scorer with twenty-three victories claimed. Among the unhappy events: two B–17s collided over enemy territory; another B–17 of the 94th Bomb Group collided with an Me 109 and both were lost; the lead B–17 from the 388th Bomb Group was hit by incendiary bombs from the 96th and lost.

George made his last entry in the diary on November 26, 1943. In that entry he expressed the determination and singleness of purpose that drove him to become the leading active air ace in the European theater of operations within a year. This mission was important to the 352nd. It was the mission on which they made their first enemy encounter, and they won three to zero. John Meyer got his first victory; there would be twenty-three added to his list by January 1, 1945. When his aerial victories are added to those he got by strafing the enemy on the ground, Meyer's score totalled thirty-seven. When that score is added to George's sum of aerial and ground victories (32), we have the highest scoring pair of aces to come from the same American group.

John Bennett and Robert Berkshire, the two who shared a victory, were flying in George's flight. If George had not had to turn back due to mechanical trouble, he undoubtedly would have made his first encounter with the enemy. Perhaps he would have gotten his first victory. In any event, he knew he had been robbed of his first chance at the Luftwaffe and he was looking forward to his next opportunity.

72

*Chapter 9*

# The First of
# Many Victories

During the latter part of 1943, German fighter forces in the west were augmented in an effort to counter continuing daylight precision bombing. This move by the Luftwaffe was costly to the American bomber and fighter forces. Four days of daylight raids in October resulted in tremendous losses on both sides. A total of 1,174 bombers attacked targets deep in Germany—Bremen, Anklam, Münster, and Schweinfurt—with precision, but 148 of them never returned. The most costly raid of the four occurred on the fourteenth when the Americans lost sixty bombers out of 229 attacking, a loss of twenty-six percent. Losses of this magnitude made for poor morale to say the least. And the average rate of loss was staggering. Bomber crews were calculating their slim chances of living through twenty-five missions.

Serious damage had been wrought against important industrial targets feeding the Luftwaffe. But, in spite of such losses, the Germans seemed to be increasing their inventory of war materials—especially fighter aircraft.

*George's long list of victories began with his successful destruction of an Me–109 on December 1, 1943 while flying Lt. Ralph Hamilton's P–47 named*

Frances B. *Hamilton's Thunderbolt was coded HO-H.* R. Hamilton and J. Bleidner

At the same time, a crisis was developing in the Eighth Air Force. Bomber crews and long-range fighter aircraft could not be supplied fast enough to meet the needs generated by the greatly expanding German fighter forces in the west. The few American P-47 fighter groups in England at this time were equipped with long-range tanks which were carried until empty or until the enemy was encountered. If carried until empty, their range was 340 miles—still not enough to allow escort all the way to some of the deep German targets.

On December 1, George led a flight of P-47s into Germany to meet a force of bombers and escort them home. The target for the day was the industrial area of Solingen; 299 bombers were dispatched and 281 made the attack. George met the bombers about ten miles south of Rheydt as they were withdrawing from the target area.

As he rendezvoused with the bombers, he sighted his first victim of the war. When he returned he filed a report explaining his encounter with the enemy—a standard operating procedure adopted by the Eighth Air Force.

> I was leading Crown Prince Red Flight in a section of twelve ships. We came in over the bomber formation at 30,000 feet and went into a left orbit. I saw one Me 109 behind the rear box of bombers about 3,000 feet below me. I started a quarter stern attack and when about 1,000 yards from the enemy aircraft, it started a steep spiral dive to the left. I followed closing to 400 yards. As I closed from 400 to 200 yards, I fired and saw strikes on the wing roots and cockpit. The airplane began smoking and fell out of control at about 7,000 feet. I fired another burst closing to about 100 yards. After I broke off the attack, the enemy aircraft disintegrated.
> The Me 109 was carrying a belly tank which he did not drop.
> CLAIM: 1 Me 109 Destroyed

The destruction of his first enemy aircraft was witnessed by his wingman, Lt. William T. "Whiz" Whisner, in his encounter report. His gun cameras also recorded the event; hence there was no doubt about his claim. The enemy pilot was apparently killed by the first burst which hit the cockpit; he never bailed out.

Enemy fighter resistance was not overly intense on this mission. The 487th claimed three enemy aircraft destroyed, and they were the only squadron of the 352nd to net a victory. Lt. Virgil K. Meroney got one Me 109 by himself and shared in the destruction of an Me 410 with Lt. Richard L. Grow. These victories were also firsts for both Meroney and Grow.

Lieutenant Meroney became the first ace of the 352nd Fighter Group. By April 1944 he had racked up nine aerial victories. He was shot down by enemy ground fire while strafing an airfield in northwest Germany. Taken prisoner, he finally made his escape good one year later, just before the war ended. Meroney started his career somewhat like George; both served in the National Guard before entering active duty. Meroney, however, did not earn his wings until October 1942.

Meroney flew F-84s in Korea and F-4s in Vietnam; in both he flew fighter-bomber missions. Among the distinctions he holds is the flight through a hydrogen bomb cloud collecting samples; he and his wingman were the first human beings to fly through such a cloud. During the last month of his tour in Southeast Asia, Colonel Meroney took his son, Lt. Virgil K. Meroney III, on his first combat mission in an F-4. It was Colonel Meroney's last combat mission—his 141st.

"B" Flight, 487th FS, assembled outside a favorite watering hole "Ye Olde Auger Inn." Little did they know at the time this photo was taken what all they would accomplish before VE-day. The flight accounted for 75.83 aerial and ground victories. Virgil Meroney would become the first ace, Richard Grow would be the first squadron casualty. Back row, with individual scores for air and ground victories, left to right—Sweeney 0.5, Grow 0.5, Bennett 6, Whisner 18.5, Meroney 10. Front row—Preddy 31.83, Berkshire 6, McMahan 3. P. Grabb

Back to 1943. The bombers, sometimes referred to as Big Friends, didn't fare as well as the fighters—the Little Friends. Twenty-four were shot down, most of them during penetration to the target. The Luftwaffe tactic at the time was to wait until the bombers were starting on their bomb run and then hit. Their aim was to break up the bomber formations and make precision bombing of the target most difficult. In many cases they succeeded in destroying the precision necessary to demolish a target. Accurate bombing from high altitudes was tough enough without continuous harassment of enemy fighters. Weather more often than not also worked against bombing accuracy.

Due to dwindling bomber forces, slow replacement of crews, and poor weather, only ten missions were flown by the 487th during December. With the exception of one fighter sweep, all missions were flown to escort the Big Friends either to or from the target. George flew all but one of the missions, and that one netted the squadron five enemy aircraft destroyed—more than any one mission to date. The 487th suffered no casualties on that mission to Bremen on the twentieth.

Two days later a force of 574 bombers was dispatched to hit the marshalling yards of Osnabrück and Münster. The primary target for the day was Osnabrück. The 487th Squadron was to provide withdrawal support for the bombers on their return from the primary target. George took off shortly after 1300 hours and headed for the planned rendezvous point east of the Zuider Zee between Linden and Zwolle. Clouds were 9/10 topping out at about 18,000 ft. Visibility was excellent above the clouds. His encounter report follows:

> I was leading Crown Prince Blue Flight. As we made rendezvous with the bombers, Yellow Flight [led by John C. Meyer] bounced a Me 109 and my flight gave them top cover. Shortly after that, I noticed three Me 109s coming in to the rear of the B-17s. I bounced two of them and they immediately went into a dive straight down and I went into compressibility following them. I pulled out at 8,000 feet and sighted one of the enemy aircraft just above a cloud layer. I gave him a short burst and he went into the clouds. No damage was noted.
>
> My wingman, Lt. Grow, and I began climbing back up with everything to the firewall. When we reached 15,000 feet, I noticed another Me 109 above us positioning for an attack. He made an attack on the two of us and we turned into him. We battled him for almost 15 minutes getting short deflection shots but we were unable to gain an advantage. He finally broke off the engagement and disappeared in the clouds below us.
>
> We resumed climbing and picked up Lt. Bennett, our Blue 3. We sighted the bomber formation about 25 miles west of and above us. We continued climbing towards the bombers and leveled off at 26,000 feet on the down-sun side still quite a few miles out. I saw a B-24 straggling to the left and below the formation. He was being attacked by six Me 210s, but they saw me coming and immediately dispersed. I began closing on one of them and fired from out of range with 80 degrees deflection. I saw no damage before he ducked into the clouds.
>
> I pulled back up and attacked another Me 210 which was attacking the B-24. I started firing at 60 degrees deflection from 400 yards. I came on down in stern continuing to fire and closing to 200 yards. I noticed many strikes on the center section, fuselage and engines. The enemy aircraft began to disintegrate with large pieces flying off and he went down into the clouds in flames. I broke back up and Lt. Grow called that a Me 109 was on my tail. I threw the stick in left corner and saw the enemy aircraft behind me and out of range. I continued down skidding and slipping. Grow then called that an enemy aircraft was on his tail but I was unable to locate him. I told Grow to hit the deck, then I went into a cloud and set course for home on instruments. I stayed in the clouds for about 15 minutes and broke out over the Dutch coast at 3,000 feet.
>
> I could not contact Lt. Grow and did not see him again.
>
> CLAIM: 1 Me 210

Apparently the 109 on Lieutenant Grow's tail got him before he could duck into the protective cover of clouds. He never returned.

With two Thunderbolts trying to scare off six twin-engined Me 210s protected by another ten Me 109s, it is truly a miracle that either one got back. As it happened, both George and the crippled B-24 made it home.

For this remarkable display of courage George was recommended for the Distinguished Service Cross by his commanding officer, Maj. John Meyer. He was awarded the Silver Star, his country's third highest award for heroism. His claim for one Me 210 destroyed was recognized on the basis of his gun

*Lt. Richard L. Grow was Preddy's first wingman. He was killed in action during a mission on December 22, 1943, when he became separated from his flight. Lieutenant Grow was a great pianist and often entertained the other pilots. P. Grabb*

camera film, and so noted in his award. However, the Fighter Victory Credits Board, which convened in 1956 and 1957 to appraise fighter kills and compile official records of Korean and top World War II aces, failed to give Preddy credit for this victory. It was an oversight on their part, and that oversight was corrected in 1978 when the US Air Force published their Historical Study Number 85, *USAF Credits for the Destruction of Enemy Aircraft, World War II*. It was the first edition of this book that brought that omission to their attention. And proof of the credit was given in the form of General Order Number 59 dated February 16, 1944, and issued by the Eighth Air Force. That order awarded Preddy the Silver Star and contained the following:

> George E. Preddy, Jr., 0-430846, Captain, Army Air Forces, United States Army. For gallantry in action, while escorting bombers withdrawing from a mission over Germany, 22 December 1943. While proceeding towards his home base, accompanied by two other fighter aircraft, Captain Preddy observed a lone crippled bomber being attacked by a large number of enemy fighters. Though out-numbered six to one, he unhesitatingly led his flight in an attack on the enemy and pressed it home with such viciousness that the enemy planes were scattered and forced to cease their attacks on the enemy bomber. Captain Preddy personally destroyed one of the enemy aircraft. When the enemy fighters switched their attack to his flight, he skillfully maneuvered them away from the bomber, thus allowing it to escape and then eluded them by taking cloud cover. The gallantry, aggressiveness and skill displayed by Captain Preddy reflect highest credit upon himself and the Armed Forces of the United States.

During the late 1980s, when Allan Matthews read the first edition of this book, he identified that straggling B-24 saved by Preddy's flight. It was his! He had been the copilot. Coincidentally, he was living in Preddy's hometown

On December 22, 1943, Preddy destroyed an Me 210 for his second victory flying Meroney's P-47 named Sweet Louise, coded HO-V. Lieutenant Meroney scored nine aerial victories in three months and was considered to have the potential of being one of the highest scoring aces in the ETO. Unfortunately, he was taken prisoner on his first Mustang mission, April 8, 1944. J. L. Slabe

of Greensboro, North Carolina, at the time he read the book. As it turned out, this particular incident had been well-documented in the 445th Bomb Group's history. Matthews's story is told in detail in the article "Thunderbolt Liberates Liberator" published in the January 1988 *Air Classics* magazine. Briefly, here's what happened on that B–24 on December 22, 1943.

On the way to Osnabrück, *Lizzie*—Matthews's plane for this mission—lost power in its number two engine just as they reached their assigned altitude of 22,000 ft. Its supercharger malfunctioned. They feathered the prop on number two and increased manifold pressure and rpm on the remaining three engines. But they were still unable to maintain formation. The pilot, Lt. Glenn Jorgenson, restarted number two and attempted to regain power by jockeying the supercharger controls back and forth. This procedure helped, and it enabled *Lizzie* to make the bomb run in formation.

As the 445th withdrew from the target area, *Lizzie* and two other B–24s fell farther and farther behind the formation. Knowing they were prime targets for enemy fighters, all three B–24s started diving for cloud cover. As Matthews descended he and his crew spotted about fifteen Me–109s attacking one of the other stragglers. In just seconds the enemy sent that B–24 down in flames and went after a second straggler. This one took about ten passes by the enemy fighter before they sent it crashing to earth.

The rear gunner on *Lizzie* immediately warned that the fighters were coming in from the rear. Jorgenson and Matthews started taking evasive action—diving, climbing, turning, slipping—any maneuver to thwart the enemy's aim. The gunners then reported eight Me 210s coming in at between five and seven o'clock. On their first pass they hit number one engine with 20 mm cannon shells, causing it to overspeed, and they hit number three fuel tank leaving a four-inch hole, but no fire. Incredible!

Now the enemy fighters were making their second pass. Two or three shells exploded in the bomb bay throwing parts of the bomb racks into the radio compartment, breaking fuel gauges and damaging radios. The hydraulic system was also knocked out leaving the tail turret inoperative. Another shell hit the nose compartment and exploded. Shrapnel from the explosion hit Lt. Arthur E. Barks, the navigator, and killed him instantly. That explosion also set the B–24 on fire; the cockpit filled with smoke. Fragments from the explosion also hit Lt. Roy Stahl, the bombardier, in his legs and ripped off his connections to the oxygen system and the radio. Nonetheless, Stahl went for the fire extinguisher. He did this at 22,000 ft. without oxygen, without gloves, and with damaged legs.

The gunners continued to fire at the enemy fighters. One fired a rocket through both rudders leaving a hole the size of a basketball in each. The engineer operating the top turret, Sgt. Charles Jones, scored a direct hit on one of the fighters; it burst into flames and went down through the overcast. The right waist gunner got off a few good bursts hitting another fighter, leaving him smoking. After that pass the enemy fighters suddenly and for no apparent reason ceased the attack on *Lizzie*. The reason, as Lieutenant Matthews learned later, was that a flight of three P–47s had intervened and chased the enemy away from the crippled bomber. But, *Lizzie* still had 300 miles between it and home base and only two engines with which to make it—numbers two and four.

*Capt. George E. Preddy, Jr., receiving the Silver Star medal from Brigadier General Anderson for his exploits on December 22, 1943. J. Sabanos*

As they approached the North Sea, they started throwing everything overboard that would come loose—steel helmets, flak suits, radios, ammunition, guns, and finally the body of the dead navigator. With all radio equipment either abandoned or inoperative, and the gyros tumbled, they flew on by the seat of their pants descending through an overcast. Over the North Sea at 1,500 ft., they prepared to ditch. It looked as if they just would not be able to make it to England. But they well knew that ditching in December in the North Sea would be most hazardous, so they tried to restart number three, which had no oil and a hole in its fuel tank. It started and they gained a bit of altitude before the engine got red hot. They shut it down to avoid another fire.

By the time they spotted the coast of England they were back down to 1,800 ft. and still losing altitude. Crossing the coast Matthews spotted a long runway ahead which turned out to be Manston. They quickly prepared for a landing, putting their gear down and going through the checklist. Only the right main gear went down and locked. The other two refused to go down, and the right main refused to come back up. So they slipped *Lizzie* out over the grass rather than land on the hard surface. The plane came to a violent stop with the left wing tip acting as a landing gear and brake. During all this the pilot had been nursing his fuel supply which was now essentially exhausted. So no fire on landing, and the remaining crewmen jumped out of the plane safely.

Lieutenant Matthews said, "Although I went on to fly a total of thirty-six combat missions, thirty as pilot-in-command and the last six as squadron leader, I'll never forget that first mission. I had always wondered why the enemy fighters left us so suddenly, for surely we were easy prey. Forty years later I unexpectedly found the answer. My daughter was on the Board of Directors of the Greensboro Historical Museum, and she had formed a group of junior historians at the museum. The group decided to call themselves the Major George E. Preddy Chapter. In connection with her research for the chapter, my daughter read Preddy's biography and thought I might enjoy reading it. So as I read about Preddy's mission on 22 December 1943, chills went up my spine. I had discovered without a doubt that it was George Preddy who drove the enemy away."

Throughout George's diary, entries have shown that he had great respect for many of his leaders. There was the remark about his flight leader, Joe Kruzel, one about the 49th Group commander, Paul Wurtsmith, and one about the commander of the 352nd Fighter Group while they were stationed in the States, Colonel Ramage. Whether he was blessed with good leaders or just had an inborn respect for leadership, the result was the same. A letter written home during the last month of 1943 expresses this same respect for his squadron commander, John Meyer.

December 29, 1943
Dearest Mother,
    . . . I'm enclosing the Christmas greeting our CO sent to all of us in the squadron. He is a few months younger than I am but has been flying about one and a half years longer. He has studied tactics and leadership and has been very tough and demanding in getting his principles established. At first many of the men didn't like him, but since we have been overseas and seen our squadron out-perform the others, we have come to have great respect for him. We believe we have a great outfit; the ground crew as well as the pilots have the fighting spirit to a high degree. . . .

*Another view of George's first P-47. Note the black and white wheel covers on main landing gear. Gun barrels were also highly polished. "Cripes A'Mighty"* *was a phrase that Preddy yelled when he played craps as he released the dice!* J. McVay

George made no mention in his letter of his two recent victories. There was no censorship rule against this sort of thing. Perhaps he just didn't want to tell his mother anything that would bring the reality of war so close.

When Ralph Hamilton was interviewed during the 1980s for a videotape on Preddy's life, he found in his files a copy of the Christmas greeting George referred to above. Here's what it said.

25 December 1943
Subject: Christmas Greeting
To: All Personnel
It's about 2:00 AM Christmas morning, and as I am writing this a large number of you men are lying on your backs beneath airplanes. With cold bodies and frozen hands, you are working outside my office. You are working yourselves on Christmas Eve so that in case our Squadron is called upon to perform its mission tomorrow, on Christmas Day, we will be ready. To you men especially I extend my Christmas greetings. Also, I extend my Christmas Greetings to you, the pilots of this organization, who have fought the war in the past few weeks and made in that time an outstanding record for the 487th. To you Lt. ——, who quitted yourself like a man; to you, Lt. ——, who spends Christmas in a foreign hospital; to you both who have given yourselves for us, and of whom the rest of the 487th are justifiably proud, I extend my heartiest Christmas Greetings. To you others of the 487th; you administrative officers and men who have made it possible for us to do our part in bringing this inferno to an end I extend my heartfelt wishes for a Merry Christmas.

I offer also, my sincere thanks for the manner in which you have performed the arduous duties that this six months of service in a foreign land has demanded. Neither the rigors of the climate, the efforts of the enemy against you pilots in the air, nor the constant high pressure to which you have all been subjected, have dimmed your enthusiasm or blurred the sparkle of your excellence.

I know that at times it must irk you—those of you who do not fly—to learn about your comrades in arms, who are engaged in more spectacular fields of glory, and that you are impatient to join them. I also know that at times you long to be with your loved ones at home.

But I also know, because you have shown me, that yours is the courage and stout-heartedness that can meet any demands cheerfully and willingly, without hope of reward other than that which comes with a job well done; and with your determination to apply your every effort to the task at hand, the successful offence against this important objective in which we are making such a vital contribution, will lead to the successful conclusion of this war.

I thank you again for your superb performance. It is a great privilege to be able to serve with such a fine body of men.

Merry Christmas to you and your families.

John C. Meyer,

Major, Air Corps Commanding

Ralph Hamilton, a lieutenant at the time and a very close friend to John Meyer, penned a note at the bottom of the Greeting, "From our very swell CO, a really capable leader." The two names that were censored out of the Greeting were those of Lt. Richard Grow, shot down on the twenty-second, and Lt. David Kramer, who on November 30 had to bail out after being bounced by the enemy. He was on the way in to pick up the Big Friends and escort them home. As Kramer prepared to jump he radioed to his flight, "So long boys, see you at Christmas." He didn't make it back for Christmas, but he did make it back.

*The right side of the fuselage was considered the chief's side. Crew chief Lew Lunn chose not to place his individual markings on the right side of* Cripes A'

Mighty. *Lunn is squatting on the wing root with other ground personnel from the 487th.* J. L. Slabe

*Chapter 10*

# Down in the Channel

The pilot's abode, Clermont Hall, resembled an old man's home even though it was filled mostly with youngsters. But they were young only in age; most were seasoned veterans of war and quite mature as a result. At twenty-four, George was one of the "old men" in the group.

During evening hours following quiet days—days when the pilots didn't make the trip over enemy territory—the hall took on the air of a very elite and gracious men's club. One group of men usually played snooker, a game similar to but more difficult than billiards. That group played quietly but fervently. And another group of pilots played bridge with equal enthusiasm and calmness. Of great importance to all was the time spent just sitting around talking.

At least five minutes before mealtime, most of them wandered to the table to engage in gentle conversation. Another five or ten minutes after the meal found the pilots shuffling around to make ready for card games, snooker, a movie, or more conversation. A stranger walking in on such an atmosphere would never have taken the men for an eager, young and spirited group of fighter jocks.

In his letters home, George described many things he did in his spare time and much about the new country he was seeing for the first time. He seldom talked of his flying.

England
January 18, 1944
Dear Mom and Dad,
The last few days the weather has been foggy and damp. It's hard to imagine how thick the fogs get sometimes. In London they are worse than any other place, and all the taxis stop running and a bus driver will lead a bus down the street with a torch.

I was talking with an Englishman last night and he can hardly conceive of a country like America where people are plowing through snow at the same time others in a different part of the country are going swimming. He thinks we all have the life of 'Riley' and never worry about taxes or money.

I went to a meeting recently and Jimmy Stewart was present. I recognized him immediately by his long slim frame and his voice. He seems to be a straight guy.

We had a good dinner with ice cream for dessert last Sunday. We don't get real ice cream here, but it's a fair substitute. I think it's made from powdered milk.

Some fellow in the nearby town bet another the war would be over before New Years. He lost £20 ($80) on the deal, so the winner threw a party at the local pub last Saturday night. Several of us from the field were invited and joined in the English dancing and fun. We had a big time and a big buffet dinner with turkey.

My room mate is on detached service for ten days and I'm taking care of his dog while he's gone. She is one of the little Spaniels I was telling you about and she is growing up to be real pretty. Every night she pulls our shoes out in the middle of the floor. If there is any paper for her to get hold of, you can be sure of having it torn up and scattered all over the place. I'm thankful she is pretty well house broken. That was the big headache for a long time.

We now have a small gym and a director who has done a lot of athletic work. I've been going down quite a bit and working out on his bars. I've laid off so long that I'm rusty compared to what I used to do.

I'm feeling fine and hope all at home are the same. Looking forward to a letter. Best love ever,
George

Due to poor weather during January, only eleven missions were flown and three of these were against Crossbow targets, German long-range weapons in the Pas de Calais area. On the tenth mission, an unprecedented force of 800 bombers was sent to Frankfurt—the Chicago of Germany—to bomb their industrial area. George's squadron was assigned the job of giving withdrawal support to the bombers, and it was his first encounter with the enemy for the month.

Fighter tactics still called for close direct support. American fighters had to stay close to the bombers so they could fend off enemy fighter attacks on the bomber formations. Unable to take the offensive often put our fighters at a disadvantage. Later, tactics were changed to allow for aggressive free-for-all fights in the approach sector. It was often quite difficult for George and others with his tenacity to refrain from taking the initiative during these early days before effective tactics were developed.

Shortly after 1000 hours, George took off leading his flight in formation through the thick overcast. Actually, this was a most difficult feat for a group of young men with minimal flying hours in the heavy, high-performance P-47s. Often, as on this day, they had to climb through six thousand or more feet of solid overcast. The task demanded the utmost in skill; given half a chance, the fighter would drop off on a wing and spin to earth if not caught in time. In fact, this happened on a number of occasions during World War II—and since. In one case when caught in a violent storm, twenty-two out of thirty fighter planes and their pilots disappeared forever. Back to this mission; clouds were 10/10 (completely overcast) and the ceiling was relatively high at two thousand feet. But the tops were between eight and ten thousand feet. His January 29, 1944, encounter report says:

I was leading Crown Price Yellow Flight and we were escorting two boxes of bombers. The Group Leader called for everybody out and I started to join him when my number two man, Whisner, called that the bombers were being attacked. I turned back coming in behind the bombers and saw a FW 190 below and behind them. Whisner had started a bounce on another enemy aircraft so I went down on this 190. He went into a steep dive and I closed to about 400 yards and started firing. I was closing rapidly and saw a few hits and a little smoke before I broke off. I lost the enemy aircraft momentarily but picked him up again on my left at about 4,000 feet. I started after him and he made a steep turn to the left. I turned with him and started firing at 300 yards and 60 degrees deflection. He straightened out and started down at about 45 degrees. I got a good long burst at 300 yards and saw hits all over the ship. The engine was evidently knocked out as I closed very rapidly after that. The last I saw of him he was at 1500 feet going down at an increasing angle to the left.

I made a steep climbing turn to the left and saw Whisner. He joined me and we climbed back to 10,000 feet. It was past time to go home so I picked up the heading as we didn't have enough fuel to do any more fighting. We went below

George expressing his appreciation to Lt. William T. Whisner for his efforts in helping him survive the freezing Channel. Whisner was George's wingman on many missions. They worked well together. USAAF

George with Lt. Fred A. Yochim, the official spotter the day George went down. Yochim provided air-sea rescue with Preddy's location. P. Grabb

the clouds and came out on the deck crossing the French coast somewhere north of Calais. Suddenly, a concentrated barrage of flak opened up. I began kicking the ship around but felt hits. She began smoking but didn't lose power so I climbed to 5,000 feet and gave a Mayday. Shortly afterwards my engine cut out. I bailed out at 2,000 feet. A P–47 spotted me and I was picked up out of the drink by a Walrus.

CLAIM: 1 FW 190 Destroyed

Lt. William Whisner was George's wingman, and he wrote an encounter report for this mission. He also wrote the author a letter about the return trip. Here is Whisner's encounter report.

I was flying Yellow 2 on Captain Preddy's wing. As Group Leader ordered us out, we were at four o'clock to a box of bombers, and several miles away. I spotted an E/A attacking the bombers. I called it in, and started a shallow dive. As I closed, a bomber dropped out of the formation, and I identified a FW 190 attacking it at 15,000 feet. He saw us coming and as he broke away I saw one chute below the Fort. I got in a short burst just as he broke, and followed him down to 1,000 or 2,000 feet. He took violent evasive action—skidding, turning and throwing everything into one corner. At 3 or 4,000 ft. I was able to get a good shot, and observed strikes on wing and engine. He went into an overcast (1,000–2,000 feet) while I was firing, and I held the trigger down even when I couldn't seen him in the cloud. When I came out below, I was beside him at 100 yards, and he was in a dive smoking badly at 800 ft. above the ground. I was certain that he couldn't recover before crashing, and being all alone, I pulled up hard with everything on the fire wall. Reaching 7,000 ft., I saw another P–47, which turned out to be Captain Preddy. We came home together on the deck.

CLAIM: One FW 190 DESTROYED

For some reason not mentioned by either Preddy or Whisner, the standard operational procedure which calls for a wingman to protect his leader's back side was not followed. Preddy and Whisner split up and each went after their own targets, and each scored. Fortunately, neither was hit during the engagements. But this encounter had to remind George of his December mission in which he lost his wingman, Lieutenant Grow, when they split up. Note that Bill Whisner makes no mention in his encounter report that George went down in the Channel. It's interesting to learn what Whisner had to say about this mission in 1983 in response to the author's query. Whisner wrote:

With regard to George's Channel adventure, we were withdrawing together after an encounter with FW 190s. I had joined with George and we were low on fuel. George never talked on the radio—nor did he talk much ever. I called him on the radio and asked his intentions, as we were approximately 100 miles inside the Continent. No Answer.

He proceeded to head west at 1,000 feet altitude, with reduced power. Shortly, I saw an airfield ahead, and as we were flying about 250 mph, I suggested to him that we change course or increase speed. No answer.

We crossed the airfield and to my surprise drew no AA fire. A few minutes later I could see the Channel and North Sea Coast and again called George on the radio. My words to him were that we needed to increase speed and hit the deck. [To avoid the 88 mm batteries which were prevalent along the Dutch Coast, as well as the Belgian and French Coasts.] No answer and no change in George's course of flight.

At this time I had approximately 150 gallons of fuel left and had no reason to feel that George had more or less. When we reached a point approximately two miles short of the coast, I made a right/starboard turn of 90 degrees and shoved on full power, and hit the deck, keeping George in sight to my left. He was obviously intent upon keeping the low airspeed and maintaining his altitude. After turning north for about 30 seconds, I turned back west at full power on the deck, keeping George a bit ahead of me off to my left. Crossing the coast, I saw a gun battery and I was fired upon as I crossed the coastline. My evasive action was to jam in full left rudder and right stick—keeping my wings level. I received four rounds of 88 mm fire and looked to George. He received four 88 mm rounds which missed and then four more which bracketed him. He was still flying slow at 500 to 1,000 feet altitude.

At this point I want to say that George Preddy was disdainful of the enemy. He had no respect for nor fear of enemy AA or fighters. Thus, his disregard of my warning.

His radio was working as I heard his emergency transmittals to the Marston Controller. The events were as follows: after George crossed the coast and was hit by the 88 mm fire, he began emitting white smoke from his engine. As I closed on him, I observed that he opened the canopy and heavy smoke was coming from the cockpit as well as from the engine. I called him and suggested he should bail out as the aircraft could explode. No reply.

I remained on his wing at about 100 feet distance and called him again suggesting that he abandon the aircraft. At this time he began calling Marston for an emergency steer. I had switched to the emergency "D" channel, and made no further calls until later—after his bailout.

He began slowing and reducing altitude and finally descended into the cloud (an undercast which topped at about 1,000 feet and rose to the west in multiple layers as there was a front moving in). At this time, as he disappeared into the cloud, he was flying at an indicated airspeed of 180 mph, and he couldn't possibly have seen his instruments due to the heavy smoke in the cockpit. He was flying by the seat of his pants and was in no way panicked.

Rather than stay on his wing after his penetration into the cloud tops, I elected to do a 360 degree turn and enter the cloud in a descent at approximately the same point which he had done. We had not obtained an altimeter setting since before take-off on the mission, and I knew that the low pressure system which had moved in would cause a significant change. I determined therefore that I would penetrate at 180 mph until I reached an altitude of 100 feet, and no lower. At just above 100 feet I observed waves/foam/water below and suddenly—to my right—I saw a P-47 strike the water. Then, there was a parachute opening and even before I could start a turn, George swung once in the chute and was in the water. He had waited almost too long to bail out.

The weather was miserable—the wind and waves high, the visibility low, and the cloud was almost on the water. I made a tight, low-airspeed 360-degree turn and when I again picked him up visually he was in the dinghy. He'd obviously followed standard procedure, despite his difficulties, and inflated the dinghy before entering the sea. I circled him several times while calling Marston for a radio fix on his position. Marston directed that I must obtain more altitude as I was too low for a fix. Then I climbed through the cloud on a turn which I calculated to remain over his position. Marston then confirmed a positive fix and advised that a Dumbo [air-sea rescue amphibian] was on the way.

During this time, the 352nd Group "Spotter" (P–47) was . . . en route to pick up Preddy in the Channel as an air spotter. He arrived just as I left, above the cloud, and how he found George is a miracle. The upshot was that the Dumbo RAF rescue aircraft landed and picked up George and on take-off in the rough sea lost a pontoon. It was therefore incapacitated and was subsequently towed in by an RAF power-launch boat.

Meanwhile aboard the Dumbo, George was consuming a quart of brandy which the air-sea rescue people carried for the purpose. At the time, the air and water temperatures were below 40 degrees F. and how Preddy survived is perhaps another miracle.

But George was tough, and as I recall, two days later we were drinking in the bar at the Officers Club, speculating on George's rescue and health, when he walked in wearing an RAF uniform. He shrugged off any hardship and advised us that he had laid the gal whom we all knew from her voice on the Marston Control Radio. She had a lovely sexy voice and we had all speculated on how great it would be to meet her.

That's the end of Whisner's story about Preddy's going down in the Channel. He summarized with a few remarks which include a comment that George never gave him any credit for his rescue. Perhaps George never learned that Whisner led the P–47 Spotter to his position. Lt. Frederick Yochim flew the Spotter P–47 and called in fixes on Preddy's position. But why didn't Preddy respond to Whisner's radio calls? Possibly Preddy's radio was not receiving, only transmitting. We'll never know the answers to these questions. Perhaps they are not important now. What is important is that Bill Whisner flew Preddy's wing on many successful missions during which neither one was lost to enemy action. They made a good team, and both proved to be outstanding fighter pilots. Carl Luksic said that when George returned to Bodney, he told the guys that, "the Walrus ran over me three times before they could get me inside. They damned near killed me! They felt so badly about it they gave me a bottle of brandy to drink on the way to shore."

This was Whisner's first victory. Bill's final tally was 15.5 aerial victories, and he went on to fight again in Korea flying F–86s. He added 5.5 MiGs to his credit, giving him a grand total of twenty-one victories. Whisner was the first pilot to become an ace in both World War II and the Korean conflict and is one of seven aces so distinguished. The others are John F. Bolt (6 in World War II and 6 in Korea), George A. Davis, Jr. (7 and 14), Francis S. Gabreski (28 and 6.5), Vermont Garrison (7.33 and 10), James P. Hagerstrom (6 and 8.5), and Harrison R. Thyng (5 and 5). Whisner remained on active duty with the air force after Korea. He won the Bendix Trophy in 1953 when he flew his F–86F Sabre Jet from Edwards Air Force Base in California to Dayton, Ohio, in what was then a record time of three hours five minutes and forty-five seconds—an average speed of 603.5 mph. He flew fighters with the Royal Air Force, served nuclear weapons duty at Sandia, New Mexico, and just before retirement served a tour in Vietnam. In 1989 he died of complications resulting from bee stings. He was 65 years old, the last survivor of the three top aces of the 352nd Fighter Group—Preddy, Meyer and Whisner.

The English Channel is very cold in January; so also is the city reservoir in Greensboro, North Carolina, on New Year's Eve. And it was on a New Year's Eve several years earlier that George and two of his close friends—Otto Gaskins and Goat Matthews—went swimming in the reservoir. They didn't, however, stay in the freezing water for an hour as George had to do when he bailed out in the Channel. His dinghy no doubt saved him; about fifteen minutes of exposure is the limit of human endurance in such icy waters.

George missed only one mission as a result of his swim in the icy waters of the English Channel. Just two days after the dunking he was back in the air flying support missions to Germany. While George continued to fly escort missions interrupted occasionally by area patrols over the hardened missile installations, Bill Preddy was in Waco, Texas, taking basic flying training. The two corresponded regularly.

England
February 8, 1944
Dear Bill,

Not long ago I got my third Jerry, an FW 190. Got hit by flak coming home and had to bail out before I could get across the Channel. It was a cold time of the year to go swimming, but the Air Sea Rescue picked me up in an hour.

I'm getting to the place that I would like to shoot down a Hun every day. I've had some damn good friends go down over there, and that is enough to make a person pretty sore. My outfit is way up on the Luftwaffe, and I hope we can increase our lead.

I'm always pulling for you, Bill, and when you think you are ready for a little duel, just let me know.

Best luck,
George

When George went home on leave seven months later, Bill was ready for that duel. George visited in Florida where Bill was stationed for his final training in combat aircraft. So they had their duel in two P-40s—Mustangs weren't available to them—and Bill gave his brother, the experienced combat pilot, quite a challenge. After the dogfight, George said he would hate to meet Bill over Germany and have the task of shooting him down. This not only spoke well of Bill's abilities, but it said much for the improved pilot training being given by the Army Air Corps in 1944.

While the Allies were not entirely sure about their target, the awesome looking T-shaped airplane without a cockpit mounted on elevated ramps in the Pas de Calais area appeared to be important enough to warrant immediate attention. What were they? The answer to this question was not learned for certain until June when the first German pilotless aircraft flamed through the darkened sky and exploded on a railroad bridge in the heart of London.

Anything connected with these mysterious weapons became known as Crossbow targets. There was more connected with them than the photographic eye could tell. The large sites were mainly underground and constructed with steel and concrete walls 25–30 ft. thick. Our bombs were almost like firecrackers to these hardened installations. Nonetheless, our B–17s made many raids in an attempt to stop the Germans from doing whatever they were doing.

George's next encounter with the enemy occurred on a Crossbow mission on February 13, 1944, a mission to the "Rocket Gun Coast" as the public knew it. He took off just after 1400 hours; it was a beautiful day and the visibility was unlimited.

I was leading Crown Prince Red Flight at 18,000 feet in the vicinity of Armentiers when I saw several airplanes at four o'clock low who appeared to be climbing. I called them in and told the squadron to follow me. As we approached them, they made a 180 and passed under us. I recognized them as about twelve FW 190s. They all dived for the deck and I dived on the last enemy aircraft. I was closing slowly and opened fire at 500 yards. The enemy aircraft took evasive action as we passed right over Lille. I broke off the attack as I could not get close enough for a kill. I attacked another FW 190 on my left but could not close on him either.

CLAIM: Nil

The 190 was superior in many respects to the Thunderbolt. Its superior speed enabled it to break off combat almost at will. The Thunderbolt, because of its ability to withstand considerable punishment, was later used extensively as a fighter-bomber. Several pilots, however, compiled impressive records flying this machine; most notable were the records of Francis Gabreski, Robert S. Johnson and Hub Zemke of the 56th Fighter Group.

Cpl. Joseph J. "Red" McVay, Preddy's assistant crew chief, was sleeping on a stack of drop tanks waiting for *Cripes A'Mighty* to return, as usual. Red, having gotten up well before daylight to preflight *Cripes A'Mighty*, would nap while Preddy flew. Red depended on George to buzz him on that stack of

*No, that's not George in the cockpit. It's the squadron artist, S/Sgt. Sam Perry, with crew chief Lew Lunn looking on. This photograph was taken after George had survived his ditching incident on January 29, 1944. Interestingly,*

*Perry has added a yellow gold fish and caterpillar to the aircraft's individual markings denoting George's induction into the Gold Fish and Caterpillar clubs. S. Perry*

tanks to awaken him and to let him know that he had been victorious. This time there was no buzz job, and Red was awakened as George taxied in to park. Although Red was the assistant crew chief, he performed the duties of the crew chief most of the time, according to other crew chiefs who knew the division of labor on Preddy's aircraft. Sgt. Al Geisting, Virgil Meroney's crew chief for a time and later line chief, said in a letter to Red many years later, "I can still see you working on Preddy's plane, and Lunn ordering you to do things. I think maybe you should have been the crew chief and Lunn the assistant, as you did more of the work. But that's bygones, and everything turned out well." One thing seems very clear: Preddy held Red McVay in very high regard. He took time out to write Red's mother while he was home on leave, and he was one of the first guys George looked up when he returned to Bodney.

As a result of their demonstrated ability and top scores at this time, John Meyer, Virgil Meroney and George Preddy were asked to pass on their knowledge of combat flying to others with less experience. Each of them did this in a letter to the requesting Assistant Chief of Staff. All three gave serious expositions with many common points. Here is George's reply.

6 March 1944
Dear Sir:
In reply to your letter dated 3 March 1944, I am writing down a few principles of operational flying. All of these facts or ideas are based upon experience in this theater while flying the P–47 on fighter sweeps and escort missions.

To begin with, it is an old story that the pilot who doesn't get across the Channel will not see any action. One of the big problems in this theater is weather and since a good 50 percent of our flying is done in instrument conditions, it is necessary that all pilots be proficient at instrument and close formation flying. The formation used going through an overcast is as follows: In the flight, the # 2 man flies on the leader's left wing with #3 and #4 on the right. In the squadron, the flights fly line astern stacked down. The whole outfit is in very close, and if each man flies a steady position it is possible to take 16 or 20 ships through an overcast. If visibility in the soup is very bad or if turbulence exists, it becomes necessary to split the squadron into two or more sections.

On the climb out, the flights and individual ships fly close formation as this reduces throttle-jockeying and saves gas. When we approach the enemy coast, everybody moves out into battle formation; i. e., line abreast and 5 or 6 ships length apart for individual ships and line abreast for each two flights. This is an easy formation to fly when flying a straight course and offers excellent cross-cover.

When escorting several large boxes of bombers it is impossible to keep the groups together, so squadrons and sections of squadrons are assigned a particular section of the task force. We usually fly two flights of four planes each. The flights fly line abreast to offer cross-cover, but if the lead ship is turning a lot, it is necessary to fall in string. Normally the flight leaders and element leaders look for bounces with the wing men on the defensive. This doesn't mean that leaders never look back or wing men never look down. It is impossible to see everything, but each pilot must keep his head moving and look to find.

When a member of the flight sees something suspicious, he calls it in and the leader takes the flight to investigate. When it is identified as enemy, we notice the number and formation and try to make a surprise bounce. The first flight of four goes down and the second flight stays up for top cover. It is necessary to have this protection as a decent bounce cannot be made when trying to protect your own tail. If only one flight is in the vicinity, the second element acts as top cover. If a surprise can be made on several enemy aircraft, all ships in the flight can pick one out and drive up behind them and shoot them down. If the Hun sees you coming from above he usually starts diving and turning. It is necessary for the wing man to stay with his leader as the leader cannot follow the Hun through evasive action and do a good job of shooting unless the wing man is there to guard against attack by another enemy aircraft. Should the attacking flight or element get bounced, the wing man turns into the attack immediately and calls the leader.

When the leader is preparing to make a bounce he should inform his squadron of his intentions. If a wing man sees an enemy plane which would get away if he didn't act immediately, he goes down on the bounce calling in as he does so. In this case the leader becomes the wing man.

When being bounced the first thing is to always turn into the attack. The flight does not follow the leader into the turn, but each ship turns into the attackers.

If a pilot sees an enemy aircraft behind him in firing range he must take evasive action immediately. He slips and skids the ship as much as possible giving the Hun maximum deflection. It is a good idea to turn in the direction of friendly planes, so they can shoot or scare Jerry off your tail.

There will be times after a combat that you are down on the deck. If you are alone and can't find a friend to join with, the best thing to do is head for home taking advantage of clouds for cover. If there are two or more they should climb back up providing they still have speed and gas. They should push everything to the firewall, and keep speed in the climb; the leader must do a lot of turning in order to keep the men behind him up. Each man must be on the lookout for a bounce and watch each others' tail. If there are only two or three of you, you should find friends and join them.

As a conclusion, in escorting bombers it is a good idea to range out to the sides, front and rear and hit enemy fighters before they can get to the bombers unprotected.

Meroney departed from the serious commentary at the end of his letter. He said, "That . . . for what it's worth. I believe the main things are . . . teamwork . . . confidence in your leaders, your ship, and that old fighting heart.

KILL THE BASTARDS ! ! !"

In an effort to determine the enemy's firepower near Pas de Calais for purposes of making invasion plans, General Kepner ordered a mission for a low-level attack on enemy airfields in that area. George went on this mission and penetrated to fifty miles, but finally the intensity of ground fire forced his group to withdraw. Eight ships suffered flak damage and two pilots were lost. The purpose of the mission was not revealed to the pilots until after its completion. Naturally, they thought the mission had been a complete flop, but costly as it was, the purpose was accomplished. We learned just how much firepower the nazis had in the area—it was one hell of a lot! Guns were spotted in open fields, church steeples, haystacks, and many other less-than-obvious places.

George's next letter home made no mention of that hair-raising mission.

England
March 13, 1944
Dear Mother and Dad,

. . .
I told you in my last letter that I had been transferred to Group Headquarters. Well, I am now back in the squadron. Shortly after I went to Group, the squadron operations officer, Donalson, was transferred to take command of another squadron, so now I have his job. I like being back with the outfit and the new job is one step up the ladder.

Today I received my membership card to the Gold Fish Club. It's a club for airmen who have been saved in the water by a dinghy and is similar to the Caterpillar Club for those who have made an emergency parachute jump.

I received a letter from my good friend, Larry Smith, who I flew with in Australia. He got back to the States last fall and immediately went to Boston and married his old sweetheart. Now he says his wife is expecting twins before his first anniversary. Looks as if he kinda made up for those 18 months in the Pacific.

Things are rather quiet tonight. Some of the gang are playing cards, others are reading, writing, shooting snooker and one guy is even building an airplane model.

Best love,
George

George qualified twice for the Caterpillar Club, and once for the Gold Fish Club. And his good friend from Australia scored a victory on 8 February 1943—about ten months before George got his first. But Larry Smith decided eighteen months and one victory was enough. He went home and got married.

George got orders to go on R and R at Coomb House (about twenty-five km west of Salisbury). The orders read "will proceed on or about 20 March 1944 to Coomb House, Semley, Dorsetshire for the purpose of carrying out instructions of the commander." Carl Luksic said that Doc Anderl gave them a fifth of scotch for medicinal purposes, and sent them off. Luksic, George, John "Tarzan" Bennett and Bill Halton were sent there together. When they arrived the Red Cross receptionist offered them some hot chocolate, a set of bow and arrows for recreation and bicycles for transportation. So Bennett and Halton—the two largest guys—formed a cross with their arms. Preddy—the smallest and most agile—used it as his springboard to do a flip. He landed on her desk and proceeded to deliver a speech. He said "Don't want no cocoa, don't want no bow and arrows; we want bicycles, we're going to town." And they got their bicycles and headed for town.

And it was 22 March 1944, while George was at Coomb House, that he was promoted to major by command of Lt. Gen. James Doolittle. Upon return to Bodney George was made 487th Squadron operations officer. Jack Donalson was transferred to take command of the 328th.

*Chapter 11*

# The Switch
# from Jugs to Mustangs

During March several of the fighter groups in the Eighth Air Force received the new P–51 Mustang. Even with its initial bugs, the new Mustang's superior performance gave many pilots a heyday against the Luftwaffe the first month they had it. The Germans had been achieving excellent results against our bombers; with the new long-range Mustang accompanying the bomber formations the story began to change. As enemy fighters became engaged in dogfights with the P–51, they soon discovered they had more than met their match. The first operational P–51B Mustangs were soon replaced by the superior D models. The bubble-canopied P–51D had 1490 hp available for takeoff which compared to 1475 for the Me 109G–6 and 1700 for the FW

*Scores depicted on aircraft were applied by the crew chiefs. The number of crosses reflected the sum of aerial and ground victories in the ETO, and frac-* *tions were usually rounded up. That's Preddy in* Cripes A'Mighty 2nd *talking with Lew Lunn after a mission in April 1944. J. Sabanos*

190A–8. The Me 109 was the lightest of the three when loaded—6,950 lbs. compared to 9,750 for the FW 190 and 10,100 for the Mustang. But the P–51D's maximum speed of 430 mph far exceeded the performance of the two German fighters. The best speeds the Me 109 and FW 190 could muster were 386 and 408 mph, respectively.

While not having the firepower of the P–47 or the P–38, the P–51 was superior on almost every other measure. Although generally not able to outclimb the Me 109 or the FW 190, the Mustang could outdive and outrun both at any altitude. And it could outturn them as well. When the K–14 gunsight was added, the P–51 became without doubt the best fighter in the ETO. The British-designed gyroscopic sight significantly enhanced accuracy in deflection shooting and allowed shots to be taken which previously would have been a waste of ammunition. But in the final analysis it was the skill of the individual pilot that made the difference in aerial combat.

On one of the early missions in March, the Luftwaffe lost twenty-six out of forty-three aircraft that took off to intercept in the area of Augsburg. Another ten were forced to land due to battle damage. Only seven were able to make it back to base unscathed. With results such as these being publicized, George was anxiously awaiting the switch to Mustangs for his squadron. It had been two months since he had destroyed his third enemy aircraft and he wanted more—many more! The longer range of the Mustang meant longer exposure to the enemy which translated into more opportunity to engage the enemy. And that meant more opportunity to get the Hun.

The 352nd Fighter Group traded their venerable Thunderbolts for new Mustangs in April 1944; George named his *Cripes A'Mighty 2nd* and his long-stagnant score quickly rose with the help of his speedy new mount.

With broken clouds and good visibility, George took off on April 11, 1944, to provide the Big Friends with penetration support to Berlin. After the long haul to the prime German target, his group left the bomber formation. His encounter report follows:

> After being relieved of bomber escort, the group made a strafing attack on an airdrome containing 30–plus medium and heavy bombers. On my first pass, I fired at a He 111 on the edge of the field and noticed strikes and a burst of flame. I turned after passing the field and fired at another He 111 but saw no results. As I departed, I saw many large fires from burning aircraft.
> On my second pass I crossed a row of hangars and saw many planes inside.
> CLAIM: One (1) He 111 Destroyed
> One (1) He 111 Unknown

His gun camera didn't record results of the second pass because he was credited with only one enemy aircraft destroyed on this mission. Aerial combat during the month of April was most limited because the German losses had been quite high. Many of their experienced pilots had been lost, forcing them to go on the defensive. Many of their remaining pilots banked and dived away from dogfights, concentrating their attacks on the bombers.

As a result of these defensive tactics, which kept most of the Luftwaffe out of the air, our fighters made strafing attacks as they returned from escort missions. At noon two days later George took off destined to get his second ground victory. The visibility was good with 5/10 cumulus clouds. Here is his encounter report:

> After leaving the bomber formation, we set course for home and sighted an enemy airdrome with about 15 trainer and transport aircraft parked on it. White

*John C. Meyer looking over his first Mustang, named* Lambie. *Coded HO-M, Meyer had accumulated 10 victories at the time the switch was made to the P-51. George's first "student" was Capt. J. C. Meyer. Meyer credited George with forcing him to become more proficient than he would have if George hadn't egged him on while they were training in New England.* J. Sabanos

Flight attacked ahead of us leaving fires on the field. I led Blue Flight into the field and sighted several single-engine biplanes parked on the south side. I put my sights on one and fired about a three-second burst. The enemy aircraft exploded. I pulled up and left.

CLAIM: One (1) Buecker 133 destroyed

George's discourse on ground victories was much more cryptic than those on aerial ones. Perhaps he had belittled the significance of destroying enemy aircraft on the ground even though it was often a more dangerous task than knocking them out of the sky. Strafing stationary targets didn't require the same level of skill needed to hit a moving target from a moving target; successful air fighting demanded quick response to quick thinking. Credit for ground victories was not held in as high esteem by fighter pilots in general. In a letter to Bill, George compared ground strafing to dogfighting.

England
April 17, 1944
Dear Bill,

Was glad to hear you went to a single-engine school. There are several pilots in my outfit who graduated at Moore Field (Texas) and a couple who instructed there. They all say it is nice country down that way.

I guess you are finding the AT-6 a lot nicer to fly than the BT. It is truly a nice airplane as are all North American ships.

I'm now flying your favorite, the Mustang, and I sure like it. Our missions run very long, sometimes five and six hours and the old fanny gets pretty sore.

I've destroyed two more airplanes recently, both on the ground. They blow up pretty on the ground, but it isn't as much fun as air fighting.

Bill, if you graduate about May 23, that will mean over two months in advance. Seems that you boys will get more training than those ahead of you got. I'm glad to hear it and hope you get some fighter time before graduation. Also, you should take advantage of all the instrument time you can get because when you get to your theater of operations you will fly in weather you wouldn't walk outdoors in at home.

Another pointer for you, Bill. When you begin flying fighters, know your airplane and how to operate it. There is nothing tricky or mysterious about a fighter but pilots get in trouble by overlooking little things like changing fuel tanks, using the wrong mixture, etc.

I hope you get the P–51 or the P–47 when the time comes because I know they are both good ships.

Keep up the good work, kid, and lots of luck.

Your bro,

George

Bill answered George's letter on May 1. Among other items written about, Bill said:

. . . let me offer another pat on the back, Ace, for tearing up two more of Jerry's sky wagons. I'd sure love to be behind six fifties and disintegrate a few. By golly, you've got the plane to do it, too. What I wouldn't give to get one of those babies in a couple of months! There may be a chance.

So far I'm doing okay, I think. I've finished instruments and gunnery. I haven't seen my last gunnery films yet but if they are pretty good and all goes well, I think my instructor will recommend me for combat training. That means I'll get two weeks on P–40s, two weeks in actual gunnery in the Gulf, then be assigned to a tactical squadron. Those are my hopes. Only 17 more hours on this buggy [AT–6] and I'll be ready for more horses. . . .

Write soon and thanks for your tips. I heed them religiously. And please leave a few for me to knock down!

April 17 was a day for George to catch up with some of his writing tasks. Besides writing Bill, he completed his request for his first extension to the normal operational tour of 200 flying hours. Before approval came back from Eighth Fighter Command, he was involved in several more missions. On the thirteenth mission for the month of April he got his first opportunity to fly as squadron leader. It was a radar-controlled mission to Paris; that is, radar was used to spot enemy aircraft so that the nearest Allied fighter group could be vectored to intercept. Visibility was good with only scattered cumulus clouds. Here is his encounter report:

The Group was vectored to the vicinity of hostile aircraft by Type 16 control. We were flying at 20,000 feet when we sighted about 15 single-engine planes climbing at three o'clock below us. We dropped our wing tanks and headed for them but, when still several miles away, they all dived for the deck. I took my flight down following the main body of 11 Me 109s. I was using full boost and closing slowly. After about ten minutes chase on the deck, all enemy aircraft pulled up sharply over an airdrome. We pulled up after them and they hit the deck again. We resumed the chase for five minutes, and the last one on the right pulled up while the others continued straight. By this time only my wing man, Captain Hamilton, and myself were around so we climbed after this one. He headed for a cloud so I opened fire at 30 degrees deflection and 500 yards. I fired until he went into the clouds and then picked him up again on the other side. I got another burst at him and saw strikes on the fuselage. He headed for another cloud and I didn't see him again after he entered it.

CLAIM: One (1) Me 109 Damaged

Even with the new Mustang, George was unable to close on the Messerschmitts with appreciable speed. A target 500 yards away is not considered duck soup; in fact, it was out of normal range of P–51 armament. Since he couldn't close on the 109 he figured it was worth a try even at 500 yards. Capt. Ralph Hamilton spoke of this mission many years later when interviewed. Hamilton said that Preddy really got upset that he couldn't close on the Me 109 and bring him down. He also said his Mustang wasn't developing full power so George should go ahead. While trailing behind, Hamilton spotted a flak tower and blew it up.

The next mission two days later found John Meyer back in the lead. Encounter reports for the mission vividly illustrate just how badly outnumbered the Germans were at times during this period. It was a clear day and visibility was unlimited as the 487th took off in mid-afternoon to escort bombers to the targets—Hamm, Soest, Bonn, and Koblenz, Germany. George's encounter report follows:

> Lt. Col. Meyer took his section down to strafe the airdrome at Stade and I stayed up to give him top cover. After the first section pulled up from the field, I took my flight to the deck and, as we approached the field, Captain Hamilton called in a Ju 88 on our left. I turned into him and he made a steep turn. I closed in and began firing at 500 yards and 90 degrees deflection. I closed to 100 yards and 30 degrees deflection and got many strikes on his bottom side and the plane began smoking. I broke off my attack as Lt. Kessler, who had been on his tail and also firing at the same time I was, broke off. The ship was smoking badly and one of the crew was getting out of the top. The ship flipped over to the left and went straight into the ground and blew up.
>
> After reforming with the squadron, we headed southeast and saw another airdrome with airplanes on it. We went down to strafe and I picked out a Ju 52 and blew it up.
>
> CLAIM: One (1) Ju 88 destroyed in the air, shared with Lt. Kessler.
> One Ju 52 destroyed on the ground.

Later, and to the surprise of both Lieutenant Kessler and George, a third pilot claimed to have shared in the destruction of the Ju 88. As a result, George told the squadron scorekeeper to credit this one to the other two pilots. Therefore his squadron records did not reflect this victory as either one-half or one-third credit. But on the basis of the gun camera film and Preddy's encounter report for this mission, the Fighter Victory Credits Board gave him credit for one third.

Close inspection of all encounter reports submitted concerning this particular engagement throws doubt on the validity of the third pilot's claim. Besides Kessler's report, which claimed to have shared the kill with George, and George's report which claimed to have shared the kill with Kessler, there was another by a witness, Ralph Hamilton, who was flying wing for George.

Hamilton's report stated, "I was flying Yellow Two on Major Preddy's wing. We were going down to make a second attack on Stade Airdrome when we spotted a Ju 88 over the field at about one thousand feet altitude. Our flight pulled up to attack the Ju 88 in the air. As Yellow Leader [Preddy] closed in on it, the pilot started a steep turn. At this time, Yellow Leader opened fire and the right engine of the 88 started burning and a second later the center section of the plane blew up and burned. Then the plane dived straight into the ground."

The third pilot who claimed to share in this victory said in his encounter report, "I was flying Yellow Three when we peeled down to strafe Stade air field. On the run a Ju 88 came across the field and I immediately turned into the attack. Yellow Leader (Preddy) fired and I followed with a 2 to 3 second burst. Top gunner was trying to bail out when the ship rolled over and crashed."

Less than one week later, George went on another radar-controlled mission to Bourges, France. This time the Germans didn't come up to fight, so George strafed an airdrome with over twenty enemy aircraft dispersed around the field. He claimed one He 111 destroyed pending film assessment. He had passed his target before he saw it explode and hoped his camera had recorded the destruction. Gun cameras often saw things the pilot couldn't see because the pilot is concentrating on his next move rather than his last one. But in this case the camera saw no more than Preddy had seen. He was given credit for a probable.

To substantiate their claim for ground victories, some pilots made a second pass at the aircraft they had just destroyed. On the second pass they would record the results of their first pass with their gun cameras. This was often a foolish thing to do because enemy ground gunners would usually have all guns manned and ready for the second pass.

On April 24, 1944, George assumed command of the 487th Fighter Squadron during the temporary absence of Lt. Col. John Meyer, who was taking his leave in the States. However, Meyer flew several more missions— May 1, 7, 8, and 12—before departing on the fourteenth.

On April 28, 1944, the target was an airdrome at Bourges, France. George, in addition to destroying a Ju 52, also strafed this very rare He 177 Grief, one of the Luftwaffe's newest medium bombers. The paint scheme was mottled gray with black side and under sections. Note the turret at the rear and on top of the fuselage. Preddy gun camera film via Sox

Official documents provide conflicting information concerning the mission of April 30, 1944. First, the Squadron's Operational Diary for the month states that the Ramrod mission accounted for enemy casualties including an airdrome, aircraft on the ground, and installations. However, the 352nd Group S-2 (Intelligence) Journal listed the following for that day:

April 30, 1944 Mission: Ramrod, Penetration, Target Support. FO 321.
   Claims: 1-0-0 (air) 0-0-5 (ground) Hangar, Barracks Damaged
          1 FW 190 Destroyed by Lt. Whisner
          2 S/E U/I A/C Damaged by Lt. Hall
          3 T/E U/I A/C Damaged, Barracks Damaged by Capt. Davis
          Hangar Damaged by Lt. Fowler.
   Losses: Nil.

As noted, Bill Whisner claimed an aerial victory for April 30. No credit was given to Whisner in the 1978 USAF Historical Study Number 85. When asked, Bill Whisner was unable to explain the anomaly. To make matters even more suspicious, Preddy's gun camera film contains the results for a mission on April 30. The Eighth Fighter Command inserted a title frame into Combat Film Number 3641 which shows Preddy attacking an FW 190, and the film shows the 190 going down in smoke. Preddy was not given credit for this victory by the Fighter Victory Credits Board in 1955 or in Study 85.

So we pursued the matter in an attempt to learn whether he should or should not have been given that credit. In 1987 Whisner responded, "What happened to the encounter report and film is a mystery to me. I have difficulty believing that an error was made in titling. Why not let the situation stand as is? If George flew a mission that day, [George led the mission] it could be simply stated in your new book that he was credited with a 190 kill for that mission." Unfortunately, it's not that simple. For George or Bill to get credit for an aerial victoy that day, we must get the air force to officially recognize it. And we can't get them to do that without better evidence than we have. The evidence we now have is conflicting.

The only plausible explanation we can find is that the title frame was in error. The mission on the thirtieth included 295 B-17s and B-24s dispatched to Lyon, Clermont-Ferrand and Siracourt. Mustangs from six fighter groups including the 352nd escorted the bombers. According to Roger Freeman's *Mighty Eighth War Diary*, the 352nd accounted for two enemy aircraft destroyed. USAF Historical Study Number 85 credits those victories to two pilots from the 486th Squadron of the 352nd Fighter Group, Capt. Stephen W. Andrew and 1st Lt. Woodrow W. Anderson.

Tom Ivie, who graciously agreed to read this manuscript before it was sent to the publisher, pursued this matter further. He found the microfilm copy of an encounter report which was filed by Bill Whisner for the April 30 mission. Even Whisner didn't have a copy of it. Here's what it said:

I was flying Red 3 in a seven ship section. We were about 17000 ft. at 5 o'clock to the bombers when I saw a lone ship in a shallow dive at about 8 o'clock at 15000 ft. I called it in and peeled off after it and the rest of the section came with me. As I closed on the A/C I identified it as a FW-190 and gave him a short burst out of range, missing him. Evidently he saw me and steepened his dive and started turning left. I gave him another burst at about 500 yards, missing again. I noticed my airspeed passing 500 and the 190 pulled out and led me right across Clermont-Ferrand A/D, right on the ground. I began closing rapidly, so I

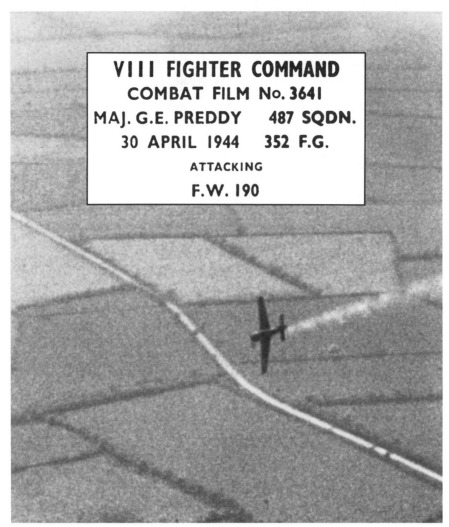

# VIII FIGHTER COMMAND
## COMBAT FILM No. 3641
## MAJ. G.E. PREDDY    487 SQDN.
## 30 APRIL 1944    352 F.G.
### ATTACKING
## F.W. 190

*Title frame to George's gun camera film for April 30, 1944 mission, and one*   *frame showing the FW 190 going down trailing smoke.* USAAF

centered my ball, and began firing from dead astern at 100 yards. Strikes covered him and pieces began to fly back. At this time we were 100 ft. or below. I had to pull up to miss him, though I didn't see him hit the ground, due to the 4 to 5/10s low cloud in the area. I'm certain of his destruction on the basis of the concentration of hits and the many pieces of his plane falling off, and the further fact that Captain Davis saw a fire on the southwesterly side of the field which would be the general location where the E/A would have crashed, judging from its course when I pulled up. [See statements of Capt. Clayton E. Davis, and Lt. Marion Nutter which follow.]

   CLAIM: 1 FW-190 Destroyed

   Although the encounter report by Clayton Davis adds little to the validity of Whisner's claim, the one by Marion Nutter does. Lieutenant Nutter wrote: "I was Red Leader and heard Red 3 call in and saw he was going down at 8 o'clock to check a bogey. I called, told him he was covered, and proceeded to go down astern of him and watched him close on the bogey who turned out to be a bandit. I observed one long burst along both sides of the fuselage and canopy. The bandit then went into a stricken side slip violently at very low altitude and disappeared into the smoke and dust of the field that had just been bombed. Red 3, 2, and myself pulled up together."

Apparently the air force, in Study 85, concluded that the above was insufficient evidence to substantiate Bill's claim. Preddy's gun camera film remains a mystery! One thing seems clear, however, and that is that the FW 190 Whisner claimed is not the same one shown on Preddy's gun camera film.

*Lt. Carl Luksic holding up five fingers designating his victory over five enemy aircraft on one mission. He was the first ETO pilot to destroy a quintet in one day.*

The month of May started out very slowly for George. He flew his first mission on the seventh and his second on the ninth with no encounters on either day. He stood down on the eighth when John Meyer led the 487th on their biggest day yet. They got fourteen victories! Lt. Carl J. Luksic got five of those and became the first pilot in the ETO to destroy a quintet of enemy aircraft on a single mission. Capt. Clayton Davis was Luksic's flight leader that day, and he didn't do too badly either. Davis scored four victories, later adjusted to 3.5.

The mission was to Brunswick, Germany, and that's where Luksic met the enemy in great numbers. "They were in packs of 15 and 20–plus," Luksic said, "and they weren't up there for a joyride. They were headed for the bombers— and trouble." The five that Luksic shot down brought his total victories up to 15.5, 8.5 of which were scored in the air. On May 24 he had to bail out over enemy territory and was taken prisoner. He later met Clay Davis in the same prison, a prison they shared with the famous and legless Gr. Capt. Sir Douglas Bader. Bader was an RAF pilot who lost his legs as a result of an accident while performing a foolish daredevil stunt in 1931. He was given tin legs, time to recuperate and then discharged from the RAF. At the outbreak of World War II, Bader was taken back into the RAF and made a flight commander flying Hurricanes. He became a legend. He fought during the Battle of Britain and on until August 9, 1941, when he was rammed by an enemy aircraft and bailed out only to be taken prisoner. He made several attempts to escape, all foiled.

After a few more uneventful missions escorting the heavies to Paris, France, and Troyes, Shuppinstedt, Berlin and other targets in Germany, George's first extension to his combat tour was about to end. So he applied for a second extension. Normal procedure required that the squadron surgeon

*Capt. Clayton Davis with colonels John Meyer and Joe Mason, from left to right, after the victorious May 8 mission.*

102

certify to a pilot's physical and mental fitness. The certificate then accompanied the formal request through channels to Eighth Fighter Command for approval. This chain of events usually took about two weeks if all went well. So George made the request after completing 230 hours of his 250 hour tour. The doctor found Preddy to be in good shape physically and mentally; the request was approved in normal time.

On May 12 while on an escort mission to Halle, Germany, Preddy and his flight encountered no enemy aircraft in the air. As they left the bombers to return home, they spotted an enemy airdrome and went down to strafe. Whisner, the number four man this time, blew up a Ju 52 while George sent a burst into an unidentified single-engine airplane. He saw many strikes, but there was no explosion; he claimed a damaged enemy aircraft.

Except for the mission on April 22 and perhaps the one on the thirtieth, George had not experienced any real air-to-air combat since the end of January—almost three and a half months earlier. He was undoubtedly getting anxious to meet the enemy in the air since he was on his second extension. He knew that fighter command wouldn't give him extensions indefinitely.

On May 13, 1944, the enemy solved his problem. They came up in great numbers willing and ready to fight. And fight they did! Here is George's encounter report:

> Leading a flight of six ships, I noticed one box of bombers being attacked so went to their assistance. When we got near them, I saw a formation of 30–plus Me 109s paralleling this box of bombers at 20,000 feet. Having the advantage of sun and altitude, I led the flight down behind the formation completely surprising the Huns. I pulled up astern of one and opened fire at 300 yards. The enemy aircraft burst into flames and the nose dropped and he went straight down. We had a fast closing speed which left us right in the middle of the Hun formation;

*So low that he could read the labels on the supply cartons, George located this Ju 87 Stuka and a rare four-engine FW*   *200 Condor transport at the Halle airdrome. Preddy gun camera film via Sox*

*Of all the aircraft George flew, documenting his first Mustang has been the most illusive. No photograph of the name* Cripes A'Mighty 2nd *has been located. The serial number is known to have been 42-106451. The 10 victory marks dates this picture around mid-May 1944.* R. Preddy Harris

we were badly outnumbered. They began breaking in all directions and I singled out one who was making a climbing turn to the left and on the tail of a P–51. I fired a long burst at him at 30 degrees deflection closing to 200 yards. I had to break off the attack as other 109s were coming in on me. I did not notice the results of my attack on the second enemy aircraft. Lt. Garney, my number four man, said he saw a 109 at this time who was being attacked in a left turn lose his left wing and spin down. He believes this to be the one I was attacking.

    CLAIM:  One (1) Me 109 Destroyed
                One (1) Me 109 Pending Assessment of Film

    The film, along with Lieutenant Garney's supporting statement, left no doubt about the results of Preddy's second attack—the Me 109 was indeed destroyed. And now George was an ace with 6.5 aerial victories. In addition he had destroyed three enemy aircraft on the ground, and probably destroyed others and damaged some.

    During an interview in 1970 with Gen. John C. Meyer, Vice Chief of Staff of the US Air Force, he reminisced about this mission when an Me 109 got on his tail but out of range. Meyer said he put his Mustang in a tight circle and the 109 did the same. The enemy was gaining no advantage, but neither was Meyer—it was a stalemate. But the thought of running out of fuel put Meyer at

Gun camera footage of the May 21 Chattanooga mission near Neubrandenberg, Germany. Note that George fired at the engine to take care of the military engineers and firemen. Because George's dad was a freight-train conductor, he never fired at the caboose of an enemy train, for that's where civilians rode. The head-on pass indicates how low he made his passes before firing. The engine exploded. Preddy gun camera film via Sox

a great disadvantage. There was no way he could continue to circle with the 109, and Meyer's adversary knew that. Just then Meyer noticed another P-51 on the tail of the 109. Making radio contact with that most welcome Mustang, Meyer recognized George's voice. However, Meyer also noticed that George was out of effective range of the enemy aircraft. So, based on his confidence in Preddy's gunnery skill, Meyer pulled back on his throttle giving the enemy an opportunity to close but also giving Preddy an opportunity to close on the 109. It appeared to Meyer that the 109 pilot was not aware that a P-51 was on his tail. The scheme worked. As soon as Meyer reduced speed, Preddy was able to gain an advantage on the enemy and with one short burst destroyed him.

With the recent change in fighter tactics—abandonment of the close defensive role to a role of offensive tactics—the future promised to bring more action to the boys flying Mustangs. Also, the Luftwaffe was bringing up their reserve fighter strength. With orders to search out and destroy the enemy wherever he may be found, George's score was bound to increase dramatically.

J. C. Meyer left for the States on May 14 and Preddy took over as acting commanding officer. Cpl. Joseph J. "Red" McVay, George's assistant crew chief, said that Meyer chewed him out one day when Meyer took George's plane on a mission and found the guns fired low. McVay had Sergeant Kuhanek, the armorer, check the guns. Kuhanek found that Meyer was right, they fired low. Red said that Preddy would never say anything about it for two reasons: he didn't want his plane taken out of action, and he usually drove in close before firing anyway. Red also said that Meyer called him every name in the book the day he chewed him out, but that Major Preddy would never do

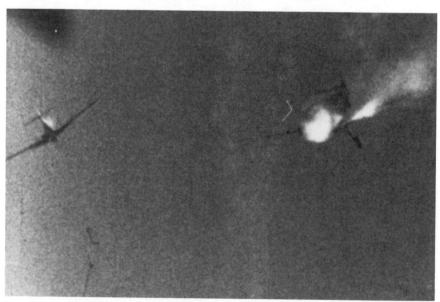

On a Ramrod mission May 30, George and Whisner jumped three 109s. Preddy got two and shared another with Whisner. Preddy gun camera film via Sox

a thing like that. And that was why the troops liked Preddy so much. McVay said, "Meyer was a tough man with no smile. But the major they loved. He never bragged, and they just loved him. When Meyer went on leave, the major was selected as the acting CO of the 487th. The top sergeants called all the enlisted men together and said that, look, while the major is CO no one is to foul up. If anybody fouls up—even in London—we're going to tear you apart. They didn't worry about Meyer because he would tear you apart. They just didn't want any reflection on the major while he was in command."

As acting squadron commander for the 487th during Meyer's rest and recuperation in the zone of interior, Preddy had many more ground duties than before when he was operations officer. So, during the next two weeks he missed out on four missions, each one of which netted the Squadron aerial victories. He didn't, however, miss the mission that cost his squadron two pilots and cost George two of his very close friends—Lt. Carl Luksic and Lt. James D. Hannon. Preddy had just appointed Luksic to be flight commander the day before. Fighting mad for the loss that occurred on a sweep on the twenty-fourth, the new ace and squadron commanding officer scheduled himself to lead an escort mission, the twenty-first mission of the month. The Luftwaffe paid dearly for his anger.

As the bombers were approaching the vicinity of Magdeburg, I was leading a section of seven ships giving close support to the rear box which was quite a distance behind the main formation. I noticed 20 to 30 single-engine fighters attacking the front boxes so we dropped our tanks and headed towards them. We came up behind three Me 109s in rather tight formation. I opened fire on one

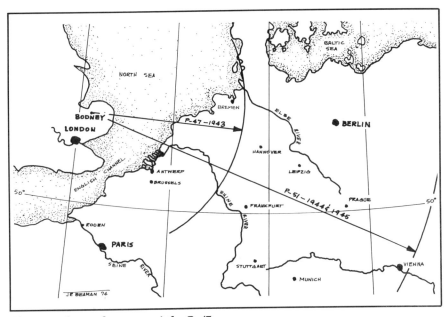

*The map shows the range of the P–47 during 1943-44 and compares it to the range of the Mustangs during 1944-45.*

from 300 yards and closed to 150 yards. The 109 burst into flames and went down.

I then slipped behind the second 109 and fired while closing from 200 to 100 yards. He started burning and disintegrating immediately. He went down spinning.

The third enemy aircraft saw us and broke down. I followed him in a steep turn, diving and zooming. I got in many deflection shots getting hits on the wing and tail section. I ran out of ammunition, so my element leader, Lt. Whisner, continued the attack getting in several good hits. At about 7,000 feet the pilot bailed out.

CLAIM: Two (2) Me 109s Destroyed
One (1) Me 109 Destroyed (shared with Lt. Whisner)

When George told Whisner to get the third Me 109, it wasn't because he was out of ammunition as he said in his encounter report. He was low on ammunition, but he had fired only 900 out of his 1,200 rounds. As a result of his lead position, it was up to him to do the shooting while Whisner protected his wing, or backside. After the first two 109s were destroyed, George apparently thought it only fair to give his wingman a crack at the third 109. As usual, Whiz made good; he also made it plain in his encounter report that George was not out of ammunition when he forfeited the privilege of finishing off the damaged Me 109. Whisner reported, "Thinking he was low on ammo he called me and told me to get the 109. I had a hell of a time turning with him but I got some hits in a deflection shot, which loosened him up. I got in directly astern and gave him a good burst and his canopy flew off. I waited a few seconds and when he did not bail out I gave him another good burst. Pieces flew back and the Jerry bailed out at 7,000 feet. I confirm Maj. Preddy's claim to two others destroyed prior to this engagement. I claim one Me 109 destroyed, shared with Maj. Preddy." Whisner expended 229 rounds.

At this point in time George was just short of being a double ace with nine aerial victories.

*Chapter 12*

# D-Day Plus

As May drew to a close, George had completed his normal operational tour of 200 hours plus two extensions of fifty hours each. He had destroyed more than his share of enemy aircraft. He could have elected to go home at this point with a feeling of pride in a job well done. Instead, he requested a third extension. Again, Capt. George C. Dodson, the squadron surgeon, found that Preddy was physically fit for another combat tour.

There were perhaps several reasons why he elected to stay and continue the fight. First and probably foremost, he had a keen sense of devotion to duty. Second, he was acting as squadron commander in Meyer's absence and naturally wanted to stay until Meyer returned. Meyer left the United Kingdom on May 14 and would not return for two and half months. Third, Preddy probably wanted to avenge the lives of his close friends lost during the last few months. The way his score was soaring gave every indication he could do just that. And he had heard rumors of the impending invasion.

As a member of Eighth Fighter Command, his primary function was to provide fighter escort to heavy bombers. In preparation for D-day, however,

*George was in the cockpit of* Cripes A'Mighty 2nd *a total of 9.5 hours on D day. Among the targets his flight destroyed were supply truck convoys and* Tiger tanks. *Note the accuracy of George's gunnery as seen by the strikes on the truck.* Preddy gun camera film via Sox

George and his squadron mates devoted much effort to low-level strafing and dive-bombing. That effort paid handsome dividends when time came to support D-day operations. Locomotives and trains, trucks and buses, bridges and airfields fell prey to the guns, bombs and belly tanks of the fighter pilots. The Luftwaffe was not to be found in the air. The Allies held air superiority and the Hun dared not come up and fight.

Rumor gave way to fact when on the afternoon of June 5 orders were given that caused the base at Bodney to be closed as tight as one could close an open base—but guards were posted and maintenance crews started painting black and white stripes around the fuselage and wings of each aircraft. The stripes were designed to make our aircraft easily identified by Allied ground forces.

The 487th Squadron flew nine missions within the short space of three days, D day and the two days immediately following. Five pilots from the 487th were shot down by ground fire during these missions. This was a heavy toll to pay, but considering the many lives of ground troops they were undoubtedly instrumental in saving, the cost was justified.

On one mission well worth remembering, a unique tactic was employed. Spotting a train of 100–plus cars on a rail siding, the Mustang pilots skip-bombed the train with their partially-filled belly tanks. On their second pass across the gasoline-soaked train, they strafed with incendiary ammunition causing the entire train to be immediately engulfed in flames.

FO Cyril Doleac had just transferred into the 352nd/487th two days before D day. He had joined the RAF in 1939 and flew with the Eagle Squadrons until he transferred to the US Army Air Force and became the private pilot for General Clark. When interviewed in 1984, Doleac said:

*Having flown* Cripes A'Mighty 2nd *for over fourteen hours on June 6 and 7, George flew Capt. Ralph W. Hamilton's beautifully maintained P-51B named* Frances B, Too! *on June 8. Hamilton is reported to have exclaimed "Who the hell messed up my airplane" after seeing it with D-day stripes. Hamilton's World War II score is five victories—four in the air and one on the ground. R. Hamilton*

During the week of D day, every available aircraft was in the air, with multiple missions being flown daily. On June 8, for his second mission, George borrowed Capt. Walter E. Starck's Mustang named Starck Mad!, coded HO-X, serial number 43-24807. Starck was officially credited with six aerial victories. Note the Malcolm hood modification. Starck is second from the left. W. Starck

When General Clark went home three or four weeks before D day, he asked me where I wanted to go. I told him I wanted to get back to a combat outfit. I asked to go to a Mosquito squadron at Watton which happened to be located about eight miles from Bodney. When I got to Watton . . . I discovered that right next door they had P–51s and I had been trained as a fighter pilot. So I jumped in a jeep and went over to Bodney to see Colonel Mayden who said, "We need pilots real badly. I'll have a transfer for you tomorrow." So I moved to Bodney just two days before D day. The next day Major Preddy, the acting CO, took me out and put me in the cockpit and told me to go ahead and take it up. I flew that morning, and that afternoon we went out and flew formation. That evening after supper we were told that the bar was closed; go home and go to bed. No one could figure out what was going on, but at 10:30 that night George Preddy came into the barracks and said, "Okay, get up, briefing is in fifteen minutes." So we took off that night at 11:30 P.M. and flew our first mission. We flew two missions that day, for a total of 5.5 hours. That was the first and only time we had a night takeoff. It was no problem to me because I was trained in the RAF to fly at night, but a lot of American pilots weren't so trained. In fact, when we took off four abreast on the grass strip, this new young Second Lieutenant [Robert Frascotti] was outside wingman. We were waiting to make a 90 degree turn onto the runway when they gave the signal to go. Frascotti failed to turn; he took off straight into three oil pots marking the boundary of the field and flew right into the new control tower which was still under construction. His plane blew up immediately.

That was a sad start to what turned out to be a highly successful effort supporting our invading ground forces during the next few days.

After three days of fierce fighting came a most welcome day of rest—a stand down necessitated by poor weather. The weather had been poor during the period they flew, but on D day plus three it was absolutely awful. George took this opportunity to write a letter of commendation to the troops.

487TH FIGHTER SQUADRON
OFFICE OF THE SQUADRON COMMANDER
AAF STATION F-141
9 June 1944
SUBJECT: Commendation
TO: All Personnel

1. The first few hectic days of the initial phase of the invasion have passed. In preparation for that momentous event and in the accomplishment of the mission of this squadron in the great offensive thus far, it has been necessary that each of you, pilot, ground officer and enlisted man alike, work long hours with little or no sleep and extend yourself to the limit of physical endurance to perform your assigned duty.

2. Without exception all of you have carried on with enthusiasm, cheerfully and uncomplainingly doing your part in the accelerated operations of the squadron attendant upon "D" day. In the critical times immediately ahead you will be called upon to keep up the increased tempo of your work to insure the ultimate success of our forces.

3. It is a pleasure and a privilege to have you serve under my command. In the words of the Supreme Commander, General Eisenhower:

I have full confidence in your courage, devotion to duty and skill in battle. We will accept nothing less than full victory.

*Sgt. M. G. Kuhaneck, George's armorer, received a letter of commendation for his excellence in preparing the weapons on* Cripes A'Mighty 3rd. *As a result of Kuhaneck's skill, George never suffered a weapons stoppage on any of his combat missions. P. Grabb*

Good luck. And let us all beseech the blessing of Almighty God upon this great and noble undertaking.
George E. Preddy
Major, Air Corps Commanding.

George also took this opportunity to write home, and he spoke of what was foremost in his mind—the invasion.

England
June 9, 1944
Dearest Mother and Dad,
By reading the papers I suppose you can realize what is going on over here. Naturally, it has kept me very busy, but it is just a continuation of the war for the airmen; it is the beginning of action for a lot of infantrymen.

We all hope this big invasion will be a success and everybody in the air is doing all that is possible to aid the men on the ground. We have the highest respect for those boys, and it is our duty to them to clear the way and protect them from the Luftwaffe.

We feel proud of our leaders and confident of their ability. Although nobody doubts that the Luftwaffe and German Army are strong and the fight will be tough, I don't think there is any doubt that we can beat them.

The invasion is a big moment for the English people and one they have been waiting for for years. They are taking it in their customary calm, quiet manner.

All of the pilots and ground crews in the Group are doing a superb job and we are succeeding in doing considerable damage to the enemy.

I hope all are well at home. I'm getting along fine and feeling very good.
Lots of love,
George

Cripes A'Mighty 3rd *qualified for seventeen victory marks when it was newly assigned to George in June. The 3rd was a P-51D, serial number 44-13321. It would ultimately have more aerial victories scored in it than any other Mustang during World War II. J. Sabanos*

And he wrote a letter to Bill congratulating him on making fighters; George said he hoped that Bill would get in a P–51 outfit, and gave him some more tips. And he noted that Bozo had not made fighters; he had been assigned to twin-engine school and was quite disappointed since both George and Bill had made fighters.

Where had the Luftwaffe been during the first days of the invasion? They had been at their positions defending the Reich. But why weren't they at the front opposing the invading forces? Plans made in expectation of the invasion called for a quick transfer of the German fighter force to the front line as soon as the invasion started. But communications were badly disrupted by the continuous strafing attacks by Allied fighters and bombers. Airfields selected for use when the invasion began had to be changed at the last moment, too, because of the severe raids made against the ground organizations prior to D day. Confusion resulted in a delay of several days; the Luftwaffe was unable to muster a force of a size felt to be necessary to pose any significant threat to the invasion.

As confusion among enemy commanders subsided, the Luftwaffe once again became an organized and potent fighting force from front-line airfields. The invasion had already succeeded in establishing firm entrenchments on enemy soil, freeing up our fighters to give escort to their Big Friends, the Liberators and Fortresses.

On the morning of June 12, 1944, George took off shortly before 0700 hours leading the entire group on an escort mission to St. Jacques, France. Broken cumulus clouds hung at about 8,000 ft. Three and one-half hours after takeoff he met in the air his first enemy plane since the invasion began. Here is his encounter report:

> I was leading the Group giving area support to bombers on various targets in the vicinity of Rennes. A group of about 18 B–24s were last out and withdrawing in the vicinity of Rennes when 12 Me 109s made a quarter stern attack on them from out of the sun. We headed for them on the same level and some turned into us; others broke for the deck. I followed one down firing from various ranges and angles. I got a few hits and the enemy aircraft lost most of its speed causing me to overshoot. I pulled above him and was starting another attack when the pilot bailed out at 8,000 feet.
> CLAIM: One (1) Me 109 Destroyed

To put this mission in perspective, the distance from Bodney to Rennes, France, is about the same as that from Preddy's hometown of Greensboro, North Carolina, to Atlanta, Georgia—a bit over 300 statute air miles. The flight to Rennes took just over an hour, so considerable time was spent in the area waiting on enemy action.

In 1970, 448th Bomb Group bombardier Ben C. Isgrig, Jr., wrote a letter about his experience on June 12, 1944, the day his B–24 was shot down near Rennes:

> While dangling in my parachute on the way down an Me 109 made a pass at me. Just as he passed me a P–51 came in on his tail and shot him down. The German pilot bailed out. I have always been extremely grateful to the P–51 pilot that very possibly saved my life, but never made any effort to find out who it was. Recently I read *The Mighty Eighth*, and in it found that members of the 352nd Group reported shooting down three Me 109s on June 12 over Rennes. In trying to find out the individual pilot that got the Me 109 [that fired at me], I wrote the Air Force and received the reply that Major Preddy was the only pilot who reported that his adversary had bailed out. He was the one.

*Squadron artist Sgt. Sam Perry liked to use script in the markings on the aircraft he painted. Here George's name is dis-played on the canopy frame of the* 3rd *in red with blue outlines.* P. Grabb

The initial success of the invasion allowed fighter units to return to flying a normal schedule—one mission a day. Missions escorting the Big Friends took place every day until June 19—the mission had to be scrubbed due to lousy weather. To make up for this, two missions were flown on the twentieth. One was an early morning takeoff and the other in the late afternoon. The early mission resulted in the first aerial encounter with the enemy since George got his twelfth victory just about one week before. Here is his encounter report:

> I was Group Leader and leading a squadron of 12 aircraft supporting the first combat wing of B-17s bombing Magdeburg. Just after the bombers reached the target I saw 15 Me 410s forming up in the sun at 28,000 feet. We flew out and intercepted them from one thousand feet above. All enemy aircraft went into a tight Lufbery except one who broke down. I followed him and after he leveled off at 6,000 feet just above a cloud I fired a short burst and he went into the cloud. I picked him up again on top and back down through he went. After following him through the cloud five or six times, I lost him altogether.
>
> My wing man, Lt. Wood, and I started climbing back up and saw an FW 190 slightly above us. He turned down and fired at Wood and I got a head-on shot at him. After several deflection shots, I got on his tail and got a long burst into him. The pilot bailed out at two thousand feet.
>
> Again we started climbing and saw a Me 410 above us. I managed to get on his tail and scored a few hits before overshooting. Lt. Wood pulled in and got a good burst into him and one of the crew bailed out. The 410 lost a lot of speed and went into the ground. It exploded.
>
> CLAIM:  One (1) FW 190 Destroyed
>           One (1) Me 410 Destroyed (shared with Lt. Wood)

Lt. James N. Wood, Jr., saw the pilot still in the doomed 410 as it whizzed by, and surmised that the pilot was dead or unconscious at that time. Other-

115

*Lt. James Wood named his Mustang*
The Fox. *Coded HO-Z, its serial num-*
*ber was 42–103758.* Ed Howe

wise he too would have bailed out. This was the first victory for Lieutenant Wood. He went on to get two and one half more aerial victories, and one by strafing. When interviewed in 1989 Wood said, "He was an incredible leader, dedicated to doing the job the absolute best he possibly could—he just stood out! He would have done anything he could have done to have ended the war one moment earlier."

After flying a five-hour mission that morning, George stood down for the uneventful late afternoon patrol. He scheduled himself for an early takeoff the very next morning. This time he gave bombers escort to and from Berlin. On the way out, according to his encounter report, he again encountered the enemy in the air.

While leading a section of seven Mustangs escorting B–24s on withdrawal, I saw three Me 109s at 23,000 feet make a stern attack on a straggling bomber ahead of us. They saw us coming and turned into us. I singled one out and he started down turning and taking evasive action. He went into a thin cloud and I went below after him. He turned into me and I dropped 20 degrees of flaps enabling me to out-turn him. He then went down right on the deck and tried to out run me, but I closed in on him and began firing from 400 yards dead astern. I got hits on the fuselage and left wing and he began smoking. As I pulled up past him, he ran into the ground and blew up.

CLAIM: One (1) Me 109 Destroyed.

As usual, Red McVay was waiting on the stack of drop tanks when George returned. This time he got the hoped for buzz job which meant that George had scored a victory. Red took great pride in Preddy's performance; it was almost as if Red had shot down those enemy aircraft himself.

George returned from this mission landing just after noon. Once again he had been in the cockpit for over five hours. His score was now 14.5 victories, three of them on the ground. He had flown 344 hours of operational time meaning he had only six more hours left on his third extension. To put it another way, he could only fly two more missions without getting a fourth extension. And it usually took a week or more to process the paperwork involved in getting a request for extension approved. Further, to ensure two more missions George had to make sure he didn't stay up more than six hours

George's ground crew preparing his most famous Mustang for another mission. George was blessed with an excellent ground crew. He never had to abort a mission because of mechanical failure. P. Grabb

on the next one. As long as he had any time at all left before completion of his tour, he could take off and fly a complete mission even if it meant he would exceed the 350 hour limit.

Tired as he was after the morning trip to Berlin that netted him one more aerial victory, he spent the afternoon tending to duties expected of a squadron commander. He also started his request for a fourth extension through channels. Since he had to limit his flying until his request was approved, George spent the next few days catching up on his ground duties. He also visited John Latham again, this time to let him know that he didn't appreciate being shot at when he was escorting the 96th Bomb Group's B-17s. Latham said, "You know, Mouse, we try to tell you fighter jocks that if you're going to point your nose at us, we're going to shoot at you!" What happened was that the 352nd boys had chased the Germans down through the 96th's formation. With closing speeds exceeding 600 mph the gunners on the B-17s weren't too interested in making positive identification before shooting. George told him that he would have to go home soon on a thirty-day R and R, but that he was coming back. Latham said, "Well, you've done pretty good so far, why do you want to come back? And he said that he wanted to be the Rickenbacker of World War II, and he meant it—he beat Rickenbacker's record!"

On June 24 he flew an uneventful mission to Lüneburg, Germany, using up five of his six hours remaining. The very next day he finished his tour with a mission to Troyes, France. Thus, he had to stay on the ground for the mission of the twenty-seventh which netted the squadron four aerial victories. That mission also cost George one of his best friends, Lt. Robert H. Berkshire. Berkshire had 4.5 victories when he met with one of the greatest dangers facing fighter pilots—the unpredictable accuracy of ground fire while strafing. He was hit in the right thigh and received second-degree burns on his face when he crashed. Fortunately, he evaded capture and made it back to England two and one-half months later. He underwent plastic surgery and a rather long convalescent period. Unfortunately, the 352nd Fighter Group Association has been unable to locate Bob so he couldn't be interviewed for this story.

On June 27 Preddy still had not heard a reply to his request for an extension. Of course, he was quite sure his request would be approved so he decided to fly a mission the next day. He led his squadron to Saarbrücken, Germany, on June 28 as they escorted heavies to the target. The Luftwaffe stayed on the ground, so George had to content himself with blowing up a locomotive.

When he returned from this mission he started a follow-up action on his request for extension. As acting squadron commanding officer he couldn't be expected to sit on the ground while others flew. He called wing headquarters and asked if his approval had been returned from Eighth Fighter Command. He was told that it had not, but that the wing commander had recommended approval. On this news, George again decided to fly the next mission. He had already violated regulations so now it would only be a matter of degree.

The June 29 mission took him to Liepzig, Germany, escorting the Big Friends. It was a beautifully clear day with only scattered stratus cloud formations. He took off at 0700 hours. Here is his encounter report:

> I was Group and Squadron Leader. After P-38s relieved us of escort, we saw
> an airdrome with a plane taxiing down the runway. My flight consisting of four
> ships went to the deck well north of the field and came into it at tree-top level. I

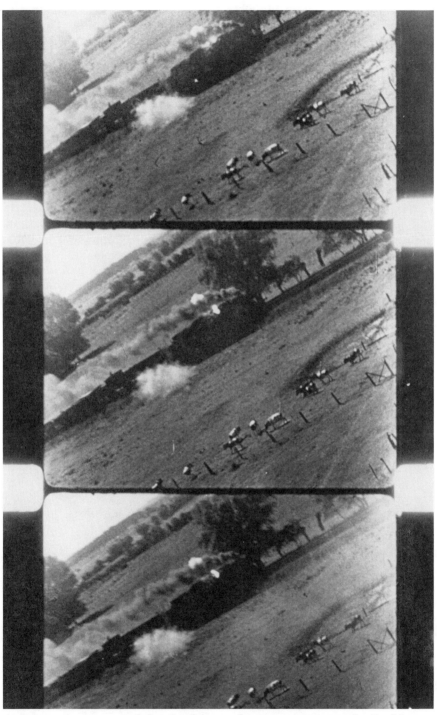

*And the cows never raised their heads! Another Chattanooga mission on June 29 near Saarbruken, Germany. White* *dots are tracer rounds.* Preddy gun camera film via Sox

119

took the left side of the field with Lt. Moran on my left and Lts. Pickering and Wood on my right. Moran and I fired at two Ju 52s setting both on fire. Pickering damaged a Me 110 and clobbered a He 111 at the end of the field. Lt. Wood scored many hits on a He 111 parked near the hangar line. Just as we passed the field I saw many tracers go past us. We continued on the deck for about two miles and attacked a locomotive. From my first hits, the side of the boiler blew up. All four of us attacked and left the locomotive steaming badly. We pulled up and started climbing. We could see the airdrome and four fires burning and throwing up columns of black smoke.

    CLAIMS: One (1) Ju 52 Destroyed—Major Preddy
              One (1) Ju 52 Destroyed—Lt. Moran
              One (1) He 111 Destroyed—Lt. Wood
              One (1) He 111 Destroyed—Lt. Pickering
              One (1) Me 110 Damaged—Lt. Pickering
              One (1) Locomotive Destroyed—shared by the four of us.

Having used up thirteen hours of his not-yet-approved fourth extension, George decided it would be prudent to attend to ground duties until the approval came through. As a result he missed the next three missions over enemy territory. Finally on July 4, formal approval reached the squadron. With more than one-fourth of his extension already flown, and with John Meyer due back from his R and R soon, George contemplated going home after this extension. Bill Whisner left the United Kingdom the day George got his last victory. Virgil Meroney was missing in action and Donalson had gone home. In fact, most of the original contingent not shot down had returned to the States by the end of June 1944.

At this time in his tour only one man in the 352nd Group had destroyed more enemy aircraft than had George—Capt. John F. Thornell of the 328th

*Capt. Jack Thornell, ultimately second only to George in the 328th FS. He was officially credited with 17.25 aerial and two ground victories. He named all his aircraft* Pattie Ann *and they were coded* PE-T. *E. Briggs*

*Some stock photos of George's squadron mates. Top row, left to right: George Arnold and John Bennett. Center row: Bob Berkshire and "Red Dog" Nutter. Bottom row: Clarence Palmer and Walter Starck.*

Squadron. Thornell came to England with the original contingent and fought his way through twenty aerial claims for enemy aircraft destroyed. The Fighter Victory Credits Board of 1955 gave him official credit for 19.25, and the USAF Historical Study of 1978 reduced his score even more—to 17.25. In any event, Thornell had more victories than George had at this time.

Occasionally the squadron and group scorekeepers recorded victories before they received the official verdict from higher headquarters. Upon receiving notification of disallowed claims, records were adjusted. That's what happened to the claim George made for one He 111 destroyed on the mission of April 28 when neither he nor his gun camera was able to witness the final result; the 487th carried this victory on the books until higher headquarters notified them that it had been disallowed.

Preddy completed his fourth extension in less than two weeks after it was approved, so he decided to ask for a fifth extension and this time request 100 hours. He wrote on July 14 and received formal approval on July 28, but for only fifty hours. Disappointed, George knew he had to make the best of the next fifty hours because it would likely be his last chance. The Eighth Fighter Command would certainly turn down any more requests from him for additional time. And Meyer would most likely return before George completed this tour.

*Chapter 13*

# Six Down

The Luftwaffe was far from out—they had not taken the ten-count by any means! Although they had been rather scarce since the invasion started, all signs pointed to a revival of the German fighter presence in the air.

Bitter ground fighting at St. Lo had stopped the invading forces in their tracks. To help counter this phenomenal defense by the Axis forces, the heaviest bombing raid of the war was dispatched on July 18, 1944. Targets included enemy battlefields; some of the bombs fell short and caused casualties among our own and Allied troops. However, it is generally accepted that many more casualties would have resulted had the fighting been allowed to continue without the aid of air support. This was the first of several large raids that most likely prevented the invasion from becoming the greatest single Allied disaster of the war.

The raid of July 18 comprised 1,600 heavy and 350 medium English and American bombers. They dropped 7,700 tons of bombs within a matter of minutes causing mass killing and wounding of enemy troops. The effectiveness of the mission reverberated all the way back up the enemy chain of command through von Kluge to Hitler himself. The bombers were escorted by more than 500 fighters, over half of which were P-51s. The others were P-38s. The 352nd Fighter Group had a big day accounting for twenty aerial victories. Preddy had his biggest day of the war also!

At 0900 hours, northeast of Rostock with 9/10 clouds and tops at 1,000 ft., the 487th encountered enemy aircraft. George's July 18, 1944, encounter report follows:

> I was leading the Squadron on a sweep south of the bombers and heading north to intercept the bombers. Yellow Leader called in bandits at four o'clock low. I made a right turn up sun of the enemy formation which consisted of a mess of Ju 88s with many Me 109s as top cover. I took my flight of three—Lts. Vickery, Greer and myself—to attack the Ju 88s, about 50 in number, while the rest of the Squadron dealt with top cover. As we approached the formation, I saw a single Me 109 ahead of me and attacked it from quarter stern. I opened fire at 400 yards and drove up his tail. The enemy aircraft was covered with hits and went down burning and falling apart.
>
> I continued to attack the 88 formation and opened fire on one of them knocking off many pieces and setting the plane on fire. Lt. Greer then called a break to the right as an Me 109 was pulling up on my tail from below. After we broke, the 109 stalled out and went back down. During this maneuver Lt. Greer became separated. Lt. Vickery and I then made a 360 and launched another attack on the main formation and I damaged one with a few hits and drove up the rear of another getting hits all over this one. I believe the pilot and crew were killed as the enemy aircraft began smoking badly and went down out of control with parts of the ship falling off. I broke off the attack and pulled out to the side

Cripes A'Mighty 3rd *as it appeared with twenty-one victory crosses on or about 19 July 1944. The occasion was a display* *prepared at Bodney for a visit by Secretary of War Henry L. Stinson.* Goodner

before the third attack on the formation. I came in astern again. In this attack I plastered one Ju 88 causing both engines to burn and the enemy aircraft disintegrated. I got a few hits and damaged a second 88. I was out of ammunition—or so I thought, but later learned that my guns had a stoppage on one side—and I had been hit in the engine by the rear gunner in one of the Ju 88s. My ship was covered with oil sprayed from the enemy aircraft which had been shot down, so I set course for home with Lt. Vickery.

CLAIM: Three (3) Ju 88s Destroyed
One (1) Me 109 Destroyed
Two (2) Ju 88s Damaged.

The Luftwaffe was back in the battle but at this rate of loss their revival would be short-lived. And Preddy was certainly making the best of his last fifty-hour tour.

The claim for enemy aircraft destroyed on this mission is still controversial. For many months credit for all four victories claimed was recognized and included in his score. In fact, credit for all four was included in his score at the time he met his death on Christmas Day 1944. He was given much publicity on the basis of this quadruple and another triple he scored. Nevertheless, the general order awarding him an oak-leaf cluster to the Silver Star that came out some months later gave George credit for only three destroyed, one probably destroyed and two damaged.

Of the fifty Ju 88s and fifty Me 109s attacking, not one got through to the bomber formation. The 352nd accounted for twenty-one enemy aircraft destroyed and eleven damaged. George was the high scorer for the day.

George's next mission was on July 20, 1944, and took him to the vicinity of Nordhausen. Cloud cover was 4/10 between 4,000 and 10,000 ft.—no factor in

*July 18 was a big day for George. Previously he had claimed a double and a triple. On this day, he claimed the destruction of three Ju 88s, one Me 109 and the damage of two more Ju 88s. This photo was taken after July 19, probably between July 21 and July 29. J. Sabanos*

this combat which occurred at about noon as the 352nd approached an enemy airdrome on the deck. Here is his encounter report:

> I was Group and Squadron Leader on this mission. I sighted about 20 twin-engine aircraft around the edge of a field. They were painted silver or a very light color. White Flight—including Lts. Greer, Graham and I—strafed while the rest of the Squadron gave top cover. I attacked an Me 410 or He 111 on the south side of the field and after a good concentration of hits it blew up. I continued across the field and got hits on another enemy aircraft near the hangar line.
> Lt. Greer attacked two He 111s getting hits on both. Lt. Graham got strikes on another He 111.
> CLAIMS: One (1) Me 410 or He 111 Destroyed—Major Preddy
> One (1) Me 410 or He 111 Damaged—Major Preddy
> Two (2) He 111s Damaged—Lt. Greer
> One (1) He 111 Damaged—Lt. Graham

Preddy's claim was confirmed to be one Me 410 destroyed and one damaged. Gun camera film allowed the specialists at headquarters to determine the types of aircraft his flight had hit. George flew HO-E with serial number 413406 on this mission and fired a total of 388 rounds of API (armor-piercing incendiary ammunition).

The very next day Preddy led his squadron to Dingolfing, Germany, on another escort mission. Visibility was excellent and clouds were thinly scattered. It was 1030 hours, just east of Munich at 30,000 ft. when he encountered the enemy:

On July 20, George—accompanied by Lieutenant Greer in Lilli Marlene and Lieutenant Graham—paid a surprise visit to the airfield at Juvincourt near Rheims, France. George later noted the presence of numerous twin-engine aircraft around the airdrome. Immediately identifiable are two Ju 88s in the foreground and an Me 110 beyond and left of center. In his haste to make his initial pass without getting shot up, he failed to see the real prize. The intelligence folks even missed it on careful examination of the film. Stashed away in the open bay at the left corner of the hangar were the first two production Arado 234 twin jet Blitz bombers, numbers V5 and V7! One Staffel stationed at the field for the purpose of establishing a new reconnaissance unit had just taken delivery of these brand-new jets during the previous two weeks. They were left unscathed. Preddy gun camera film via Sox

The Group was north of Munich at our rendezvous point but the bombers were late and way south of their course, so the Group Leader made a 180 degree turn to pick them up. I was Squadron Leader and we saw one contrail very high and eight aircraft in formation below it. We were heading east at the time and the enemy aircraft were northeast of Munich heading south. I took our Squadron to intercept while the rest of the Group turned back to rendezvous with the bombers. We were at 27,000 feet and the enemy aircraft were 3,000 feet above us. We climbed towards them and came in dead astern. Our closing speed was very great considering a climbing attack. I opened fire on one of the enemy aircraft at the left of the formation from 300 yards and 30 degrees deflection but noticed no strikes. As I passed him I pulled over to the right and fired at another from 100 yards but spun out in the prop wash without noticing the results. The enemy aircraft began jettisoning their belly tanks and breaking for the deck. When I pulled out of the spin I was at 15,000 feet and saw a P–51 with a Me 109 closing on him. The enemy aircraft broke for the deck and I followed him down closing easily. I fired from dead astern getting strikes and knocking his engine out. Lt. Moats from my flight made an attack at this time and the enemy aircraft looked as if he were going to belly in. Instead, the pilot pulled up and bailed out.

CLAIM: One (1) Me 109 Destroyed (shared with Lt. Moats)

Things were really beginning to get hot. The Luftwaffe had moved most of their reserve forces to participate in the great conflagration taking place in the west. Massive bombing attacks were now aimed at a breakthrough at St. Lo. Not until the evening of July 27 were our ground troops able to break German resistance and make significant penetrations. Then they made their breakthrough largely because of successful Allied bombing raids.

On July 28 George led his squadron on an escort mission over Gera, Germany. There were no casualties, friendly or enemy. But on the twenty-ninth while escorting bombers over Naumburg, Germany, the enemy displayed their buildup of fighter forces in the west by coming up to meet the attack with great fighting spirit in the form of the recently-developed storm-fighter tactic. The storm fighter's aim was to shoot down the heavy American bombers at any cost. Some of these pilots had proposed suicidal ramming attacks patterned after the Japanese kamikaze tactic; German High Command turned them down. The storm fighters adopted the tactic of attacking in tight formation as close to the bomber formation as possible. With extra powerful armament they were almost sure to break up any bomber formation as they waded into it. Occasionally when a storm fighter got hit by one of the bomber's guns, he rammed another bomber as he passed through the formation. Whether the ramming was on purpose or not is a moot point. The attacks on our bombers were best made while Allied fighters were busy elsewhere. The storm fighter had no desire to tangle with the American fighter pilots. Their mission was to disrupt the bomber formations and thereby render them less effective.

On the twenty-ninth the storm fighters came up to intercept the heavies. As it turned out their fighting spirit was far greater than their fighting ability. Here is George's encounter report for this mission:

The Group was assigned to cover the 2nd Task Force of B–17s consisting of ten combat wings bombing Merseburg. We rendezvoused with the last combat wing and swept up to the lead box. We were southwest of the target covering

*A perfect approach. Low, from dead astern in his blind spot, and a windscreen full of 109! This July 29 victim in* *the making never knew what hit him.* Preddy gun camera film via Sox

bombers going in and coming out. After one box came off the target, I saw 20 Me 109s in formation come in behind and high to them. I led the Squadron in astern of the enemy aircraft and came in range just as they began firing on this box of B–17s from astern. I saw one B–17 get hit and start burning so led the flight right into the middle of the 109s. I came up astern of one enemy aircraft on the right side of the formation and opened fire from 300 yards, five degrees angle-off, and got hits. I continued firing as I closed to 100 yards and the enemy aircraft began smoking badly and went down falling apart. The whole formation began splitting up and diving for the deck. I followed one down but lost him in the clouds. I picked up Lt. Sears and we climbed back up towards a box of bombers. While still several thousand feet below them I saw a B–17 peel out of formation and explode. There were enemy fighters above the B–17s but other P–51s chased them away before we got up to them.

CLAIM: One (1) Me 109 Destroyed

Some attacks made by storm fighters were far more successful than this one. They made the mistake of pressing their attack on the bomber formation while American fighters were in the vicinity. Even so, they brought down several B–17s. Often more vicious as enemies of the Allied fighters and bombers were the deadly flak the Germans threw up and the weather conditions under which missions were flown; missions that would have been scrubbed due to foul weather a year earlier were now being flown without hesitation.

While the enemy was experimenting with new tactics, the Americans were trying diligently to knock out German installations suspected of housing launch pads for Hitler's vengeance weapons, or V-weapons. Those installations were protected by iron and concrete domes as thick as thirty feet, and required an extraordinary amount of concentrated explosives to damage them. The Americans and British came up with competing answers to the problem. The British bombers carried six-ton blockbusters streamlined to achieve speeds of about 750 mph as they hit the installation. The Americans loaded battle-worn B–17s and B–24s with 20,000 lb. of high explosives, had a pilot and copilot fly the bombers out over the Channel and fuse the bomb load. Then the crew bailed out and the bomber was guided to its target by remote control from a "mother" plane. Seven of these missions, called *Aphrodite*, were flown by the Americans during August, but several blew up prematurely—perhaps as they were being armed. Joseph P. Kennedy, Jr., President John F. Kennedy's older brother, was one of the pilots killed in this way.

George led the 487th on Ramrod missions of August 2 and 4. On the second the squadron penetrated to St. Quentin, France; on the fourth to Cape Arkona, Baltic Sea. There were no losses on either side.

Lt. Raymond Littge went along on both these missions. At this point in his career, Littge had not scored a single aerial victory. He had, however, scored four ground kills—two on 25 August 1943, and two more on 11 September 1943, Littge claimed his first aerial victory on 27 November 1944. He went on to get 9.5 more before the war ended, and one of those was an Me 262 jet fighter. Here is how Littge described that victory: "We had finished a pass through the bomber formation. There was nothing funny about these jet jobs, but this one was having trouble with his landing gear. It kept dropping down and reminded me of a kid who was running away from someone, and whose pants kept dropping down. He was trying to fight, fly and at the same time keep working his gear up. This factor decreased his speed, and I was able to close and clobber him."

Littge was one of America's best fighter pilots, admired for his flying skill. His score does not fully reflect his abilities because he got a late start. Even so, he is Missouri's top ranking ace. He so idolized George Preddy that he named one of his sons George Preddy Littge. Ray Littge lost his life on 20 May 1949 while flying an F–84 jet. Coincidentally, when his wife remarried it was to a pilot from the 339th Fighter Group, James R. Starnes, who was an ace with six aerial victories. The 339th is the group to which Bill Preddy was later assigned. Jim Starnes was most helpful to the author in tracking down information about Bill Preddy and Ray Littge.

Since getting his last extension George had claimed 6.5 enemy aircraft destroyed in aerial combat. He had claimed these within a space of two weeks. But the next several missions escorting the Big Friends over Germany were uneventful for the fighter jocks; there were no encounters with enemy fighters. The ever-present flak was there, however, taking its normal toll of our fighters and bombers. George was getting somewhat anxious; his extension was about to run out and Meyer was back from his Stateside leave. At this point George was the leading ace in the group with twenty-two enemy aircraft destroyed.

It was just before noon on 5 August 1944, the ceiling and visibility were unlimited and George was leading the 487th Squadron south of Hamburg at 28,000 ft. He had just enough flying time left for one more mission after this one; he was hoping to make the best of them both. As his encounter report shows, he did.

*Capt. Raymond Littge on the right with Capt. Henry Stewart, and Maj. William Halton. J. R. Starnes*

*Returning to the 487th in early August 1944, Lt. Col John C. Meyer was assigned this bubble canopied Mustang. Upon seeing that its name* Petie 2nd *had been painted in bland white, with yellow victory marks, he instructed unit artist Sgt. Sam Perry to brighten up the name and make those kill marks bright enough "to scare the hell out of the Germans." The name was subsequently painted bright yellow with horizontal bands of orange yellow outlined in black. The victory marks were orange yellow.* H. B. Ross

We had just made rendezvous with the bombers southwest of Hamburg. I led the Squadron out ahead of the lead box. We were five miles ahead of them when I saw 12 to 15 Me 109s coming towards the bombers. They saw us at the same time and jettisoned their belly tanks. We pulled in behind them before they could reach the bombers and I opened fire at one from 400 yards and got many hits. The enemy aircraft began burning and losing many pieces. He went down out of control and on fire. At this time 40–plus enemy aircraft were sighted above us at 30,000 feet. They were the top cover for the aircraft I had just attacked. They began coming down. A big dog fight ensued with just a few enemy aircraft diving away from it; the rest remained to fight. I got behind another one and scored many hits on him. He began pouring out white smoke and went into the clouds. At this time I looked back and saw an Me 109 in range and firing at me so I pulled into a steep turn. I lost this one and then saw another being chased by a flight of P–38s. He went into a spin and was still spinning at 15,000 feet when the pilot bailed out. By this time there were 50–plus enemy aircraft in the sky and many P–38s and P–51s. I picked out an Me 109 in a steep left turn and fired at him with 50 to 30 degrees deflection without results. By this time only my left inboard gun was firing so I drove up behind another Me 109 very fast. I fired to 75 yards and 5 degrees deflection without getting hits. Finding no friendly aircraft to join with, I decided to go home as I had only a little ammunition left in one gun.

CLAIM:  One (1) Me 109 Destroyed
One (1) Me 109 Probably Destroyed

In an interview, John Meyer recalled this particular engagement. He said that George was definitely not obsessed with his score. He said many pilots were and would do anything to increase their score. On many occasions, he said, George would fly as wingman to a pilot in his squadron merely to observe if that man was suitable to become a flight leader. As wingman, he gave up his opportunity to shoot down enemy aircraft because a wingman's job is to protect the man whose wing he is flying on.

With reference to the mission of August 5, Meyer pointed out that George shot down an Me 109 which fell into the clouds. He didn't observe the enemy aircraft breaking apart or exploding but merely observed smoke. Therefore, he claimed a probable rather than a kill. Upon returning to base Meyer asked Preddy why he didn't claim a victory, and George explained that according to the rules he could only claim a probable. Meyer said, "You and I both know that you shot that airplane down, and I'm willing to corroborate your claim." But George insisted on leaving his claim as a probable. He knew that headquarters would not see the kill in the gun camera film because it wasn't there. So when he decided not to claim a sure thing, he knew it wouldn't be upgraded at a later date.

That night at the gaming tables in the officers club, George's luck took a turn for the better. He and his good friend Harry Kidder broke up a crap game. After winning all the money on the table, they started collecting pants and blouses. When he had yelled his final "Cripes A'Mighty!" and made his final roll of the dice, George had won $1,200. He purchased a war bond with the proceeds and mailed it home to his mother. Incidentally, this was the month the Eighth Air Force put on its War Bond Drive. The quota for Bodney was $53,000. George's purchase—over 2% of the quota—gave the drive its initial impetus.

Missions were not planned the next day because the weather was predicted to be rotten. So the evening turned into one big blast. After the party and several drinks too many, George returned to his quarters a bit tipsy and prepared for the sack. No sooner had he settled down than the officer of the day appeared and announced that there would indeed be a mission. The briefing would take place in twenty minutes. It was George's turn to lead the group, so he was expected to give the briefing. John Meyer came by George's quarters and saw his predicament. Meyer offered to take the mission. According to Meyer, George said, "No, damn it, I'll take the mission. It's my turn." So Meyer accompanied him to the briefing room.

Normal procedure called for the briefing officer to stand on a platform about the size of a large coffee table while giving his briefing. Normal procedure did not, however, call for the briefing officer to fall off the platform. But that's exactly what happened to George. The group commanding officer looked to Meyer the first time it happened and whispered, "George is drunk!" Meyer said to the officer that it would be several hours before they had to take off and he felt sure that by that time he could get George in condition to fly.

As soon as the briefing was over, Meyer and others made sure George breathed an adequate amount of pure oxygen before takeoff time. George led the mission to Berlin flying *Cripes A'Mighty 3rd* through high scattered clouds on what turned out to be a beautiful day with excellent visibility. This would be a six-hour mission, and since he didn't feel the best, George sort of hoped for a milk run. Here is his encounter report:

I was Group Leader. We were escorting the lead combat wings of B–17s when 30–plus Me 109s in formation came into the third box from the south. We were a thousand feet above them so I led White Flight—consisting of Lt. Heyer, Lt. Doleac and myself—in astern of them. I opened fire on one near the rear of the formation from 300 yards dead astern and got many hits around the cockpit. The enemy aircraft went down inverted and in flames. At this time Lt. Doleac became lost while shooting down an Me 109 that had gotten on Lt. Heyer's tail.

*Single frames from George's gun camera of the record-setting feat of destroying six fighter aircraft in a single mission.* Preddy gun camera film via Sox

Lt. Heyer and I continued our attack and I drove up behind another enemy aircraft getting hits around the wing roots and setting him on fire after a short burst. He went spinning down and the pilot bailed out at 20,000 feet. I then saw Lt. Heyer on my right shooting down another enemy aircraft. The enemy formation stayed together taking practically no evasive action and tried to get back for an attack on the bombers who were now off to the right. We continued with our attack on the rear end (of the enemy formation) and I fired on another from close range. He went down smoking badly and I saw him begin to fall apart below us. At this time four other P-51s came in to help us with the attack. I fired at another 109 causing him to burn after a short burst. He spiraled down to the right in flames. The formation headed down in a left turn keeping themselves together in rather close formation. I got a good burst into another one causing him to burn and spin down. The enemy aircraft were down to 5,000 feet now and one pulled off to the left. I was all alone with them now so went after this single 109 before he could get on my tail. I got in an ineffective burst causing him to smoke a little. I pulled up into a steep climb to the left above him and he climbed after me. I pulled it in as tight as possible and climbed at about 150 miles per hour. The Hun opened fire on me but could not get enough deflection to do any damage. With my initial speed I slightly out-climbed him. He fell off to the left and I dropped down astern of him. He jettisoned his canopy as I fired a short burst getting many hits. As I pulled past, the pilot bailed out at 7,000 feet.

I had lost contact with all friendly and enemy aircraft so headed home alone.

CLAIM: Six (6) Me 109s Destroyed

George's claims were supported in the following report filed by Capt. Seymour Joseph, Capt. Gerald Costello and 1st Lt. Sheldon Heyer: "I was flying Maj. Preddy's wing when we made the attack on 30 plus enemy aircraft. The first one he shot at, I observed many hits around the cockpit and the enemy aircraft went down burning and spinning. I think the pilot was killed. Again we attacked and Maj. Preddy opened fire on an enemy aircraft which burst into flames. After about one and a half turns of a spin the pilot bailed out. At this time I became engaged with one and shot it down. On our third attack Maj. Preddy got hits about the canopy and wing roots and the enemy aircraft went down spinning and in flames. I then had to break and lost Maj. Preddy as he continued the attack alone and went after another 109 of the remaining 15 or so."

Lieutenant Heyer wrote his own encounter report for the mission, claiming one Me 109 destroyed, and Preddy wrote a supporting statement for his claim. Lt. Cy Doleac, White Three, also claimed one Me 109 destroyed on that mission. White Flight became quite famous after this mission, and it is the subject of a painting done by artist Darrell Crosby. Four aircraft flew in White Flight, but one aborted, leaving Preddy and Doleac flying P-51Ds and Heyer in a B model.

On his return to Bodney after the mission, George buzzed a stack of drop tanks where he knew his assistant crew chief would be snoozing. Red McVay knew Preddy had been successful when he was awakened by the roar of a Mustang passing low—very low—overhead.

McVay, John Meyer and half the squadron gathered around *Cripes A'Mighty 3rd* as Preddy taxied up to his hardstand. Word had gotten back by radio that George had really gotten into the thick of battle on this mission. Fortunately, Lt. George Arnold had a camera and took photos of a very sick-looking George Preddy. George said he would never again fly with a hangover. According to Meyer, George had thrown up last night's party while flying at 32,000 ft. just before engaging the Me 109s.

On August 6, 1944, White Flight origi-
nated as a flight of four with George in
Cripes A'Mighty 3rd *as leader and Lt.
Sheldon Heyer in* Sweetiface *as his
wingman. Heyer scored a single victory
on the mission. Heyer's aircraft was*
*coded HO-N, serial number 43–6958.
He so loved the olive drab B model that
Lieutenant Colonel Meyer had to
threaten him with a court martial before
he would give it up in exchange for a
later model.* McEwen

Reporters, photographers, correspondents, commentators and writers
were at Bodney the next day to congratulate Preddy and get his story. He
performed some aerobatics, a few victory rolls and landed, rolling out on the
hardstand where his proud crew were waiting to congratulate him as they had
done the previous day. Editors spliced into this publicity film the actual gun
camera footage made while Preddy was shooting down six Me 109s. It's
interesting to note that Preddy didn't fly his *Cripes A'Mighty 3rd* for the
photographers on the seventh. Rather, he flew Lieutenant Greer's new P–51D
while performing the aerobatics and landing, but taxied up in *Cripes
A'Mighty 3rd* for the benefit of the cameras. Perhaps his plane had not been
completely serviced after the mission, or maybe George just didn't want to
put any unnecessary flying time on his aircraft.

Next on his list of public events was a broadcast interview by CBS. Bill
Shadel interviewed George just three days after his spectacular dogfight.
Edward R. Murrow was head of the European Bureau of CBS, and on the
evening of George's interview Murrow was chief announcer for the program
on which George was to be featured. Here is how the interview went between
Bill Shadel and George Preddy:

**Shadel:** "It is our pleasure to bring you from London this evening one of
the VIII Fighter Command's greatest fighter pilots, twenty-five year old Maj.
George E. Preddy of Greensboro, North Carolina who just this last Sunday
turned in the most amazing record of Fighter Command to date—six German

*This page and next*

August 6, 1944 sequence—the way it really happened. No official unit photographer was present when George returned from his record-breaking mission, but Lt. George Arnold was there with his 35 mm camera. The following pictures were taken as the event unfolded. George lands and taxis up to revetment with Cripes A'Mighty 3rd showing signs of the encounter. Note: the 3rd has 21 crosses on the top and three on the bottom; one cross was added after the victory scored on July 29. Pilots and ground crews gather to hear how he did it and to congratulate him. George's face reflects strain of the fight and the effects from the preceding night's activity.

135

fighters shot down out of a group of thirty Me 109s who were trying to break up our bomber attack against Berlin.

"Some people would like to think the days of the Luftwaffe opposition are over. Major Preddy can tell you how determined they are on occasion to ward off the blows of our heavies. The protection against just such determination is the job of the Fighter Command. It is still a tough job, a job that calls for all the experience and technique our men can muster—especially when there are only three of our fighters against thirty Germans . . . . as was the case on Sunday.

"Major Preddy has plenty of that experience, and plenty of Jerry fighters to his credit. With his latest performance on Sunday, he now has 24.5 shot down out of the air, five destroyed on the ground . . . only 3.5 to go to equal the present record of Lt. Col. Francis S. Gabreski of Oil City, Pennsylvania, with 28 shot down in the air. [Author's note: This is a clear indication that Eighth Fighter Command had recorded 24.5 aerial victories at this time for Preddy and twenty-eight for Gabreski. The 1978 USAF Historical Study Number 85 still shows twenty-eight for Gabreski who was a POW at this time and until the war ended. If one adds the four undisputed aerial victories claimed by Preddy after this date, then his score as reflected by Fighter Command is 28.5 aerial victories.]

"Major Preddy has been shooting down Germans for nearly a year, but before that he had some twenty-five combat missions against the Japs. Within a month after Pearl Harbor he was chasing off Japs that were attacking the northern tip of Australia. Back there the odds were terrific. He was used to being outnumbered; perhaps that's why he and his two wingmen dared tackle the thirty Germans. He was flying a P–40 out of Darwin when the Japs were coming in from New Guinea with their bombers and heavy escort of fighters. He bailed out once back there, over the jungle, fortunately was spotted by his

*This public relations photo was taken moments after the Arnold shots were recorded. The real strain of the preceding 24 hours is most evident.*

own buddies and was rescued within a few hours, but still had to spend three months in a hospital recovering from his injuries.

"He bailed out once in this theater over the Channel and again was spotted by friendly planes. He's had enough experiences to make him grey-haired I would say, yet as he sits here in the studio before me you would never guess such a background . . . . He's quiet, mild-mannered, almost shy . . . in fact protesting more about reciting his story for you than facing a flock of Jerry fighters. But from his decorations you know he's been around.

"Major, before we get into your story of the big day, Sunday, would you give us a briefing on the Silver Star decoration, and also the Distinguished Flying Cross you're wearing, and I notice, with three clusters. [Preddy's award of the Distinguished Service Cross came three days after this interview.]"

**Preddy:** "There have been several days similar to this last one. I hardly know just how the decorations fit in, but the Silver Star represents a fight three of us had with twelve Me 410s and about fifteen Me 109s who were attacking one of our bomber formations. I got one single-engined fighter and three twin-engined Ju 88s in one day, three single-engined fighters on another day and two fighters on two other days."

**Shadel:** "This record of six last Sunday then, sounds like it is just a build-up from other days. Apparently there is no limit to your fighting once you get started—but of course, you run out of ammunition and out of gas at some time during a fight, so we won't go on expecting the impossible from you. But whether you realize it or not, you're a hero in the eyes of your own fellows as well as your countrymen back home. I know we would like to hear about Sunday's hunting."

**Preddy:** "Our job was the usual one, escorting the bombers. We were meeting them north of Hamburg, escorting them on to their targets east of Berlin and part of the way back. About fifteen minutes after picking up the bombers we saw these thirty Me 109s come in for a stern attack on the third box of B-17s. Our flight of three was the only protection around at the

August 7, 1944—the way it was recorded for the press! A camera unit from Eighth Fighter Command arrived on August 7 and had George put on an air show for the troops. George and another pilot really beat up Bodney, making many low-level, high-speed passes across the field. Careful screening of the motion picture footage revealed that George did not fly Cripes A'Mighty 3rd during the show. It hadn't been fully serviced following the mission on the sixth and he didn't want to risk a mishap with his favorite plane. A separate taxiing sequence was edited into the film with George at the controls of Cripes A'Mighty 3rd. Assistant crew chief Cpl. Joe "Red" McVay, armorer M. G. Kuhaneck and several others staged a reception as soon as the prop unwound. Note: Seven victory crosses were added to the 24 displayed on August 6. He had received confirmation for the Me 109 destroyed on August 5. Eighth Fighter Command via Sox

moment, although I was leading the group escort. We had altitude on the Jerries, so we went down after them. They saw us coming and although they showed no intention of leaving the bombers alone, they did pull out to the left in evasive action.

"We came up on their tail and each one of us picked out a Jerry. From about 300 yards I gave mine a burst and set him on fire. I saw him go down in flames. They were trying to hold their formation, but were sending singles and doubles out to slip up on us from behind.

"At about 26,000 ft., one that slipped out and was trying to get on our tail had to be dealt with by one of my wingmen, FO Cyril Doleac of New Orleans. Lt. Sheldon Heyer of Pearl City, Illinois, and I kept after the main formation. I got in a burst at another Me 109 and the pilot bailed out. Lieutenant Heyer, to my right and below me, set another one on fire. Then Heyer had to leave me and take care of those strays from the enemy formation. By this time another single that had slipped out was down below me with the idea of coming up under me. I throttled down and slipped behind his tail just as he started up. Right after giving him a burst, he went into a spin and then fell apart.

"Luckily, just after that four more of our fighters came into the fight. It was now five of us against about twenty that were left in the formation after they had sent out their decoys and counted their losses. The Jerries were still intent on holding formation. I got behind my fourth target and shot him down in flames. Then they gave up on the bombers and went down fast in steep turns. I got one on the outside of a turn and closed in on him for a shot that sent him down.

"As they started breaking their formation for the first time our fighters scattered out in the chase. As a 109 pulled up to get on my tail I had to turn into

*War correspondent Arch Whitehouse visited George several days after his great mission and was shown around the ace's revetment. Note the Donald Duck patch on George's A-2 jacket.* J. Sabanos

139

him . . . that was the first time I left off chasing the formation . . . and by this time our fighters were off on their own. I got a short burst at the Jerry but missed. It was just the two of us then, and after I missed he had the edge on me. I went into a steep climb into the sun and as he tried to follow me I could see him firing everything he had. He couldn't stay with me in that climb and dropped off. Then it was my turn again. I got behind him, and he must have known then that his game was up. Before I could get in a shot I saw him fumbling with the hood above his head, trying to get out. When I hit him, the plane quivered a bit and started down, but he was out by this time, so I saw him float down without bothering him. By that time the bombers were over their target and I was almost to Berlin, so I set my course for home."

**Shadel:** "That is truly a great performance, Major."

**Preddy:** "Well, I have told only my part in it, but I'd like to give my wingmen lots of credit. You just can't watch your tail and concentrate on your shooting, too. That's why my wingmen are due as much credit as I am."

**Shadel:** "Major, that's fine of you to say that. But you'll have to get over some of that modesty as this latest exploit of yours becomes better known. It's one of the most outstanding fighter jobs of the war and that's on the record. Thank you for coming here this evening to let us hear about it in your own modest terms. And the best of luck to you."

Colonel Meyer recommended George for the Congressional Medal of Honor for his unequaled feat of destroying six Me 109s in one mission. Much to Meyer's surprise and disappointment, Preddy was awarded the second highest medal for his extraordinary heroism and disregard for his own safety

*Lt. Col. John C. Meyer recommended George Preddy, Jr., for the Medal of Honor for destroying six enemy aircraft on one mission on August 6, 1944. On*   *August 12, 1944, wing commander Gen. Edward H. Anderson awarded him the Distinguished Service Cross at Bodney. USAAF*

140

*The last victories scored in 44-13321 as* Cripes A'Mighty 3rd *were scored by Squadron Commanding Officer John* *Meyer at the controls. He added four ground victories to his total on 10 September 1944.* McVay

against overwhelming odds—the Distinguished Service Cross. Meyer also recommended George for a regular Army commission by letter dated August 17, 1944.

*Cripes A'Mighty 3rd* now displayed thirty-one white Balkan crosses which included George's ground victories and partial victories. The authors tried with mixed success to equate the number of crosses on Preddy's aircraft with the number of victories confirmed for him at various times during 1944. Photos taken showing seventeen, twenty-one and twenty-three crosses were not dated. But the photos taken showing thirty-one crosses were indeed dated; that number equates to the number of victory credits Preddy had accumulated through August 6. Appendix A shows that the number of victories tallied at Squadron level accumulates to thirty-one; that list of victories includes one for April 30, which was later omitted, perhaps disallowed. It also excludes the one-third shared victory which was added by the Fighter Victory Credits Board. In short, all the victories Preddy had chalked up through August 6 including the five he got while strafing totalled thirty-one. At this time George had scored twenty-three aerial victories, shared three other aerials (crosses were painted on aircraft for fractions of kills), and destroyed five enemy aircraft on the ground. He would add four more aerial victories to bring his unadjusted total to 28.5 aerial plus five ground victories.

This was the last time George would fly *Cripes A'Mighty 3rd*. It was assigned to Capt. Henry Stewart, who changed her name to *The Margarets*. It is known to have been flown by Col. John Meyer (who scored a quadruple in it on September 10), Lt. Marion Nutter (who claimed three aerial victories with it), Lt. F. C. Reading, Jr., and finally Lt. Walter Padden, who was killed in it while strafing on 15 April 1945. The name was changed to *Sexshunate*

(Section Eight) some time before it went down on the fifteenth. *Cripes A'Mighty 3rd* probably had the longest Mustang combat career, serving continuously for more than ten months.

Now that George's extensions had run out and Meyer was back to take command of the 487th, it was time for George to go home on a well-deserved and overdue leave.

*By September 11, 1944, while George was on 30 days R and R in the zone of interior,* Cripes A'Mighty 3rd *was stripped of her markings and reassigned to Capt. H. Malcolm Stewart who named her* The Margarets. *The individual aircraft code was changed to HO-N.* H. Stewart

*Chapter 14*

# And Glory

George's homecoming was a glorious event for him and those who knew and loved him. His mother and dad met him in Washington, D. C. where the Army Air Force had scheduled a stopover for a couple of days for interviews with the Press. This was the custom for all leading aces upon their return to the States. All had to go through the rigors of interviews, back-patting and handshaking, all designed by the public relations folks to keep America behind the war effort. Some aces relished the attention, others didn't take to it too kindly. The officials of the news bureaus said that George "made the best

*George's mom and dad met him in Washington. There's no welcome greater than that!*

subject of any of the aces to come through Washington." He gave the newsmen and the Army Air Force what they wanted without hamming it up.

When he arrived in Greensboro there was a big welcome party awaiting. He was treated as a distinguished guest the entire time he was home. A ceremony in his honor was held at the World War I Memorial Stadium which happened to be just a block from George's home on Park Avenue. The Chamber of Commerce invited Captain Eddie Rickenbacker to attend the ceremony, but he declined via the following telegram dated 25 September 1944.

> Please convey my genuine regrets to Major George Preddy, one of America's leading and outstanding hero pilots of World War Two. Nothing would give me greater pleasure than to grasp Major Preddy's hand and offer my heartfelt congratulations and appreciation for his great contribution and stimulating inspiration to all Americans and to the citizens of your community. Well may you be proud of being able to call Major Preddy one of your own.
> Eddie Rickenbacker.

Besides the speech he gave at the stadium, George was asked to address the Boy Scouts, high school students, the Chamber of Commerce and other organizations in Greensboro. He announced his engagement to Joan Jackson, his Australian girlfriend. Their correspondence had resulted in plans for marriage following the war.

One Sunday while attending the church of his childhood, First Methodist, the Reverend E. H. Neese quoted a sonnet in George's honor. The sonnet had been written by a nineteen year old American flyer of the Royal Canadian Air Force whose parents were the Reverend and Mrs. John G. Magee of Washington, DC. It is familiar to most airmen today, but is well worth repeating here.

High Flight

Oh, I have slipped the surly bonds of earth
   And danced the skies on laughter-silvered wings;
Sunward I've climbed, and joined the tumbling mirth
   Of sun-split clouds—and done a hundred things
You have not dreamed of—wheeled and soared and swung
   High in the sunlit silence. Hov'ring there,
I've chased the shouting wind along, and flung
   My eager craft through footless halls of air.
Up, up the long, delirious, burning blue
   I've topped the windswept heights with easy grace
Where never lark, or even eagle flew.
   And, while with silent, lifting mind I've trod
The high untrespassed sanctity of space,
   Put out my hand, and touched the face of God.
—John Gillespie Magee, Jr.

After the service, the Reverend Mr. Neese recalled that he spoke with George who said, "Preacher, I know what 'Put out my hand, and touched the face of God' means. I've done it."

"George," said Neese, "what do you expect to do with your expressed desire and determination to go back and help complete the job?" George said, "Reverend Neese, I must go back—

*George said to the photographer while posing with his younger cousin, Joe "Buddy" Noah, that we should be celebrating Buddy's solo flight. Incidental-* *ly, that solo took place about the same time George got six enemy aircraft on one mission.* Greensboro Daily News

Back to do my part,
  Back to fly and give again;
And I am not afraid.
  My plane may be shot away;
But I shall not fall,
  For I have wings—
Wings not of wood or steel or stuff,
  But wings of a firmer kind—
Wings God gave my soul.
  Thank God for wings."

Neese said he wrote down George's words several months after hearing them, which was in fact a few days after he received word that George met his death over Belgium. Some time after George's death, Neese sent George's mother and dad a copy of the sonnet he had quoted during his sermon along with his recollection of his conversation with George after the service. And, of course, it was a line from the above sonnet that gave title to the first edition of Preddy's biography—*Wings God Gave My Soul.*

Perhaps the most memorable event that occurred while George was home on leave happened when he met Bill in Venice, Florida. Bill was taking his final training in fighters there. George and his mother, dad and Rachel all went down to visit Bill. George and Bill each took a P–40 up for a friendly duel in the sky. The P–40 was the only type of fighter available at Venice. The result of the dogfight between brothers was that George was absolutely amazed at Bill's flying ability and knowledge of air tactics. Bill gave his brother, one of the top aces of the war, a real scrap that almost ended in a draw. George said to Bill, "Boy, you're ready to take on the best the Luftwaffe has to offer, but just don't get too cocky!"

When he returned to Greensboro, George was asked to participate in another radio broadcast, a local one this time. After a lengthy introduction citing all his recent feats and awards, George was given the microphone and asked to tell the folks about himself. He spent the entire time talking about Edward R. Murrow:

> When my group sailed for England many months ago we had aboard ship a man who is well known by radio audiences the world over. Every evening the officers would gather in the lounge while one of America's leading radio commentators, Edward R. Murrow, gave the straight dope on the war news of the day. It was a real pleasure having Mr. Murrow on the trip and to hear him give a fifteen-minute newscast each day.
>
> It was over a year after sailing that I ran into Ed Murrow again. I was called to the CBS studios in London to participate in a broadcast to the States. When I arrived at the studio I found that Edward Murrow was head of the European Bureau of the Columbia Broadcasting System. On this particular evening he was to be chief announcer for the program in which I was taking part. To sit beside this famous commentator at the same microphone was a great privilege.
>
> After the program we stepped outside to smoke a cigarette and he began asking about Greensboro and some of the people here. I couldn't understand why he was so interested until he told me that this section of North Carolina was his home until he was a young man and went away to school . . . then, of course, I was more interested than ever in Murrow. We talked for more than an hour on that London street.
>
> Ed Murrow has been overseas for seven years and in that time he has had as many experiences as any soldier at the front. He has seen the Germans occupy France. He knows what it was like to live in London during the blitz. He has great admiration for the English people for the great battle they fought against the Germans when they stood alone.
>
> Ed Murrow was right there when the Allies invaded Normandy and followed them onto the beaches to bring first-hand news to the anxious people in America and England. He rode in an English bomber to Berlin on a raid at night. Ed Murrow knows what he speaks about because he has spent every available moment getting a better insight into the feelings of the war-stricken peoples of Europe.
>
> I consider it a great honor to have met Ed Murrow and hope I will have the pleasure of seeing him again. Greensboro should be truly proud of him.

At the height of his fame and glory, George took this opportunity to sing the praises of another great Tarheel. Greensboro is proud of Murrow and Preddy; they have named boulevards in honor of each of them. George also took time out to extol the accomplishment of his younger cousin, Joe Noah, who had just earned his student pilot license and soloed a J–3 Cub. That was George's nature; he was most thoughtful of others.

Although grateful for some R and R at home, George was now ready to get back to England and take up where he had left off. He didn't have to go back; many aces who returned to the States with much less combat time than

George had decided to stay home. No one would have faulted him for electing to stay in the United States for the duration. But the war was far from over, and George's love of flying and desire to bring the war to a close led him to his decision without hesitation.

*George addressing a homecoming audience at the War Memorial Stadium in Greensboro, North Carolina, while* *home on leave in September 1944.* Greensboro Daily News

*Chapter 15*

# Return to Combat

Having spent September at home with his loved ones and many friends, George returned to the 352nd Fighter Group in October. Col. Joe Mason, the group commanding officer, had plans for George; he was to take over the 328th Fighter Squadron, the squadron with the lowest total score of enemy aircraft destroyed in the group. Leaving the 487th was a bit tough on George, but many of his closest friends had departed by now—a few were downed and taken prisoner, some killed in action, and others had rotated back to the United States. Going to the 328th was accepted as a challenge; George was determined to bring out the best they had to offer.

The 328th had many different commanders during the year they had been operational; the 487th had the same leaders the entire period. Sporadic leadership is not conducive to good morale and a high fighting spirit and could very well have been the underlying cause of the "black sheep" position the

*Several days after assuming command of the 328th FS, George gave his new squadron an air show in his new Mustang. It was serial number 44–14906 and was coded PE-P. Photo was taken at the conclusion of the demonstration. Note evidence of hydraulic problem as the left main gear door has not retracted as is normal in landing configuration. This Mustang was named simply* Cripes A'Mighty. *Each squadron of the 352nd had their rudders painted a different color for easy identification. The 328th painted theirs red. R. Powell*

328th achieved. Inspired leadership by an individual who had proven himself in combat promised to put some new enthusiasm in their fighting.

Lt. Raymond Mitchell said, "The morale was a bit low because the other two squadrons were doing better score-wise, and they were looking down on the 328th. I had a good impression of George because I had heard a lot about his past exploits in the South Pacific as well as in the ETO. So our expectations were great for George before he came. In his first meeting with us he seemed to be more cold and calculating, kind of quiet. When he talked, he had something to say; it wasn't just idle chatter. Everybody respected him, but it took a while for us to get acquainted with him and know what to expect of him."

His new crew chief, Sgt. Arthur Snyder, said "Within a day or two of taking command, he gathered the squadron around a bomb shelter, and he got up on top of the shelter and gave a short talk as to what we were there for. I vividly recall him saying that the main thing we were there for was to shoot down the Hun. The aircraft they gave me to crew for him was a new model. I used to cut hair on the side, and always had the theory that it paid to advertise. So I painted a barber pole on the right side of his cowling. He never complained; he thought it was a good thing."

With George's uncanny ability to seek out the enemy and pursue them with vengeance, the 328th was sure to get every chance to boost their lagging score. Preddy took over the squadron on October 28th, and led them on their first mission on October 30, 1944. Coincidentally, Col. Don Blakeslee was leading his 4th Fighter Group for the last time. Blakeslee had been in action in England since 1941 and had flown 350 missions and more than 900 hours, half again as much as any other American fighter pilot in Europe. His final score was 11.5 aerial victories.

Col. Hubert Zemke was flying his 155th, and last, planned mission on the thirtieth, but with the 479th Fighter Group rather than the group he formerly led, the famed 56th Fighter Group. He was southeast of Hamburg escorting bombers when those bombers disappeared into towering cumulus clouds. Zemke decided to lead his group over the clouds rather than through them. At 24,000 ft. the leading flight entered the clouds and was buffeted unmercifully by the turbulence. Zemke called for the execution of a 180–degree turn to get out of there. As he banked his Mustang he was thrown over on his back violently and sent downward with great force. His wingman and his second element followed. The final result was that Zemke and Lt. Douglas Holmes were forced to bail out of their Mustangs as they broke apart. Zemke was taken prisoner and spent the remainder of the war travelling from one POW camp to another. His final score was 17.75 aerial victories. Others in his group were able to pull out of their spins just before reaching the deck. One Mustang, however, actually got bent in the 9.6 G pull-out. Had it not been for the recently invented G-suits, several pilots would have blacked out from the force of gravity as they tried to pull out of their dives.

The bombers escorted by the 352nd were recalled due to bad weather, so they turned back in the vicinity of Dummer Lake. They remained clear of the violent thunderheads and suffered no problems. Incidentally, Dummer Lake served as a landmark from the air where enemy fighters often concentrated. It's about 200 nautical miles east of and on the route to Berlin from East Anglia.

The next time up, November 2, 1944, things were a bit different for George. It was an escort mission to Merseburg, Germany, and the clouds were

*George's last Mustang was a P-51D-15NA, serial number 44-14906. His crew chief, S/Sgt. Art "Snoots" Snyder, cut hair on the side, so he became the 328th squadron barber. On each of the three Mustangs he crewed, he chose to use the right side of the aircraft to advertise his barbering services.* A. Snyder

10/10 at 4,000 ft. with occasional holes. It was half-past noon when George saw the enemy.

> I was leading a section of 20 P-51s sweeping ahead of the last two combat wings of B-17s in the target area. The rest of the Group was giving close support to the bombers. Shortly before our assigned wings approached the target I saw 50-plus contrails at 33,000 feet heading for the target area from the east. We were at 28,000 feet so we dropped wing tanks and began climbing for the enemy aircraft. I reported the bandits to the Group Leader and made contact with the enemy before they could reach the bombers. They were Me 109s flying in waves abreast, and as we approached the first wave they began diving. I got behind one of them but he went into a cloud before I could close on him. I then pulled up and began climbing for the bombers.
>
> At 15,000 feet I saw several P-51s and Me 109s in a dog fight so I pulled up behind a Me 109 which was in a left turn. I opened fire at long range but did not get results until at 150 yards. I then saw strikes on his engine and center section and the enemy aircraft began burning. He went down leaving a long column of white smoke. A P-51 from another Group went in behind him and the enemy aircraft continued on down crashing into the ground.
>
> I believe the K-14 sight is effective if the pilots know how to use it. My results were not satisfactory on this occasion because I haven't had enough experience with it. Pilots should have eight to ten hours training and continue practice tracking while on training hops.
>
> CLAIM: One (1) Me 109 Destroyed.

The K-14 gunsight was entirely new to George because the 352nd Mustangs had been equipped with them while he was home on leave. The sight was supposed to, and did for those who knew how to use it, allow for more accurate deflection shooting. The gyroscopic sight, which compensated for high G-forces encountered when pulling tight turns, was a huge improvement. But it was very sensitive and required smooth coordination of stick and rudder.

Fortunately, all the fellows in George's squadron were not as new to the K–14 sight as was he, and the record they set that day speaks well for themselves, for the new gunsight, and for his inspired leadership. The 328th Fighter Squadron downed twenty-four of the thirty-eight enemy aircraft accounted for by the 352nd Group. Both of these totals set new records in the Eighth Air Force. In reply to a news correspondent after it became known that he was still the leading active ace in the ETO, he said, "I sure as hell am not a killer, but combat flying is like a game and a guy likes to come out on top. I'm not aiming for any particular score, I just want to finish the job here in Europe so I can go back to the Pacific. I'd like to get another crack at the Japs and also see my fiancée in Australia."

When asked why the Americans were doing so well against the Luftwaffe, he replied, "It's our aggressiveness. The boys we are facing today aren't as good as the ones we battled a year ago. The current crop is not experienced. They were aggressive when we raided Merseburg the other day [November 2] but they probably had orders to stop those bombers from hitting the target regardless of cost. Well, they paid plenty. It looks to me like they're conserving their air power all the time, but on important targets they go to it."

A story appeared in *Yank* Magazine about the epic air battle that took place over Germany on November 2, 1944. It contained a few paragraphs about Major Preddy. The point of those few paragraphs was that George was the one who spotted the bandits. Sgt. Joe Sabanos, photographer, said he often heard around the field at Bodney that Preddy had the best eyes for seeing at a distance and spotting the enemy. Lt. Col. John C. Edwards, who retired as a general officer, wrote in 1987 that he recalled one mission he flew with George very vividly. Edwards was leading the group and George was leading a squadron. Edwards said, "George called on the RT asking permission to make a sweep away from our current position, which I okayed and shortly thereafter he and his squadron were in one hell of a fight. I didn't see a thing. He could smell a fight!" And that is a common characteristic among the top aces.

The Luftwaffe was putting forth another challenge that could not be countered by the best pilots in the world flying less-than-competitive aircraft. And the Mustang suddenly lost its lead over German fighter aircraft with the introduction of the Me 262 jet. It had been known for quite some time that a jet fighter was being developed by the Germans, but many of our leaders chose to belittle the significance of it by saying they would never have them in sufficient quantity to affect the direction of the war. As it turned out, they were right. But it was Hitler's blunder that made them right. He made a bomber out of the Me 262 hoping that he could return some of the tonnage the Allies had been dropping on his fatherland. Had he made it a fighter from the beginning and given it high priority for production, the direction of the war might well have changed. Battles would certainly have been hotter for the Allied fighter and bomber crews.

George's squadron first encountered the Me 262 on November 11 when they saw one cut his power and dive down and then climb up underneath an

*The 352nd Fighter Group leaders photographed about mid-November 1944. Left to right they are Lt. Col. Jim Mayden, deputy group commanding officer; Lt. Col. Willie O. Jackson, commanding officer of the 486th FS; George Preddy, commanding officer of the 328th FS; Col. Joe Mason, group commanding officer; and Lt. Col. John C. Meyer, commanding officer 487th FS. Mason's Mustang* This Is It! *is in the background. It was coded PZ-M, with serial number 44-14911. Its rudder was yellow.* P. Grabb

unidentified Mustang and shoot it down. They gave chase only to find that the jet was 50 to 75 mph faster than their Mustangs. The lone jet, not anxious to pit his wits against a group of slower but more maneuverable P–51s, escaped merely by pouring on the power. The jets were a deadly new enemy that would be most difficult to deal with in numbers.

Luftwaffe fighters were conspicuously absent for much of the rest of November 1944. George continued to lead his squadron on escorts without encountering the enemy until the twenty-first when once again the German High Command decided the target should be protected at all costs. While they didn't succeed in protecting it, their efforts to do so were obviously all-out and costly to them. Again the target was the oil center at Merseburg. It was George's 132nd combat mission.

We were sweeping behind the rear box of B–17s as they pulled off the target at Merseburg. We were at 20,000 feet and saw a big formation of FW 190s with about 15 FW 190s for top cover heading for the bombers from the northwest. The main formation was at 29,000 feet so we started climbing for the top cover. I pulled up behind a formation of three FW 190s and fired on the middle one from astern. He was leaving a heavy contrail making it hard to see him from behind. I got good hits on him and he began smoking badly and fell off to the left in a spin. The last I saw of him he was spinning through the overcast which had tops at 25,000 feet. I then attacked a single FW 190 and opened fire at 400 yards with slight deflection. After many hits he flipped over and started down in flames, out of control. I believe the pilot of this airplane was hit by my fire. I saw the airplane lose pieces of its wing and tail as it went into the overcast. I then went down on the main formation from astern and they started a turn to the left. I pulled up behind one of them as they headed for the overcast. I opened fire just as they went into the soup and continued firing part of the way into it. I saw hits on this enemy aircraft but do not know the outcome as he disappeared into the overcast. I then pulled up and saw another FW 190 above and behind us so I broke into

*George in one of his more somber moods shortly after taking command of* the 328th FS. Cropped from a group photo by Sox

him. We passed head on and exchanged fire without results. I turned to get on his tail but he dived into the overcast.

CLAIM: One (1) FW 190 Destroyed (Air)
One (1) FW 190 Probably Destroyed (Air)
One (1) FW 190 Damaged (Air).

George was officially credited with one destroyed, one probably destroyed and one damaged. That brought his score to 26.5 aerial and five ground victories according to Eighth Fighter Command records at the time. But Preddy's position as the leading active ace in the ETO was being seriously challenged by John Meyer, who had recently been promoted to deputy commanding officer of the 352nd Fighter Group. Meyer destroyed three FW 190s on the same mission to bring his total to thirty—seventeen aerial and thirteen on the ground. George still held a comfortable lead in aerial victories.

Bill Whisner challenged Preddy's record of six victories in one mission on 21 November 1944. The Fighter Victory Credits Board gave Whisner credit for five destroyed and two probables. General Order Number 9 dated January 24, 1945, however, awarded Whisner the Distinguished Service Cross for valor displayed on this mission and gave him credit for six destroyed and one probable.

Some time following the war, John Meyer wrote a story entitled "George Preddy." The story was found in draft form only and is not dated. We believe

*On November 21, 1944, Capt. William T. Whisner equaled George's August 6th record of destroying six fighter aircraft in a single mission, flying his Mustang Moonbeam McSwine. At the time, Whisner's claim of six destroyed was reduced to five and it was not until 1978 that he was given credit for the sixth victory! His P-51 was coded HO-W and was serial number 44-14237. Its rudder was blue. His final total was 15.5 aerial and three ground victories. He scored 5.5 more victories during the Korean conflict. Moralls*

it was written between 1946 and 1950. Although not the point of his story, he brings out a characteristic that Whisner and Preddy shared—a weakness for whiskey. Meyer said, "George's life with the group was a kaleidoscope of evening drunken brawls, magnificent loyalty to duty and industry as an officer, tedious and repetitious training at the art of a fighter." He said that George had a weakness for whiskey and women. George's diary tends to support Meyer's assessment of Preddy's weakness for women. However, interviews with fellow officers suggest that Meyer may have used poetic license when he used the phrase "evening drunken brawls" in connection with Preddy.

Meyer pointed out a conflict in Bill Whisner's character. It was brought out at the party immediately following the 1 January 1945 victorious mission at Y-29 (Asch, Belgium). Meyer said, "Bill sat dejectedly drinking Coke amidst the gala partying of the remaining participants in this day's events. Bill had had a serious brush with the Group Commander about three months before. He caused a hell of a scrap over at the Officer's Club and struck a high-ranking visiting officer. Under ordinary circumstances, if it had been anyone else but Bill, he would have been court martialed right then. The command was becoming fed up with his periodic soirees, and he had been told in no uncertain terms . . . that the next time would be the last . . . . Bill, since that date, had not touched a drop. However, it seemed to me that this occasion was an exception, and after arranging with two of the burliest of our Group to

In November 1944 Capt. H. M. Stewart received a new P-51D. Again old Cripes A'Mighty 3rd was stripped of the name, The Margarets and renamed Sexshunate (for section eight) by its new pilot Capt. Marion J. "Red Dog" Nutter. Three aerial victories were added by Nutter. On January 25, 1945, Lt. Ray Littge completed the long succession of victories scored in this faithful Mustang. A total of 18.5 aerial and nine ground victories were finally tallied. Final count indicates that more aerial victories were scored in this Mustang than any other serving in World War II. Lt. Walter Padden flew it on its last mission April 16, 1945, when he was killed in action while strafing on the Continent. This photo was taken on December 23, 1944, moments before Lieutenant Nutter left Bodney for Y-29 in Belgium. McEwen

be his watchdogs [Ralph Hamilton was one of the burly guards] and take responsibility for keeping him out of trouble that night, Bill joined the fun. It was not too long, however, before he was on the road he had travelled so many times before, and the watchdogs stepped in. This medium-sized youngster, however, was a wild man, driven crazy by his drink, and a battle royal ensued, glasses were broken, furniture wrecked, and whiskey bottles smashed . . . ."

Apparently, George exhibited less aggression under the influence of alcohol than did Bill. Jack Donalson was able to calm George when he had too much to drink. George's aggression was often taken out in a playful manner. Lt. Karl Dittmer, 487th pilot, told the story about George "slow-rolling the brass" when he was drunk. He would come into Clermont Hall, or into the hut as the case may be, and turn their beds over dumping them out on the floor while they were sound asleep. He said this may explain why George didn't make lieutenant colonel when he took over the 328th Fighter Squadron.

December started off rather slowly; there was little action. Weather was the most fearsome enemy and the 328th was able to get off the field at Bodney only eight times. For the most part, these were routine escort and strafing missions with little combat. Perhaps the most exciting mission for one of the 328th pilots occurred during this lull. It was on December 4th that Lieutenant Taylor, flying in George's section, was attacked by an enemy aircraft while returning from an operation over the continent. The German escaped before the rest of the 328th could bring him down, but also before he had finished Taylor. But ground fire completed what the enemy aircraft started. It knocked out Taylor's engine, forcing him to bail out of his crippled ship. He was at only 500 ft. when he hit the silk and, apparently, he was knocked unconscious as he exited the ship. When he regained consciousness he found himself suspended in a tree with his parachute still unopened. Disentangling and lowering himself from the tree, he evaded enemy soldiers for two hours—so he thought. Fortunately, he soon discovered that he was on friendly soil and reported to a hospital where he was given a checkup.

Taylor was found to be okay and was sent immediately to a front-line unit, handed a carbine and given a platoon of infantry to lead against the Germans. Explaining that he was just a fly-boy and not a qualified platoon leader served to get him relieved from this assignment. He took his carbine and went to a station about fifteen miles from the front line—somewhere south of Strasbourg, France. Finding the people at the station too busy fighting a war to pay him any attention, he left there on his own and headed for Paris hitchhiking his way in trucks. No sooner had he arrived than he was picked up by the military police; he convinced them he was a legitimate American pilot and finally got a ride back to England in a C–47.

On December 10, 1944, George wrote a letter to Bill and Wanda Teague. Recall that Bill Teague taught George to fly in a Waco before the war. Wanda had sent George a fruitcake, and he was writing to thank her. In this letter he told them that he had been given command of a squadron. He said, "I have some fine pilots and am proud of the job they are doing, particularly on one mission when we knocked down 24 Jerries to set a new record." Bill Teague's younger brother, Giles, had dropped in to see George several weeks before the letter was written. Giles' nickname was "Runt," and he had asked George to try to get him transferred from his bomber outfit to fighters. George had his group commanding officer write a letter requesting that Runt be transferred to the 352nd. That never happened. First Lieutenant Giles L. Teague, twenty-nine years old, went down in the English Channel on December 30, 1944, was reported missing in action on January 16, 1945 and confirmed killed on May 5. Runt was a B-17 pilot and had been in England since June 1944.

Goat Mathews visited George at Bodney one evening during the middle of December. Mathews was serving with a bomber group at Thurleigh near Bedford. It was an evening just before a planned mission. Goat said they had a great time that evening, and just before turning in George said, "Let's go over to the orderly room and see if I have any mail." So they went over and George discovered he didn't have a key to the room, so he peered in through a window and saw that he did have some mail. He broke the window to get in. He had a letter from his fiancée, Joan Jackson. The next morning, Goat was invited to listen in on the briefing George gave his squadron prior to the mission planned for that day. Goat said that there was no doubt who was in command during that briefing. He said, "George controlled that meeting, and it was clear that all respected him!"

George took advantage of some spare time provided by poor weather and wrote his last letter home. He wrote this letter the day the Germans unleashed a shattering attack against the weakly-held Allied positions in the Ardennes—the Battle of the Bulge!

England
December 16, 1944
Dear Mother and Dad,
    Mail [delivery] continues to be very bad. I suppose we will just have to be patient until after the Christmas rush.
    I just got back from a 48-hour pass to London last night. We drove down and the fog was so bad you could hardly see the front end of the car. It has stayed that way for the past four days.
    Last Sunday the Group had a tea dance which was pretty nice. It started at 4:00 and lasted until about 10:00 PM. The girls weren't too sharp, but we had a good band and good food.
    I was a little surprised to hear Bozo was in Italy. I'm anxious to hear about Bill's whereabouts. I kinda expect to see him turn up here any time.
    I sure hope Uncle Laurie [Joe Noah's father] is better now. He must have been hurt badly. I hope he will not be permanently injured. [Laurie was crushed between a platform and a rail box car; three doctors said he had little if any chance for survival. He spent 101 days in the hospital and survived to work on the Southern Railroad until retirement.]
    Mail from Joan is even worse than from you. I don't expect to hear from her until way after the first of the year. I believe she must think I returned home for good.
    Here's hoping everybody is fine as ever.
Best love always,
George

Bozo was a pilot with the 719th Bomber Squadron in Italy. He had made it overseas before Bill Preddy, who was just leaving the States to join the 339th Fighter Group stationed in Fowlmere, England. Bozo completed fifty missions over Europe during a seven-month period. His most exciting and difficult mission occurred when flying over Vienna. Two of his engines were knocked out by flak, forcing him to make an emergency landing in Yugoslavia. He and his crew successfully evaded the enemy and made it back to friendly territory.

# Chapter 16

# Christmas Day 1944

For what had the Luftwaffe been preserving their strength? It had been obvious for the past few months that they only came up to fight on very important occasions—when the target was quite valuable. It had not been obvious that they were building the largest inventory of fighters since the war started. In fact, it was inconceivable that they were able to build such a force in light of the repeatedly heavy bombing raids made by the Allies on their production facilities.

Inconceivable or not, that is exactly what Hitler had accomplished during late summer and fall 1944. The greatest number of aircraft assembled in any year of the war would be used in conjunction with Germany's last big offensive—the Battle of the Bulge.

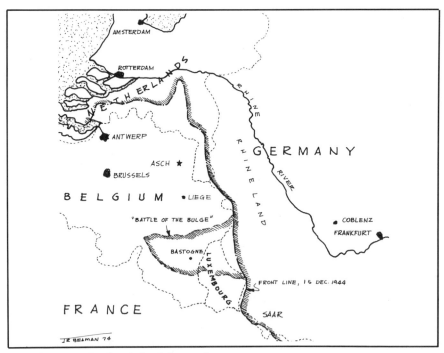

*Map depicting Battle of the Bulge and the forward airfield, Y-29 at Asch, Belgium, where the 352nd was deployed on December 23, 1944.*

When Von Runstedt launched his murderous counteroffensive in the Ardennes Forests of Belgium and Luxembourg and threatened to cut off our supply and communications lines, the 352nd Fighter Group was deployed to a hastily prepared advance base at Asch, Belgium, known as Y-29. On the morning of December 23, Preddy and his 328th Squadron took off for Y-29 under poor weather conditions. The ceiling was so low that the aircraft flew in trail rather than in squadron formation. As a result many pilots became stragglers, continually dodging slag heaps while looking for the steel mat strips that marked Y-29.

Lt. Raymond Mitchell explained what happened this day: "They called us into a briefing, and everybody was wondering what are we going to hear now. It was announced that we were needed over on the Continent. We were going to move out right away. We were to fly in and there would be little of anything there except fuel. We'd be sleeping in tents! And so right away we started wondering what's this all about. They explained that we would be there to fly close support. The Battle of the Bulge had broken out, and they need aircraft badly.

"So, they gave us a set of spark plugs and said we'd have to change our own plugs because the mechanics wouldn't be there. They said there would be fuel, and there would be a strip cleared out of the forest with steel matting on it."

Lt. J. Gordon Cartee said, "It was a rough day. I've always been so proud of Duke Lambright leading us there, because unless you're familiar with the country, slag piles going 100 to 125 feet in the air—we had to dodge around them because we were right on the deck hunting this steel mat." Mitchell added, "As we circled to land on the mat once we found it, we got shot at by the Germans from across the swamp. They weren't too far away!"

*Unfortunately, no one photo was taken of* Cripes A'Mighty *which displays all of its markings. Here is a photo showing* *the famous markings with two proud crew men.* A. Snyder

Arriving at their destination one at a time and over the course of perhaps an hour, they were greeted with tents set up in snow—quite a change from the relative comforts of Bodney. A typical tent contained six cots, a stove and a bucket of coal. A steel helmet served as a substitute for a bath tub or a shower.

George's tent contained a stove rigged to accept gasoline rather than coal, so he gave his bucket of coal to his wingman, Lieutenant Cartee. Cartee made the understatement of the day, "That was primitive living for us—tents and a bucket of coal for a potbellied stove. It was fairly comfortable considering there was snow on the ground. The most uncomfortable part was going to the latrine. It was a slit trench with canvas siding."

The pilots' tents had been placed in a straight line in a pine thicket, and guards were posted about the area at night to deter infiltrators from knocking off pilots while they slept. Some of the tents were equipped with trenches in front in case of air raids, and some were not so equipped. At about 9:30 that first night, bed-check charlie came over to greet the new inhabitants of the strip at Asch. Unaccustomed to surprise greetings of this sort, the American pilots raced for the scarce trenches to seek protection from their visitors. It became immediately obvious that the trenches were inadequate to provide shelter for all the pilots; those without trenches spent most of the night digging in. Later they became so accustomed to bed-check charlie's visits that they seldom retreated to the trenches; they just turned over, got their helmets and went back to sleep. Then, too, at Y–29 the V–1s came over frequently. As long as that putt-putt sound made by the engine continued, there was no cause to worry. When it cut out, all tried to find a trench quickly.

Sgt. Art Snyder, who got there a couple of days later, said, "There were no facilities for taking care of the planes; we just kept our stuff in a bag. We had some extra tools and spark plugs, and a few very essential things that were needed to keep the planes in operation." The 352nd was sent to Asch to conduct a continuous patrol of the area. One squadron was to be in the air, one squadron briefed as next up, and the third squadron was free to remain in the tent area. On December 24, they flew a four-hour patrol during which the

*Ditto White Flight on Christmas Day 1944 was led by George in* Cripes *A'Mighty with markings as depicted here by artist Darrell Crosby.* Crosby

weather was terrible and aircraft radios were set incorrectly. The air waves were filled with garbled static, and there was no enemy action.

On December 25, Christmas Day, the 328th Squadron was second up for patrol. The weather was still rotten but George said he knew it was going to be a good day because he had his fighting socks on. After briefing his squadron, George laughingly pulled up his pants legs and showed off his bright red fighting socks and said, "Let's go get 'em!"

Ten pilots of the 328th got into their planes, warmed up and took off in element formation climbing to 15,000 ft. at full throttle. According to Lt. J. Gordon Cartee: "We climbed like gangbusters until we got to 12 or 15 thousand because there was a real danger of being caught with our wheels down." When they leveled off George checked in with radar control. There was no action at that time, and the radios were still poor but readable. After almost three hours on patrol, radar control called Preddy, reported bandits and gave him a vector to intercept. Setting his squadron on the new course they soon came insight of a dogfight already taking place. George drawled over his radio to his squadron mates, "Looks like they started without us; let's join 'em." George drove in, picked out one Me 109 and started turning with him. He was gaining when another 109 cut in front of him. He gave the latter a burst. There were numerous hits, the canopy came off and the enemy pilot bailed out. Preddy resumed his attack on the first 109. After several more turns with him he managed to close and get many hits. This pilot also bailed out.

The brief dogfight had scattered the aircraft of the 328th, so Preddy and Cartee resumed patrol until joined by Lt. James Bouchier in a white-nosed P–51 from the 479th Fighter Group. George received a vector from radar control and proceeded to Liège, where bandits were reported on the deck. There was some talk on the radio about intense flak, and radar control said they would halt the flak so the three Mustangs could attack the bandits. Lieutenant Cartee reported the action in his December 25, 1944, encounter report:

I was flying Ditto White Two. Near the end of our patrol, Ditto White Leader was vectored to a point slightly southwest of Coblenz where bandits were reported. When we got there a fight was already in progress, but we drove in and Major George E. Preddy, Ditto White Leader, picked out a target and started turning with him. After several turns Major Preddy was gaining on the Me 109, when another 109 cut in front of him. He gave the latter 109 a burst. I observed many hits and the pilot bailed out. Major Preddy immediately swung back to the first 109 and after about another turn got on him. He got numerous hits and this pilot also bailed out.

Getting a new vector, we continued toward Liege where bandits were reported on the deck. We have a three-ship flight now, a white-nosed P–51 having joined us. Southeast of Liege we were at 1500 feet when we spotted a FW 190 on the deck. Major Preddy went down after him. The 190 headed east at tree-top level. As we went over a wooded area, I was hit by ground fire. Major Preddy apparently noticed the intense ground fire and light flak and broke off the attack with a chandelle to the left. About half way through the maneuver and about 700 feet altitude his canopy came off and he nosed down, still in a turn. I saw no chute and watched his ship hit the ground. Flak and tracers were still very thick. I went balls out until over it.

This statement can be used as confirmation of two Me 109s destroyed by Major Preddy.

*Art Snyder and Sgt. Deigman in front of the 31 crosses on George's new aircraft. These photos were taken after George* *took command of the 328th but before his first victory with the 328th—November 2, 1944.* Robling

The tragic incident was related by Capt. William S. Cross, 12th Anti-Aircraft Group:

When the Battle of the Bulge broke out, our unit moved south in Germany. Snow piled up among the trees of the Hurtgen Forest and the whole landscape was bleak and forbidding. The weather was extremely cold; the mud had frozen. It was just terrible in the fields. The skies were overcast; we could rarely see aircraft flying overhead although we could hear them and were aware of them through our communications net. It was only when they came in low and attacked ground targets that we had a chance to see them. We were in a heavily wooded area. [See map showing area D459.] The mission of our unit was to defend that area, basically the field artillery, the Corps Headquarters, bridges, ammunition and fuel dumps. The enemy tactic at that time was to make ground attacks against the artillery, the infantry if they could find them, and of course against any bridges to delay our movement back and forth. And our purpose was to deny them.

Our weapons were basically automatic weapons. We did not have the long range antiaircraft artillery guided by radar; ours required visual observation in order to fire them. These were very fast firing quadruple .50 caliber machine guns in turrets mounted on the back of half-tracks. And accompanying each one of those was a 40 millimeter Bofors automatic weapon that fired an inch-and-a-half round about 7,000 yards. The weapons were extremely effective against low-flying aircraft, but of the two the quad was by far the most effective.

The situation at that time was rather desperate from the point of view of the Army. The Germans had broken through the Bulge. We were defending the northern flank of the Bulge and trying to contain it. We set up our guns around the artillery battery we were defending. As time went on we realized it was more effective to set up in area defenses; we assigned a .50 caliber quad and one Bofors gun to a 1000–meter square area. That was our situation in December. There was a crew of six with each area defensive unit. The crew was lonesome and cold, and had little support.

162

Lt. J. Gordon Cartee was George's number two flying for the first time his new P-51K named Steph'NJane. His crew named her Bonny on the right side. J. G. Cartee

The firing units were connected by a command radio that was on all the time. It was an open-loop network so that any one unit could hear any other unit speak. From the radio, the firing unit got warnings of approaching enemy aircraft and any other data they needed. On Christmas morning, planes had been flying overhead all day long trying to attack ground targets beyond our units. There was very little enemy activity in our unit on that morning. We would hear the planes but couldn't see them because they were above the overcast. From time to time a plane would come under the overcast, would be identified and fly off. In this case, there was a flash, flash, flash warning—a first or red alert which says that enemy aircraft are approaching. They were approaching from the southeast. All the weapons swung in that direction and there was the sound of anti-aircraft firing or machine gun firing—whether it came from a plane or from the ground was impossible to tell. Anyway, the guns were alerted and swung in that direction waiting to see the planes coming. We were told there were two Me 109s flying in strafing ground targets—a typical attack.

Suddenly, over the trees, two planes appeared. The gunner on the quadruple .50 caliber machine guns fired a very short burst at these planes. He had only an instant to fire because the planes were flying so fast and low. We understand that he fired only sixty rounds, and the weapons had a fire rate of 6,000 rounds per minute, so you can see he simply touched those triggers and immediately recognized that the plane was friendly, that he had fired on a friendly plane. The plane was hit and crashed nearby. It was not a terrible crash, it didn't go in head first, and the pilot could possibly have survived the impact. The gun crew ran to

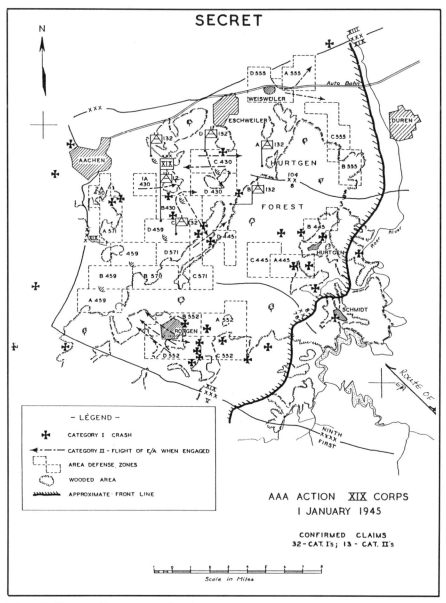

*Map of Hurtgen Forest area showing*
*AAA Action XIX Corps. George went*
*down in the D459 section.* Cross

it as fast as they could. It crashed some five to six hundred yards away. Unfortunately, the pilot had been hit by one of the .50 caliber rounds. It was then that they realized—when they got the dog tags off—that it was the leading ace of the ETO, Major Preddy. You can imagine our sorrow. The other friendly plane [flown by Lieutenant Cartee] made a wide circle and flew back overhead several times before finally departing.

William Cross spent his adult life in Greensboro where he developed and managed a successful engineering firm. He was kind enough to share this very sad experience with us.

Lieutenant Cartee saw the incident from a different perspective: After witnessing Preddy's victory over two Me 109s, we were called and told that there was an FW 190 on the deck. Radar control said they would halt the antiaircraft fire if we would go down and get the 190. Apparently communications were not as good as I thought they would be. But, anyway, we went down chasing the 190 right on the deck. We passed a little patch of trees and then we began to get exceedingly heavy ground fire. I took a tracer in the cockpit, and about the same time I saw Major Preddy start a chandelle up—but it seemed like halfway through that maneuver they gave him another burst that cinched him because he went on over and in. He just went down. The white-nosed P-51 that had joined us was so severely damaged that the pilot [later identified as Lt. James Bouchier] was forced to bail out. I was trying to flash my stars as best I could, but until I got over their area they continued to fire. I wasn't hit but once. When I got over the gun emplacement the tracer was still burning and I tried to stamp it out. I hurried back to Y–29 and landed on the mat. Colonel Mayden, who didn't normally greet the returnees, was out there perhaps because he was interested in Major Preddy. Mayden had probably gotten word that there was a mishap. His first question was, "Where is George?" The whole outfit was upset at the loss of Preddy!

In summary, here is what apparently happened on this fateful Christmas Day. Preddy, with Lt. J. Gordon Cartee on his wing, was joined by Lt. James Bouchier as he picked out his third target for the day, an FW 190 speeding along at treetop level. The flight of three dropped down on the deck in trail hoping to use their superior speed gained by diving to close on the 190. They were closing rapidly when they flew over an area defended by members of the 12th Anti-Aircraft Group. Standard operating procedures governing all antiaircraft units provided that when friendly aircraft were in their vicinity, all units in the line of flight were to be notified and ordered to hold all fire. One gunner in the 12th must not have gotten the word.

As the trio flew over the area defended by the 12th, Cartee took a tracer in the cockpit, Bouchier's P-51 was so badly damaged that he had to bail out, and Preddy—hit by two rounds—instinctively pulled up into a chandelle and released his canopy in a vain effort to escape. His survival instincts were present to the end; he brought his colorful Mustang to a survivable crash-landing in a field less than a thousand yards from the artillery unit.

Lt. Ray Mitchell, another 352nd pilot, landed and parked his Mustang. Heading for his tent and contemplating the loss of Preddy, a fellow pilot asked that he join him for Christmas dinner. Mitchell replied, "Christmas dinner! Is it really Christmas?" It had been that kind of day.

Later—after the 352nd moved to Chievres, or A–84, Bill Preddy visited and talked with a few of George's close friends. He wanted to know how his brother had been killed. Cartee said of the visit, "We had a long talk and had lunch together. He was an impressive young fellow. He wasn't afraid of flying or combat after that. He wanted to do well and was ambitious and I admired him for the way he conducted himself. I told him I thought of George as a quiet, competent type of leader. He was strictly a career pilot; he picked his career and worked hard at it. He seemed to enjoy his fun, and enjoyed his flying."

Sgt. Art Snyder, George's crew chief in the 328th Squadron, recalled Christmas morning this way:

The major used to give me his watch to hold for him while he flew combat missions. But that morning when I preflighted his plane I noticed the cockpit clock was out of order. So when he came out to the plane, I mentioned this to him. He said, "I'll just take my watch with me." When the mission was over and the planes landed and taxied in, the pilots would hold up one or two fingers indicating how many aircraft they had shot down. Then I recall this one pilot—I can still see the picture in my mind—went by with his thumb down. I knew what he meant—that the major had had it!

About three weeks after the major was shot down, his brother came in with a special service fellow in a jeep. And one question that I recall him asking was if I had any personal effects. Well, of course, I didn't. But I related the story about the watch which was lost because he took it with him that day. [The watch was never recovered even though Preddy's plane was only damaged when it crashed.] I mentioned the fact that we had a roll of film that was being developed, and I would be sure and send him a copy of it when it came back. I did this, and about a week later I got my letter back with MIA stamped on the envelope.

When asked his last impression and recollection of George, Snyder said, "Well, I thought he was very sincere, he was a good leader, and he was

*Lt. Bill Preddy visited with pilots from George's squadron at Chievres, Belgium, or A–84. From left to right, John*   *P. Kessler, unknown, Bill Preddy, Clarence J. Palmer, Ralph W. Hamilton and Raymond H. Littge.*

respected by the pilots. I cut hair in my spare time, so I got to know the pilots rather well. They would complain about different leaders, but I never heard a complaint about the major. They were always willing to go with him and have him as their leader. I think he was a fellow that was a born leader. He did a good job."

For one who had flown battle-torn skies for three years, who had narrowly escaped death on many occasions, who had given his all to the cause he believed most worthy, who had foreseen the possibility of just such an end, who had established records for enemy aircraft brought down, who had won the respect and admiration of so many, this was a terrible fate—an irony wrought by the hands of his own ground troops. Perhaps there is no finer tribute than that paid by Sgt. Alphonse H. Fradella of the 487th who wrote:

> While victories during operations from Y–29 have been many, they can never atone for the irreparable loss of Major George Preddy. . . . It was small consolation to know that before he was fatally hit by Allied ground fire, Major Preddy added two more Me 109s to his long list of aerial victories. To the world he will be remembered as George E. Preddy, Jr., Major, AC, Squadron CO, who destroyed 32.5 enemy planes, 27.5 in aerial combat, and held the DSC, Silver Star with OLC, the DFC with eight OLCs, the Air Medal with seven OLCs . . . To those of us who knew him, he will live long in our memories as "Ratsy," a man's man, a good friend and true, who lived hard and fought harder still for a cause in which he believed. In humble tribute, we dedicate these few words to the memory of a great flyer, and a gentleman.

> To George, A Toast
> It will be nice to think in years to come
>   Of all the fun we had, the escapades we dared;
> The comradeship that grew in us instinctively,
>   The wine, the women and the songs we shared.
>
> But then, there's bound to come that better time,
>   When I will get to thinking how you are . . .
> And, if we'll ever get the chance to meet again?
> And why the Gods of War picked on your star.
> And tho' it's most ironic how it came to end,
>   I'm proud I had the privilege, to call you "Friend."
> —Sgt. Alphonse H. Fradella

*Animated strip entitled* War Sidelights
*by F. K. Barnes.* J. Noah

# Chapter 17

# Bill

Bill Preddy and a number of his classmates left Boston on a converted cruise ship bound for England. Among his classmates was Lt. Philip W. Barnhart who told how they got to England, in a roundabout sort of way. Bill and Barnhart were shipped out as casual officers on the ship; that is, they were not assigned to any particular unit. The officers were quartered in staterooms while the troops were housed below. The troops were replacements so they had no officer contingent along. Therefore, the casual officers had to pull duty down below periodically. The plan was to drop the pilots off at Southampton, England, before taking the troops on to the Continent. But the Battle of the Bulge had reached a critical stage so the ship didn't stop until it docked at Le Havre, France.

Bill, Barnhart and the other pilots disembarked and immediately boarded a train to Paris—the Ninth Air Force Replacement Depot. They were supposed to fly back to England the very next day, but poor weather delayed those plans for several days. This time, rather than the luxury of staterooms, they were given tents in the woods at a Rothschild residence. Barnhart remembers that tents in the snow in January is not high living, even in Paris. The pilots were restricted to the area each day, because it was anticipated that they would be flown to England the following morning. That finally occurred after several days, so they really didn't get a chance to visit Paris.

News of George Preddy's death was withheld from the press for about twenty days while Army Air Force brass attempted to determine why such a thing was allowed to happen. Generals Spaatz and Doolittle personally investigated to find out who was responsible for violating the regulation forbidding ground troops from firing when friendly aircraft were present. They wanted to learn the circumstances surrounding this particular violation. This sort of thing had happened before and it was hoped that it would not happen again after the regulation was put into effect.

The American public accepted the news with apathy, chalking the accident up as one of the many perils of war. Maybe that's what it was. But George's family received the agonizing news with disbelief and pain, shock and grief. George had escaped death so many times they had come to believe he was truly invincible. Even with death all around, it's difficult to believe it can come to one's own—even after it has happened.

A letter telling the Preddy family that Bill had arrived in England followed closely the telegram stating the cryptic and tragic news of George's death. Of course, that made matters even worse for them. Clara and Earl Preddy could have had Bill returned to the States and excluded from combat duty; all it would have taken was a letter to the War Department. Bill was torn between what would be best for his mother and dad, what he thought George would want him to do, and what his country expected him to do. Bill, after due deliberation, would have nothing to do with the suggestion that he return to the United States; he had worked hard to get his silver wings and his assignment to fly fighters. Now that George was gone, he wanted even more to get into the scrap. The letter to the War Department was never written.

Because of Bill's circuitous route to England, the news of George's death didn't reach him until a week after it was public knowledge. As soon as he heard, he visited George's base at Asch, Belgium (Y–29) and talked with

*Lt. William R. Preddy's portrait.*

several of his brother's close friends. Then he wrote a most inspired letter to his parents.

England
January 23, 1945
Dearest Mother and Dad,

As you may know, I've been moving around pretty much but have been assigned to the 339th Fighter Group recently. It seems to be a very good outfit. The boys are tops and I'm flying Mustangs at last.

Yesterday I learned about George. Today I went to his home field and talked to many of the boys there.

What I have to say now is difficult to explain because I hardly understand it myself. There is no use to say not to grieve for I know that is impossible. It is useless to say try and forget, for we can't and shouldn't. We should remember, but in doing so we should look at it in the true light.

. . . . . . . . . . . . . . . . . . . . . . . . . . . . . . . . . . . . . . . . . . . . . . . . . . . . . . . . . .

I close offering you my eternal love and devotion. Let us carry on as George wanted and may we arrive at his standard.
Always love,
Bill

It was now up to Bill to uphold the high standard set by George. Perhaps Bill thought other airmen expected him to continue the record-setting achievements of his older brother. The task before Bill was difficult enough without having it made more so by suspecting that great things were expected

*Soon after Bill arrived and settled in at Fowlmere, home of the 339th Fighter Group, a publicity photo was taken of* *him with Maj. Harry St. G. Tucker of Lexington, Kentucky, Intelligence Officer. J. R. Starnes*

of him. Many a good man has fallen flat on his face endeavoring to live up to a reputation earned by a member of one's family. Perhaps the failure in some cases can be attributed to tension and stress brought on by the ever-present knowledge that no matter how hard one tries, any accomplishment achieved will be thought of as no more than the expected.

J. Fred Baumann of Tennessee attended flying school with Bill (Class 44-E: basic training at Waco, Texas, and single-engine advanced at Moore Field near Mission, Texas). Fred said it was only by chance that Bill's classmates learned that he was the brother of the famous ace. Bill never attempted to take advantage of that fact. Baumann thought quite highly of Bill; he said, "He was an outstanding individual, cadet, and pilot; moreover, he was our Cadet Group Commander. His personality and bearing were most commendable."

Fred Baumann and Bill received different assignments after graduating. Fred went to the 5th Squadron, 52nd Fighter Group in southern Italy where he flew nineteen combat missions before getting hurt in a crazy accident. He was flying a "training mission" in his Mustang when his oil line ruptured and the plane caught fire. Fred bailed out, hit the horizontal stabilizer, was knocked out, came to in time—just barely in time—to pull the rip cord. He sustained a fracture to the lumbar area of his back and was in a cast for three months. He was returned to the States as a litter patient and rehabilitated in Miami Beach.

Bill started flying Mustangs as soon as he settled in with the 339th Fighter Group based at Fowlmere, just ten kilometers south of Cambridge, England. With just a few hours in a P-51 he was flying escort missions to targets like Osnabrück and Nürnburg, Leipzig and Kassel. Upon completion of the escort phase of the mission, strafing attacks against trains, substations, autobahns and airfields were carried out if ammunition permitted.

The entire 339th Fighter Group accounted for only one aerial victory during February 1945. However, the victory was over an Me 262 jet fighter. The new jet fighters were becoming more numerous since Hitler finally recognized their value as fighters rather than as bombers. The Me 262 was a potent enemy for the Mustang, but on occasion the jet fighter was brought down when caught in a turning maneuver; the P-51 could not catch the 262 but it could certainly turn inside of one.

The 339th made up for their low February score by blasting the enemy on the ground in an attempt to get the Luftwaffe back into the air. It worked; as a result of tremendous losses on the ground the Luftwaffe decided to come up and fight. By the end of February Bill had not even encountered an enemy aircraft in the air. He was itching to test himself. Bill wrote home on March 1st; here are a few extracts from his long letter to his Mom:

I am in the Eighth Air Force flying the same kind of airplane George flew—a Mustang. I'm doing long escort work with bombers over Germany. We have been destroying railways and big rail centers. . . . We have gone down strafing locomotives and trains through Germany. I destroyed my first locomotive on my second mission. It blew up and burned when I hit it. I sure would like air fighting, but the enemy air force is very scarce. . . . That's about all I'm allowed to say. . . . Hope Uncle Laurie is getting along better now. Give him my best and when I come home I'd like to see him up and around as before. . . . Buddy [Joe Noah's nickname] is getting along with his flying. He's a good boy and should make a darn good pilot with the attitude he has. I'd like to fly with him sometime. . . .

171

*Bill Preddy visiting with Bill Whisner following the March 2, 1945, mission after which Bill Preddy was forced to land on the Continent. J. R. Starnes*

It was not until his seventh mission that Bill got an opportunity to see what he could do in aerial combat. Major William E. Bryan, Jr., was leading the 503rd Fighter Squadron on an escort mission to Ruhland. It was March 2, 1945. They took off at 0739 hours. Rendezvous was made over the Zuider Zee at 0840 at about 20,000 ft. Escort was provided the Big Friends to the area of Magdeburg where, at 1015 hours, about thirty-five to forty enemy aircraft were spotted at 14,000 ft. and climbing. They were FW 190s and Me 109s, and they were coming up fast to intercept the bombers; they never made it! The 503rd spotted the bandits soon after they poked their noses through the clouds. The undercast was thick, rising to about 6,000 ft. Outnumbered but with the advantage of altitude, the 503rd proceeded to make a bounce on the enemy. Bill, flying wing for Bryan, reported the action as follows:

I was flying Beefsteak Red #2 when we went down to attack approximately 20 FW 190s in the vicinity of Magdeburg. We pulled up behind the formation of enemy aircraft and Beefsteak Red Leader, Major Bryan, opened fire. The 190 he attacked peeled off into the undercast with flames pouring from his engine; I substantiate this claim for one FW 190 destroyed by Major Bryan.

Another 190 came in front of us and began turning in on our left and behind us. I turned into him and opened fire when I was in range; I kept firing until I saw his engine flame up and black smoke pour out. The Jerry then snapped over on his back and fell off into a spin burning fiercely; the pilot did not get out. I claim one FW 190 destroyed.

I was looking around for my flight when an Me 109 came in on my left from above. We went into a Lufbery to the left and I opened fire slightly out of range but closing all the time. The Jerry tightened his turn but I dumped ten degrees of flaps and got my sight back on him. I saw strikes around the cockpit and tail which I believe killed the pilot because he dropped out of the Lufbery and went into a spin to the right. I followed him down very closely and as he hit the clouds at about 6,000 feet his ship began to disintegrate and pieces were flying off. I claim one Me 109 destroyed.

I was in a tight spiral when I broke out below the clouds at about 3,000 feet and immediately climbed back up to 14,000 feet where I bounced another 109. Before I could get in range I was attacked from above and behind by two FW 190s and one Me 109 so I headed for home alone; I was forced to land on the Continent and, as my ship has not been ferried back yet, my film has not been entered and ammunition expenditure is unknown.

CLAIM: One FW 190 Destroyed.
One Me 109 Destroyed.

The Mission Summary Report said that flak was heavy, moderate and inaccurate over the target. Weather ranged from 7/10 to 9/10 and air visibility was good. One V-2 was observed in the target area at 0810 hours.

The intelligence officer, Capt. Eldred J. Carow, writing the general summary for the month of March said of this outstanding mission that, "eleven were destroyed, one probably destroyed, and seven damaged. Individually, Lt. Poutre led with three Jerries destroyed. Also taking honors were Major Bryan, Captain Gerard and Lt. Preddy with two a piece." Incidentally, Bryan brought his total aerial victories up to 7.5 on this mission, his final score for World War II. He was recalled to active duty during the Korean War, and remained in the US Air Force until he retired as a major general. Francis R.

*Bill Preddy was assigned P-51D serial number 44-11823, coded D7-A. It retained the name* Rusty *from former pilot Capt. Jeff French. That's Jeff with his left foot on the wing tank.* J. French

Gerard brought his total to seven, and added one more on 18 March 1945 for a total of eight World War II victories. He, too, retired as a major general.

Major Bryan had led his flight to attack the low gaggle of FW 190s while two other flights bounced the top cover of Me 109s. Bill had overextended himself in the fight and in so doing ran low on fuel. It was fortunate for him that the Luftwaffe ganged up on him when they did or he just might have fought until completely out of fuel. As it was, he took George's often repeated advice and landed at the first friendly airfield on the Continent when it became obvious that he couldn't make it back to Fowlmere. When he landed he found his Mustang had been hit in several places requiring repairs, so he had to leave it and hitch a ride back to England. It was reported in the press that Lieutenant Preddy was forced to land near the 352nd Fighter Group and took that opportunity to visit George's comrades. Bill said, "I thought I'd come over and visit my brother's old gang. I never hope to equal George's record of 32.5 planes, but I'll carry on from where he left off."

In scoring two victories on his first aerial encounter with the enemy, Bill had certainly lived up to the expectations of all who knew he was George Preddy's brother. In so doing, Bill had surpassed one of George's achievements. Remember, George didn't get his first aerial victory until December 1943, almost two years after he first entered combat. Bill got his first in less than two months after entering combat. George must have been sincere when he remarked, "Billy's a much better pilot than I am. I tried him on every trick I knew and he completed everyone of them. He's a wonderful pilot." George said this just after their mock duel over Florida while George was home on R and R. In all probability Bill was not a better pilot than George, but as a result of getting far better training he was a close second.

Here's how Bill explained his first successful mission to a reporter:

I don't expect any other single mission ever will be as thrilling as my seventh mission over Germany. I've been flying as a combat pilot only a few weeks, but on that mission I had my first engagement with the Luftwaffe and I came out of that dogfight with two victories . . . It gave me a wonderful feeling of satisfaction to know that I could meet the Germans in the sky and hold my own. That Mustang is really a great plane.

The action took place a few miles east of Magdeburg. We were cruising along on a bomber escort mission when below us we suddenly sighted a formation of 20 FW 190s and Me 109s. We peeled off and went down to attack, tearing into the formation.

I was flying as wingman to my flight leader, Major William E. Bryan, Jr., of Flint, Michigan, when we bounced the Jerries. It was my first scrap. Naturally I was excited, but I knew I had to stay cool. The first thing I knew I had a FW 190 in my sights. A squeeze of my trigger and the bullets from my six 50–caliber machine guns struck home. He went down for good.

That was my first victory over the Luftwaffe. But the dogfight was still raging all around me, and I managed to close on an Me 109. . . . Again my aim was good, and he, too, flopped over and down. . . . That was my second victory. But what was worrying me at the time was that as a wingman I had two kills, and I thought my flight leader had only one. . . . Things like that aren't supposed to happen in good formation flying. Later I learned that Major Bryan had shot down two planes and damaged a third, which made me feel very good.

I did have a pretty close call in the dogfight. After I shot down the first two planes I went after another Me 109. . . . I might have knocked him down also, but just as I was closing on him I was attacked from above by three German planes, an Me 109 and two FW 109s. But I poured on the gas and ducked into some clouds to get away from them. Then I headed for home.

You might say that 'I walked home' from my first aerial engagement. My engine by then was running very rough and on the return trip played out over the Continent, so I had to land over there and leave my plane to be ferried back to England later. Still, it was a great thrill for me to shoot down those two German planes and escape from the three that were trying to get me. Back in Florida when we were training in P-40s I often tried to picture my first engagement with the enemy. The Magdeburg show filled in all the details I had overlooked.

Bill made it back to Fowlmere in time to fly the mission on March 5. Captain Perry led the squadron on an area patrol to Ruhland, Germany, not far from the eastern front. Several pilots had to abort due to mechanical difficulties. The squadron took off at 0720 hours and made landfall north of The Hague at 0820 hours and 21,000 feet. They arrived in the target area at 1000 hours and patrolled uneventfully until 1130. Landfall out was made north of Ostend at 1330 hours and 12,000 feet. Heavy, moderate and inaccurate flak was encountered over Ruhland. Weather was 10/10 with heavy, persistent contrails at 25,000 feet. Lieutenant Gauger crashed at B-83 on the Continent. Although Gauger was not hurt, his plane was a total loss. All other planes returned safely, landing at 1400 hours.

Those were long missions. Sitting in a P-51 for over six hours at a time is grueling to say the least. Foul weather and rubbernecking for bandits made it even more so! Escort, patrol and strafing missions continued; Bill flew missions on March 5, 8, 11, 14, 15, 17, 20 and 24. At about six hours per mission, that amounts to more than 50 combat hours for the month of March. On March 23, Bill was promoted to first lieutenant.

Bill, in a letter home dated March 7, said, "The Memorial Service [for George] must have been beautiful and I would have given anything to have been present while tribute was being paid to the greatest fighter pilot . . . I visited his old Group again and had a whole day to talk to Whisner and most all the fellows who flew with George. The fine things they said in praise of George were things I've never heard about any one person before. They said he was a natural born fighter pilot and they always felt safe when they flew with him. . . . By the way, Dad, I got a couple for you—you'll hear more about it later." Bill was referring to the two aerial victories he had just gotten.

Toward the latter part of the month, the First and Third armies called for aerial support in their mighty assault across the Rhine. Bill participated in this one, but again the Luftwaffe failed to come up and fight. As a result, the 339th wreaked havoc on ground targets including locomotives, freight cars, oil cars and troop trains.

Bill flew missions on April 2-7 (six consecutive days), 9, 11, 15, and 16 before his final mission on the seventeenth. They were long missions to places including Kiel, Parchim, Gera, Hamburg, Munich, Ulm and Regensburg.

On April 7, the 503rd Squadron encountered twenty-five FW 190s and Me 109s and seven Me 262s in a long-lasting battle ranging from Steinhuder Lake to the area of Hamburg. The fight lasted about forty-five minutes. The German conventional fighters attacked in singles and doubles; the jets attacked in line abreast formations. This time the enemy was aggressive; they pressed home their attacks viciously. The 503rd was able to disperse most of the attacks on the bombers; they destroyed four enemy aircraft and damaged one. Cloud cover was scattered at about 4,000 ft. leaving excellent visibility above. Bill was flying as wingman to 1st Lt. Richard F. Krauss. Lieutenant Krauss reported the encounter:

> I was leading a spare, two-ship element in Beefsteak Squadron and had just rolled out of a turn when I saw an Me 109 about a hundred yards to my right and a little ahead of me. I started a gentle break into him when he broke hard left and passed in front of me. I broke after him and saw he was heading for some clouds paralleling the bomber stream. I chased him from 19,000 feet and pulled into position and opened fire at about 15,000 feet. I saw strikes and at 12,000 feet he started spewing smoke and flame so I broke off as he hit a patch of cloud. My wingman, Lt. Preddy, continued to watch the enemy aircraft and saw it crash. I claim one (1) Me 109 destroyed.

Bill made no claim on this mission. Lt. Philip Petitt got one FW 190, Lieutenant Poutre destroyed an Me 109 and damaged an FW 190; Lt. Raymond G. Johnson claimed one long-nosed FW 190 destroyed. The jets escaped unharmed.

It was on April 16 during an escort and area patrol mission to Regensburg that Bill damaged an unidentified twin-engine aircraft while strafing one of the five different airfields he attacked that day. Because of intense flak, attacks on three of the airfields were abandoned; fields at Marlenbad and Prague/Kbely, Czechoslovakia, suffered tremendous damage from repeated strafings. Bill's job for the most part was to fly top cover in the event enemy aircraft came to the rescue. But on one occasion his flight went down and made a pass which netted Bill one damaged enemy aircraft. Total claims for the 503rd were thirty-one destroyed and nineteen damaged—a big day!

Strafing ground targets continued to be the order of the day as the Luftwaffe remained scarce during April. Bill and the 503rd went on missions primarily in the area northwest of Berlin, but then his group started pushing farther into enemy territory by hitting targets in western Czechoslovakia and the Regensburg, Germany, area. It was during this period that the 339th Fighter Group, and most notably Lt. Col. Joseph L. Thury, established records for aircraft destroyed on the ground. On 10 April 1945 Joe Thury, commanding officer of the 505th Fighter Squadron, brought his total ground victories to 18.5, then on 17 April added seven more giving him the ETO record at the time.

That record was topped by Lt. Col. Elwyn Righetti who ended the war with twenty-seven. Righetti achieved this record while he was commanding officer of the 55th Fighter Group. His wingman, Lt. Carroll Henry, gave testimony to the last nine enemy aircraft destroyed by Righetti the day he was shot down. Henry also observed that his commanding officer made a safe emergency landing about twenty miles northwest of Dresden. Righetti called Henry on the radio and said, "I'm okay, broke my nose in landing. Got nine today...." The Allies thought Righetti was most likely taken prisoner; it was not until the end of hostilities that grave concern for his safety became apparent. The area where he went down lay within the Soviet zone of occupation, and efforts to get US officers to that area were impeded by Soviet authorities. Finally, after getting very limited information, it was assumed that Righetti had been killed by German civilians. That's pure speculation, but because of the casualties suffered by civilians during Allied strafing and bombing attacks, Allied flyers were not too popular among the civilian population. It was reported that the twenty-nine-year-old commanding officer often carried a revolver, unlike most of the other pilots, and he would not hesitate to use it if threatened. Righetti's body was never recovered.

Righetti established his record on April 17, the same day Joe Thury brought his total up to 25.5. But Righetti's score was not recognized until later because he didn't return from the April 17 mission. Thury's Mustang was also hit by enemy fire while strafing that day, but he managed to make it to friendly territory with the knowledge that he had added seven more enemy aircraft to his previous total.

Bill Preddy also flew an escort and patrol mission on the seventeenth, to Pilsen, Czechoslovakia. Taking off at 1135 hours, the 503rd Squadron made rendezvous with the bombers in the vicinity of Frankfurt at 1325 hours and 18,000 ft. They escorted the bombers to Selbat where they broke off and started strafing airdromes in that area. The 503rd hit the Klatovy and Eisendorf airdromes doing considerable damage. They claimed ground victories against three Ju 88s, one Me 262 and one Me 109 on the ground. In addition, one aerial victory was claimed—an Me 262.

While Bill and his flight were busy strafing, another flight in the squadron encountered and destroyed an Me 262 jet coming from the direction of Prague. Lt. John C. Campbell reported the action as follows:

> I was flying Beefsteak Blue #3 at 2,000 feet and had no wingman when I called in two jets which dived by at 90 degrees to our course. We gave chase but gradually lost distance and were about to break off when another Me 262 crossed in front of us in a shallow turn to port. I followed Lt. Ferrell and his wingman as they broke to cut him off; Lt. Ferrell fired in a steep turn and overshot the jet. I pulled six Gs and followed the 262 at about 325 IAS as he dived for the deck. I opened fire and hit his left jet engine and kept firing short bursts while he made a 90–degree turn to the right closing all the time. The blow-job leveled off at 200 feet and I knocked pieces off his left wing, corrected my fire to hit the fuselage, and the pilot bailed out. I may have hit the pilot because his chute did not open; the jet half-rolled in and exploded in a clearing in some woods. I claim one (1) Me 262 destroyed.

Bill was flying wing to the squadron leader, Capt. Raymond Reuter, an old-timer who had been with the 503rd since the middle of 1944. Ray had completed eighty missions and 300 combat hours in February 1945 and had been assigned ground duty in England rather than return to the United States. Reuter had just returned to flying duty with the 503rd on April 15, his twenty-eighth birthday. He was one of the "old men" in the squadron; Bill, in comparison, was twenty years old. Incidentally, Reuter went down because of mechanical difficulty in September 1944 over enemy-occupied France near Saarbourg. He bailed out at 5,000 ft. and delayed opening his chute until 500 ft. but landed safely. He hid in a quarry for five hours watching German soldiers search for him in an adjoining forest. Later he was picked up and sheltered by the French Marquis. He made it back to England and his squadron about two weeks later.

After strafing Klatovy and Eisendorf they investigated other airfields but found the flak too intense. It was 1440 hours and time to go home when Bill and Captain Reuter spotted two Me 262s and gave chase. Apparently the jets outran the Mustangs and left the battle area, so Captain Reuter and Bill decided to make another strafing run—the last for both of them.

Lt. Philip E. Petitt wrote Bill's parents in October 1945 and gave the following account of what happened. He said that Bill and Capt. Reuter chased the jets which eluded them. Then, he said, Bill called Reuter and reported, "There's a field to the south; let's go over." Petitt said they must have strafed that field because he could recognize voices, but no words. At this point Petitt said he was a little busy himself, and it wasn't until he got back to Fowlmere that he found out that both Bill and Reuter were missing.

*Capt. Ray Reuter leading the 503rd FS the day he and Bill Preddy were reported missing in action, April 17, 1945,* *while strafing an airdrome near Prague, Czechoslovakia.* R. Reuter

*Grave markers of Preddy brothers at Lorraine American Military Cemetery,* *St. Avold, France, approximately twenty-five miles east of Metz.* J. Noah

Also in October of 1945, Lt. Jeff French wrote to Bill's parents. Although Jeff was not on that particular mission, he was passing along the information he had gathered from others who were there. Perhaps the most meaningful information came in a letter dated September 20, 1945, from Alec Boychuck, a pilot with the 503rd who also wasn't on that mission. He said, "They both had to make crash landings because they were too low to parachute out. We listed them both MIA." Indeed, they were listed as missing in action over Czechoslovakia since April 17, 1945. Bill's parents were notified by wire followed by a letter dated May 8, 1945. The letter promised a follow-up in three months if no information was found sooner. And on August 9, 1945, another letter from the War Department arrived and told the Preddys that no new information had been found, but the department was making a continuous effort to establish the actual status of personnel who had been reported missing in action.

The Missing Air Crew Report (MACR) on Bill is dated 21 April 1945 and gives the following information of interest:

1. Aircraft Type, Model & Series:   P-51-K-5
2. AAF Serial Number:   44-11623
3. Engine:   V1650-3
4. AAF Serial Number:   V-301955
5. Airplane Nickname:   None
6. Identity of person believed to have last knowledge of aircraft:
   Lt. Joseph G. Ferrell, by Radio.
7. No search conducted.

The Casualty Clearance Plan (CCP) is dated September 5, 1945, and lists Bill's status as still missing in action (MIA). It gives a statement by Lieutenant

*Joe Noah's favorite photos of his cous-ins, George and Bill Preddy.* R. Preddy
Harris

Ferrell: "At 1430 hours we caught a good deal of 20 mm and 40 mm flak from the airfield southeast of Prague. After calling it in I broke to the left away from it, with the rest of the Squadron following. Captain Reuter (Squadron Leader) and Lt. W. R. Preddy were not seen after that, but five minutes later Captain Reuter told us to rendezvous over the river southwest of Prague. Before we could get there, Captain Reuter said he was chasing two jets. After several minutes he gave up the chase and said he was heading due south. That was at 1445 and the last time we heard from him. Lt. Preddy was flying wing position to Captain Reuter." Both Reuter and Preddy were listed as missing in action.

The CCP added the following information in Ferrell's handwriting: "Dog tag sent in by the Germans; it was bent and the Germans said he was dead. It is my guess that they tried to strafe the airdrome at Budejovice, Czechoslovakia. The flak there was terrible." Budejovice is about 120 kilometers due south of Prague.

Bill's status was finally listed as killed in action (KIA) as of October 9, 1945, in WD AGO Form 51-1 dated November 19, 1945. A response from the Department of the Army dated June 16, 1988, reveals that Bill's remains were temporarily interred in the Civilian Cemetery, Ceske Budejovice. Subsequently his remains were moved to the US Military Cemetery, St. Avold, France, and interred July 28, 1945, in Plot L, Row 22, Grave 1693. His remains were moved again—January 18, 1949—to a permanent grave next to George in the same cemetery—now named Lorraine American Military Cemetery, St. Avold, France. George's body was moved to St. Avold from a temporary grave in Margraten, Holland. His grave site is Plot A, Row 21, Grave 43. Bill's is Plot A, Row 21, Grave 42. Captain Reuter is also buried at Lorraine.

# Epilogue

It's impossible for us to give follow-up details on all the people who have been mentioned in this book, but we endeavor to give some.

Clara and Earl Preddy: Clara and Earl raised Johnny Faircloth, the son of their first daughter, Jonnice. Earl retired in 1959 and died in 1972. Clara died in 1974.

Rachel Preddy Harris: Rachel and her husband, Rigdon Harris, moved to Raleigh where they raised two fine children, Anne and George. Anne lives with her husband, Carl Gordon, near San Francisco. George lives with his wife, Barbara, in Jacksonville, Florida. Rachel retired from North Carolina State University in 1986.

Bill Preddy: One of the two claims Bill made was later allowed as a probable. Perhaps the gun camera didn't see what Bill saw as the Me 109 entered the clouds at 6,000 feet.

Bill's remains were identified by dog tags and dental work, according to John F. Manning, Mortuary Affairs and Casualty Support Division, when queried in 1988. What is puzzling about this matter is the fact that Bill was buried in Budejovice before July 28, 1945, because that's when his remains were reported to have been moved to St. Avold. Yet it was not until October 9, 1945 that "evidence considered sufficient to establish the fact of death was received by the Secretary of War from a Commander in the European Theater." Mr. Manning explained how this can happen. Recovered remains were often buried in temporary cemeteries. Upon burial, the army had various degrees of identification—some proved right and some wrong. Some were buried as unknown soldiers, and later they were identified and named. Bill fell in that category. Once identified, they knew when and where his remains had been buried earlier. But until his remains were identified, the army had insufficient evidence to establish the fact of death.

Another bit of mystery was added by a Czechoslovakian, Mr. M. F. van Eyck, who is conducting research in support of an article he hopes to publish about Americans who lost their lives in Czechoslovakia during World War II. His research turned up a gentleman who said he spent several hours with Bill after he crashed on April 17, 1945. The gentleman said that Bill died of his wounds three to four days later because the Germans refused to provide immediate medical attention.

Raymond Reuter: Captain Reuter's aircraft was set afire by hits, but continued to fly south of the airfield he was strafing. About five kilometers south and at about 150 meters above the ground Reuter's P–51 exploded, according to van Eyck's source. Captain Reuter is buried at Lorraine American Military Cemetery, St. Avold, France.

Robert J. "Bozo" Boaz, Jr.: Bozo flew B–24s during the war. After the war he moved to Wilmington, North Carolina, where he raised his family. He died in 1983.

Clyde "Otto" Gaskins: Otto has retired and lives in Greensboro once again. He served as an instructor for army primary flight training in Stearman PT–17s during the war. He spent one five-year period during the 1960s flying amphibians in Brazil where he accumulated 4,400 flying hours, bringing his total to over 10,000. At age seventy-two he has returned to flying, this time for the Civil Air Patrol.

John L. Latham: John was recalled to active duty for the Korean War and remained in the reserves. He lives in Greensboro where he has been in construction, real estate and government planning businesses. Now that he has retired he is serving as deputy commander of the local Civil Air Patrol.

Arnold "Goat" Mathews: Goat was nicknamed by a teammate on the midget football team who once said to Arnold when they met in huddle, "Man, you butt me in the back just like an old billy goat!" From that time on he was called "Goat." He served as an aerial photographer on B–17s during the war and saw George occasionally in England during the war. He attended Guilford College in Greensboro after the war and worked for Addressograph-Multigraph for many years. He then became a hospital administrator. Now he is retired and lives in Marietta, South Carolina.

Bill Teague: Teague, in 1952, was killed in a crash of a twin-engined Beechcraft near Danbury, North Carolina, in the mountains just one mile from Hanging Rock State Park.

John C. Meyer: Meyer remained in the air force after World War II, returned to combat in Korea where he downed two MiG–15s bringing his total aerial victories to twenty-six. Reaching the rank of four-star general, he commanded the Strategic Air Command and served as Vice Chief of Staff of the Air Force. He retired in1974 and died of a heart attack in 1975.

I. B. Jack Donalson: Donalson remained in the air force and retired in 1968. He lives in San Antonio, Texas. He and John Landers became very good friends.

Joseph J. "Red" McVay: Red lives in Springfield, Virginia, after retiring from his job at the Pentagon. He is an outstanding member of the 352nd Fighter Group Association, and a staunch member of George Preddy's fan club. When the Greensboro Historical Museum held an event in honor of Preddy in the 1970s, Red took the time to write the *Greensboro Daily News*. Excerpts from his letter follow.

The enlisted segment of our squadron was drawn primarily from the northeast. . . . The Major was our southern gentleman. The men idolized him. He commanded respect from all who knew him, not through his officer status, but because of his deeds, his quiet nature, and his humanity. I was the first to his plane in the morning and the last to leave after flying had ceased, to assure his equipment was in order. This was not done under an order, or out of fear, but out of love.

On that fateful Christmas Day in 1944, a keg of beer had been purchased for the enlisted men to help lessen their pangs of homesickness. Before most of us had downed our first glass, the rumor came that the Major, our Major, had been killed. After the first sense of shock, of disbelief, wore off, we emptied our glasses on the ground and returned to await further word. We would not accept this loss until we received the final confirmation. . . . I shall always revere my association with Major Preddy. I will never forget him and Christmas will never be the same for me again.

Carl Luksic: Luksic retired from the US Air Force in 1968 with over 11,000 flying hours. Carl remained in fighters during his entire air force career. Almost all of his hours were racked up in fighters. He lives in Tallahassee, Florida.

Bill Whisner: Bill died in 1989 of complications arising from bee stings. The 352nd Fighter Group Association, and specifically Robert Powell, arranged to have Bill's ashes spread from a Mustang. Vlado Lenoch, who owns a Mustang with Whisner's *Moonbeam McSwine* markings, flew down to Louisiana where he graciously spread Bill's ashes. Vlado also gave Sam Sox and Joe Noah their first P-51 ride in his Mustang at Experimental Aircraft Association's Sun 'n Fun, 1990. What a ride!

There are also a number of memorials in honor of George Preddy, some in honor of both George and Bill.

*Maj. George E. Preddy, Jr., Veterans of Foreign Wars Post 2087 located in Greensboro, North Carolina.* S. Sox

Veterans of Foreign Wars: The VFW Post in Greensboro was named for George soon after the war ended. It is the Major George E. Preddy, Jr., VFW Post 2087.

Preddy Boulevard: Preddy Boulevard was dedicated in honor of both George and Bill on Pearl Harbor Day, December 7, 1968. The invocation was given by Dr. Samuel L. Sox. Mayor Carson Bain introduced the special guests, including General John C. Meyer and the Honorable Horace Kornegay. General Meyer gave dedicatory remarks for the attendees. Clara Preddy unveiled the bronze tablet. It was an overcast and cold day. A flyover of Mustangs was provided by the US Army.

Preddy Boulevard is a section of Interstate 85 that goes through Greensboro. The monument and marker is located at the northwest corner of the intersection of Routes 421 and I85. The event was sponsored by the Greensboro Historical Museum and the Major George E. Preddy, Jr., VFW Post 2087. Sam Sox, Jr. and William Moore, director of the museum, were responsible for having the City of Greensboro name a boulevard for the Preddy brothers.

Historical Marker: A historical marker in memory of George was placed by the state of North Carolina on Summit Avenue near the home of the Preddys, 605 Park Avenue. The marker was dedicated on May 21, 1983, at the urging of Professor Alexander R. Stoesen of Guilford College. Rachel unveiled the marker after Eugene Pfaff, Greensboro Public Library, gave a biographical sketch.

Greensboro Historical Museum: Earl Preddy gave many items of memorabilia to the Greensboro Historical Museum where they are displayed from

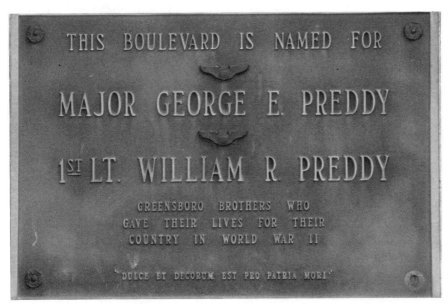

*Preddy Boulevard bronze plaque honoring George and Bill Preddy, "Greensboro brothers who gave their lives for their country in World War II." S. Sox*

time to time. A photo of one of their earlier displays is shown. William Moore, director, has done much to preserve the memory of George Preddy.

Champlin Fighter Museum, Mesa, Arizona: The American Fighter Aces Association (AFAA) has its headquarters in the Champlin Fighter Museum. A display there includes a signed photo of George, a lithograph of his *Cripes A'Mighty 3rd* made from a painting by Harley Copic, and a nameplate which George used in his office while at Bodney.

Experimental Aircraft Association (EAA) Museum, Oshkosh, Wisconsin: The EAA Museum has a display of the top aces who flew the P–38, the P–40, the P–47 and the P–51. Preddy and Meyer are both included among the top Mustang aces. George Preddy is the top Mustang ace when only aerial victories are counted (26.83 aerial and five ground); Meyer is the top Mustang ace when both aerial and ground victories are included (24 aerial and 13 ground).

United States Air Force Museum, Dayton, Ohio: The USAF Museum has a photo of George in one of their displays.

Weeks Air Museum, Tamiami, Florida: Kermit Weeks restored a Mustang using the markings of *Cripes A'Mighty 3rd*. He keeps it housed in his museum in Tamiami, Florida. It is airworthy, and Kermit flies it to air shows. He won the EAA's grand prize for the restoration in 1988.

352nd Fighter Group Association: This association has been outstanding in tracing members of the 352nd, and in planning and holding reunions. Their

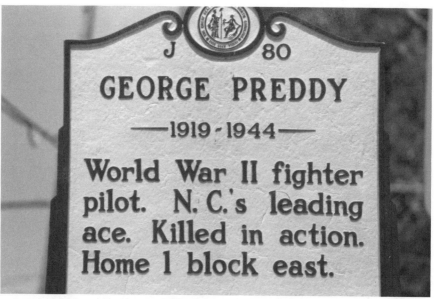

*Historical marker placed near the Preddys' home by the State of North Carolina.* S. Sox

186

Maj.

MAJOR GEORGE E. PREDDY

352ᴰ FIGHTER GROU

*Greensboro Historical Museum. Exhibit displayed in 1981.* J. Noah

187

work has made our work fun, and also quite a bit more meaningful. Many of their members have told us truly interesting stories. Some appear in this book. Robert Powell of the 328th Fighter Squadron was instrumental in putting together *Blue-Nosed Bastards of Bodney,* the 352nd Fighter Group history (with help from Tom Ivie and Sam Sox, Jr.).

*Preddy, The Mustang Ace:* A videotape on the life of George Preddy was written, edited and produced by Sam Sox, Jr., and John E. Lambeth in 1986. Joe Noah provided air transportation in his Comanche to visit and interview many of the people included in the mini-documentary.

*Cripes A'Mighty 3rd:* Harley Copic, famous aviation artist, painted a series of Mustangs which included *Cripes A'Mighty 3rd* and *Moonbeam McSwine.* Harley had lithographs made from his paintings, and Joe Noah had postcards made from the litho of *Cripes A'Mighty 3rd.*

Warbirds: Several privately-owned P–51 Mustangs carry the wartime markings of 352nd pilots. Kermit Weeks owns George Preddy's *Cripes A'Mighty 3rd,* Pete McManus owns John Meyer's *Petie 2nd,* Dr. Tony Buechler owns *Petie 3rd* and Vlado Lenoch owns Bill Whisner's *Moonbeam McSwine.*
    A P–51 which was flown by Capt. Ray Littge and later by Lt. Russell Ross (both of the 352nd) was located in a playground in Israel. Robert Lamplough bought and restored it with the markings it had when Littge flew it. It is the only Bodney-based Mustang known to exist at this time.

*Postcard made from Harley Copic's painting of* Cripes A'Mighty 3rd.
Copic/Noah

# Appendix A: The Score

## VICTORIES—MAJOR GEORGE E. PREDDY, JR.

| DATE OF VICTORY | US/ENEMY AIRCRAFT TYPE | GRND ALL | AERIAL FVCB | VIII FC | 352nd FG | 487th/328th Sqdns. | Cumulative Crosses | Study 85 |
|---|---|---|---|---|---|---|---|---|
| 01–Dec–43 | P-47/Me 109 | | 1 | 1 | 1 | 1 | 1 | 1 |
| 22–Dec–43 | P-47/Me 210 | | 0 | 1 | 1 | 1 | 2 | 1 |
| 29–Jan–44 | P-47/FW 190 | | 1 | 1 | 1 | 1 | 3 | 1 |
| 11–Apr–44 | P-51/He 111 | 1 | | | | | 4 | |
| 13–Apr–44 | P-51/Bu 133 | 1 | | | | | 5 | |
| 22–Apr–44 | P-51/Ju 88 | | 0.33 | 0 | 0 | 0 | 5 | 0.33 |
| 22–Apr–44 | P-51/Ju 52 | 1 | | | | | 6 | |
| 30–Apr–44 | P-51/FW 190 | | 0 | 1 | 0 | 1 | 7 | 0 |
| 13–May–44 | P-51/Me 109 | | 2 | 2 | 2 | 2 | 9 | 2 |
| 30–May–44 | P-51/Me 109 | | 2.5 | 2.5 | 2.5 | 2.5 | 12 | 2.5 |
| 12–Jun–44 | P-51/Me 109 | | 1 | 1 | 1 | 1 | 13 | 1 |
| 20–Jun–44 | P-51/FW 190 | | 1 | 1 | 1 | 1 | 14 | 1 |
| 20–Jun–44 | P-51/Me 410 | | 0.5 | 0.5 | 0.5 | 0.5 | 15 | 0.5 |
| 21–Jun–44 | P-51/Me 109 | | 1 | 1 | 1 | 1 | 16 | 1 |
| 29–Jun–44 | P-51/Ju 52 | 1 | | | | | 17 | |
| 18–Jul–44 | P-51/Ju 88 | | 2 | 3 | 3 | 3 | 20 | 2 |
| 18–Jul–44 | P-51/Me 109 | | 1 | 1 | 1 | 1 | 21 | 1 |
| 20–Jul–44 | P-51/Me 410 | 1 | | | | | 22 | |
| 21–Jul–44 | P-51/Me 109 | | 0.5 | 0.5 | 0.5 | 0.5 | 23 | 0.5 |
| 29–Jul–44 | P-51/Me 109 | | 1 | 1 | 1 | 1 | 24 | 1 |
| 05–Aug–44 | P-51/Me 109 | | 1 | 1 | 1 | 1 | 25 | 1 |
| 06–Aug–44 | P-51/Me 109 | | 6 | 6 | 6 | 6 | 31 | 6 |
| 02–Nov–44 | P-51/Me 109 | | 1 | 1 | 1 | 1 | 32 | 1 |
| 21–Nov–44 | P-51/FW 190 | | 1 | 1 | 1 | 1 | 33 | 1 |
| 25–Dec–44 | P-51/Me 109 | | 2 | 2 | 2 | 2 | 35 | 2 |
| **Totals** | | 5 | 25.83 | 28.5 | 27.5 | 28.5 | | 26.83 |

*Notes:* GRND denotes ground victories.

FVCB denotes the victories credited by the Fighter Victory Credits Board.

VIII FC denotes victories credited by Eighth Fighter Command.

352nd FG denotes victories credited by the 352nd Fighter Group.

487th/328th Sqdns. denotes the score kept by the 487th and 328th fighter squadrons.

Cumulative Crosses denote the number of crosses painted on George Preddy's aircraft. A full cross was painted for each victory or shared victory.

Study 85 denotes the victories credited in *Study 85: USAF Credits for the Destruction of Enemy Aircraft, World War II*.

# Appendix B: Aircraft Markings

### P–40E, SN 85, *Tarheel*

Flown by Lt. George Preddy during the spring of 1942 while serving with the 49th Pursuit Group in Northern Australia, defending Darwin. The upper surface was olive drab and the lower color was neutral gray. The name *Tarheel* is white. The number 85, the assigned squadron aircraft number is painted in white under the nose, just behind the lip of the cooler intake and on the vertical stabilizer. The dragon had a medium green body and arms with black scales; it had a red face and beard. The top of the dragon's hood was white; the rest of the hood was light green. Its horns were white, and the top of the nose and the area surrounding the eye was yellow. The eye was black, the mouth pink, the tongue red, the teeth and claws white, and the nostril yellow. The smoke was white with black highlights. All features had thin black outlines. The names Lt. George E. Preddy and crew chief Corporal Yates were painted under the canopy in white.

### P–47–RE, SN 42–8500, *Cripes A'Mighty*

Flown by Capt. George Preddy from September 1943 through the middle of April 1944. The upper surface was olive drab and the lower surface neutral gray. The cowl band, code letters and tail stripe were white. The name was white with yellow shadow shading. The names under the canopy were white. The victory cross was white with black in the center. The gold fish and caterpillar symbols were yellow, and the wheel covers were striped in black and white.

### P–51B–10–NA, SN 42–106451, *Cripes A'Mighty 2nd*

Flown by Maj. George Preddy from the middle of April through the middle of June 1944. It had a medium blue nose and upper cowl, standard for the 352nd Fighter Group. The code letters, serial numbers and tail stripe were black. Black 12 in. identification bands were on the top and bottom of the elevator and the horizontal stabilizer. The victory crosses under the canopy were black with white and black outlines. To date no photograph has been found that shows the name on this aircraft. The name was, however, *Cripes A'Mighty 2nd*.

### P–51B–10, SN 42–106449, *Princess Elizabeth*

Flown by Lt. William Whisner from April through July 1944. It had the standard blue nose and upper cowl of the 352nd Fighter Group. The code letters, serial numbers, and the Maltese cross victory marks under the canopy were black. The name *Princess* was white with a yellow border; *Elizabeth* was green outlined in red with a yellow-orange yellow floral design. The remainder of the aircraft was natural metal.

### P–51D–5–NA, SN 44–13321 *Cripes A'Mighty 3rd*

Flown by Maj. George Preddy from mid-June through mid-August 1944. The nose and upper cowl were the standard blue color of the 352nd. The remainder of the Mustang was natural metal. The serial numbers and code letters were black. The invasion stripes were black and white, also standard. The name *Cripes A'Mighty 3rd* was white shadowed in red with black outlining and red shadowed in white with black outlining on natural metal. A black 12 in. identification band was on bottom of the elevator and on the horizontal stabilizer. The small crew names were black. The pilot's name on the canopy frame was red with blue shadow shading. An earlier photo (June 12, 1944) shows Preddy's Mustang with seventeen victories (starting at the canopy and extending to the nose) and the invasion stripes completely around the fuselage and wings. The final appearance of *Cripes A'Mighty 3rd* on August 7, 1944, showed a total of thirty-one victories, twenty-one on the top row and ten crosses below, all in white. Other documented scores displayed were July 19, 1944—twenty-one; July 24, 1944—twenty-three; and August 4, 1944—twenty-four (twenty-one crosses on top row and three on bottom).

## P–51D–10–NA, SN 44–14151, *Petie 2nd*

Flown by Lt. Col. John C. Meyer from July through October 1944. It had the standard blue nose and upper cowl of the 352nd; the antenna was also blue. The code letters and serial numbers were black. The name *Petie 2nd* was bright yellow. Two horizontal bands of orange yellow were applied to lower third of the letters. The kill marks were orange yellow. The entire name and kill marks were outlined in black. The aircraft crew names were in black. The pilot's name on the canopy frame was in black letters. The emblem on the side of the fuselage was the 487th Fighter Squadron patch, which is a blue disk with red outline encircling a small boy with a machine gun under his left arm. The boy's body is flesh colored. He's wearing a white scarf with a red stripe on it, white diapers, red socks, brown shoes and helmet. The goggles and gun were gray. The lock of hair was white and the streak of lightning yellow. The swastikas around the emblem and to the side were orange yellow with black shadow shading.

## P–51D–15–NA, SN 44–14906, *Cripes A'Mighty*

Flown by Maj. George Preddy after he returned from R and R in the United States and took command of the 328th Fighter Squadron—October through December 1944. The aircraft was natural metal with the standard blue nose marking of the 352nd Fighter Group. The front canopy frame was also 352nd Blue. The squadron letters were black. The rudder was red, and the serial numbers were black. The pilot's name on the canopy frame was yellow in old English style on a red background. The code letter and bar under the P were black. The name *Cripes A'Mighty* was white with small concentric yellow letters inside. The letters were outlined in black. A barber pole on the right side of nacelle had black and white stripes with a red ball on top. The thirty-one swastikas below the canopy were black. The stripes under the fuselage were black. A black identification band was on bottom of the elevator and horizontal stabilizer. There were dual mirrors above the windscreen, and they were painted black. The antenna had red and white stripes, and all trim tabs were painted with diagonal red and white stripes. Gun covers on leading edge of wings were white with red teardrop designs covering each gun barrel. The main landing gear doors had small, red half circles applied to lower edge. There were six white diagonal hash marks slightly below the exhaust stacks on each side of nacelle.

# Index